ReFocus: The Films of Francis Veber

ReFocus

ReFocus: The International Directors Series

Series Editors: Robert Singer and Gary D. Rhodes

ReFocus is a series of contemporary methodological and theoretical approaches to the interdisciplinary analyses and interpretations of international film directors, from the celebrated to the ignored, in direct relationship to their respective culture—its myths, values, and historical precepts—and the broader parameters of international film history and theory. The series provides a forum for introducing a broad spectrum of directors, working in and establishing movements, trends, cycles, and genres including those historical, currently popular, or emergent, and in need of critical assessment or reassessment. It ignores no director who created a historical space—either in or outside of the studio system—beginning with the origins of cinema and up to the present. *ReFocus* brings these film directors to a new audience of scholars and general readers of Film Studies.

Titles in the series include:

edinburghuniversitypress.com/series/refocint

ReFocus:
The Films of Francis Veber

Keith Corson

EDINBURGH
University Press

Edinburgh University Press is one of the leading university presses in the UK. We publish
academic books and journals in our selected subject areas across the humanities and social
sciences, combining cutting-edge scholarship with high editorial and production values
to produce academic works of lasting importance. For more information visit our website:
edinburghuniversitypress.com

First published in hardback by Edinburgh University Press 2019

Edinburgh University Press Ltd
The Tun—Holyrood Road
12 (2f) Jackson's Entry
Edinburgh EH8 8PJ

Typeset in 11/13 Monotype Ehrhardt by
Servis Filmsetting Ltd, Stockport, Cheshire,
and printed and bound by CPI Group (UK) Ltd,
Croydon, CR0 4YY

A CIP record for this book is available from the British Library

ISBN 978 1 4744 2948 1 (hardback)
ISBN 978 1 4744 2949 8 (paperback)
ISBN 978 1 4744 2950 4 (webready PDF)
ISBN 978 1 4744 2951 1 (epub)

Contents

Figures

Acknowledgments

This book was made possible by the vision, enthusiasm, and encouragement of Gary Rhodes and Robert Singer. The very existence of the *ReFocus* series is a much-needed addition to the field of film studies and I feel lucky to be a part of the broader project that they have created. Many thanks to Richard Strachan, Gillian Leslie, and everyone at Edinburgh University Press for being so helpful and patient throughout the entire process. I am grateful to Rhodes College for providing the travel funding that allowed me to attend a conference in Paris, leading to key conversations that helped me conceptualize this project. Also at Rhodes, a big thank you to Laura Loth for giving me the opportunity to talk through this material with an audience for my first public lecture about Veber. Many thanks to all of my students over the past few years at Rhodes, Memphis College of Art, and the University of Memphis for serving as a sounding board for many of the ideas that appear in the following pages. Much of this project was made possible by the help I received working on my French, which started from scratch shortly before taking on this project and ramped up quickly once my research started in earnest. *Alors, merci pour tout, Émilie.* And of course, Mina deserves a special thank you for keeping me happy and healthy throughout the entire process.

CHAPTER I

Francis Veber and the Canon

The career of Francis Veber presents a paradox for auteurist film studies. A "Veber film" is as identifiable and idiosyncratic as those of any other French auteur, yet he is rarely invoked in discussions of post-*nouvelle vague* cinema. He is a filmmaker who has achieved success at home and outside of his native France, yet he is often omitted from histories of French cinema, particularly those written in English. Part of this has to do with Veber's chosen mode of address, which is popular comedy. Clearly, the critical film canon is resistant to genre practices, placing value in both the self-consciously serious and non-commercial (or, at least, a less blatant commercialism than popular genre films). Veber is also a problematic figure due to his relationship with Hollywood. Veber has writing credits on eleven Hollywood films, with his screenplays being the most prominent recipient of the French-to-American adaptation treatment in the 1980s and 1990s; a phenomenon that would be coined "le remake." Yet, other respected international auteurs have seen their films bowdlerized by Hollywood without it impacting their personal reputations as filmmakers, including François Truffaut and Jean-Luc Godard.[1] Perhaps the biggest impediment to Veber receiving the auteur treatment is that he is primarily seen as a writer, not a director. Although he has directed twelve features, his unobtrusive, almost invisible visual style suggests a writer who stepped behind the camera simply to assure that his screenplays would not be reinterpreted or altered by someone else. Veber's comments in various interviews put forth a seeming indifference toward the act of filmmaking, lacking the passion for technical details and *mise en scène* that are often associated with the director as auteur. But it is because of the ways that Veber fails to fit into traditional definitions of the auteur, not despite them, that he is such a compelling figure for analysis.

The *ReFocus* series offers the perfect venue for an exploration of Veber in that it utilizes the authorial subject while challenging the limitations of the canon, expanding parameters to welcome new directors into the broader conversation of film scholarship. Veber's career intersects with central issues surrounding film authorship, commercial and industrial practices, and national cinema, generating questions that are increasingly pressing in a globalized and fractured cinematic landscape. Veber's films look to the past, stylistically indebted to classic screen comedies and theatre. They are also incredibly prescient, as his remarkable run of box office hits in France were made within an unstable national film industry and, in turn, helped studios like Gaumont fully understand the continued need to produce films made explicitly for a French audience as opposed to, or at least in addition to, international co-productions made for a global audience. Spanning from his directorial debut *Le jouet* in 1976 to his final outing behind the camera with *L'emmerdeur* in 2008, this book will primarily cover the twelve films that Veber directed during his career while also addressing his work as a playwright and screenwriter, and the sizable body of American remakes of his projects.

Veber's relationship with Hollywood has not been completely passive. The most glaring example is Veber directing the remake of his own French film *Les fugitifs* (1986) as *Three Fugitives* (1989) for Disney's Touchstone Pictures. This transnational adaptation—which in this particular case may be more accurately labeled a transnational repetition—is just one of the many Hollywood utterances of his career that will be explored in the coming chapters. The work he has produced reinforces common American perceptions about France's poor taste in comedy while also falling victim to romanticized notions of working outside of the dominant film industry. Hollywood's tendency to Americanize his films—a practice that Veber has been alternately victimized by from a distance, and guilty of as a participant—has hurt his artistic reputation, but comparative analysis of his French originals and their English-language remakes helps to unpack intent, reception, and subtext.

In order to dedicate a single volume to Veber's career, however, there must be more at play than a need to challenge the limitations of the canon or to use him as a symbol of Hollywood adaptation of foreign films. The primary impetus of this book ultimately rests in the value of Veber's films, both in the quality of his writing and the underappreciated level of his directorial craft. It is true that Veber considers himself a writer first and foremost, but his work as a director makes a far more compelling case for an auteurist reading than his numerous outings as a screenwriter for other directors. His writing and directing function in unison, even if his approach to writing deviates from the ways in which other writer-directors think in images and camera movements when committing words to the page. Perhaps the best corollary to Veber is Billy Wilder, one of his cinematic inspirations. Considering a good script as the foundational element of any successful film, Wilder also uses an unobtrusive visual style as a director to help emphasize the screenplay. Just as a musician plays their instrument in service of the song as opposed to an outward display of their virtuosity, Wilder and Veber direct in service of their writing. Like Wilder, Veber began as a journalist and eventually found comedy as his preferred medium for making broader social commentaries. Not coincidentally, the final film of Wilder's career would be *Buddy Buddy* (1981), a remake of Veber's *L'emmerdeur* (originally a stage play, it was also made into a film in France by Édouard Molinaro in 1973). Clearly there was a mutual respect between the writers, but the conflicts and failures of *Buddy Buddy* (which will be explored in Chapter 13) speak to the importance of the independent authorship that Veber sought to create for himself as a director.

COMEDY, NATIONAL CINEMA, AND CANON

Considering the quality and artistry of Billy Wilder's directorial œuvre from the vantage point of the late 1960s, Andrew Sarris chose to keep the director out of the "Pantheon" in his book *The American Cinema*.[2] Instead, relegating Wilder to the "Less Than Meets the Eye" category, Sarris takes umbrage with Wilder's "penchant for gross caricature" and "visual and structural deficiencies."[3] Both of these criticisms have also been leveled against Veber. Although Sarris would soften his criticism of Wilder in subsequent years, the writer-director remains a figure often left out of discussions of cinema's premier auteurs despite the fact that his films and career have generated a sizable body of scholarship and critical discourse.[4] Of the fourteen directors in Sarris's pantheon, only three (Charles Chaplin, Buster Keaton, and Ernst Lubitsch) are primarily associated with making comedies. Howard Hawks, another pantheon director in Sarris's eyes, certainly made his fair share of iconic comedies—*Twentieth Century* (1934), *Bringing Up Baby* (1938), and *His Girl Friday* (1940) among them—but he has largely been championed for his ability to move between genres as disparate as Westerns, musicals, gangster films, and science fiction rather than through an isolated or even primary consideration of his comedies. Whether or not Billy Wilder deserves to be mentioned alongside the likes of Hawks, Chaplin, and Lubitsch is a question for another scholar on another day, but the fact remains that comedy and the filmmakers associated with the genre remain marginalized in the realm of film scholarship. Arguably, Sarris's pantheon is unusually inclusive of comedy directors when compared to the broader scope of auteurist studies.

The exclusion of comedy has been particularly pronounced in the scholarly consideration of French cinema. Film students in English-speaking countries could be forgiven for assuming that French cinema is dominated by auteurist art cinema, as textbooks, monographs, art house releases, film festival selections, and home video distribution largely eschew genre filmmaking and popular cinematic entertainment made for a domestic French audience. While the work of Jacques Tati is an exception of French comedy deemed worthy of inclusion in most historical surveys, a film like *La grande vadrouille* (1966, Gérard Oury) is not routinely mentioned by English-language scholarship of French cinema. The most popular film in the history of the French box office before it was unseated three decades later by *Titanic* (1997, James Cameron), *La grande vadrouille* is rarely analyzed with much rigor and remains largely unavailable on DVD in North America. This speaks to one of the biggest problems in writing about a national cinema from an outsider's perspective, as access often supersedes language as the primary obstacle to creating a complete portrait.

Subtitles may not be the most elegant or complete way to engage with a film, but there is a level of understanding that can be gained regardless of the viewer's level of familiarity with the spoken language on the audio track. While a large percentage of French films are available with English subtitles when released on DVD, only a small percentage of them are ever distributed outside of France. As Alan Williams points out in his introduction to *Republic of Images: A History of French Filmmaking* (1992), decisions regarding the films and filmmakers emphasized in his book were made with ease of access in mind.[5] At the same time as he acknowledges the problematic nature of shifting film canons, Williams concedes that in his analysis, "emphasis has been placed on films which can be seen without much difficulty."[6] Even Williams's title smartly points to the limitations of his project, creating "a history" as opposed to "the history" and choosing "filmmaking" over "film" to connote an emphasis on authorship in place of a comprehensive overview of all manner of national film production. Distribution of traditional art cinema spawns scholarship addressing the same set of films, which in turn reinforces distribution trends toward auteurist films moving forward. Subsequently, more scholarship is created on the same set of filmmakers, and so on and so forth.

Recently there has been a noticeable shift away from this closed system as broad histories of French cinema have made strides to seriously consider genre films alongside those made by the usual suspects of auteur directors. Wiley Blackwell's edited volume *A Companion to Contemporary French Cinema* (2015) includes sections relating to contemporary genre film and the current state of the national film industry, moving away from the self-consciously selective model of Alan Williams or the dense but equally selective history of Roy Armes's *French Cinema* (1985).[7] Rémi Fournier-Lanzoni's comprehensive *French Cinema: From Its Beginnings to the Present* (2002) provides a breath of fresh air as it deftly balances analysis of major auteurs and film movements with the sort of popular genre films that equally define the national cinema within France, giving readers a more complete account of film history from a French perspective as opposed to a cherry-picked overview based solely on the types of films that gain traction abroad.[8] Fournier-Lanzoni extends this project further with *French Comedy on Screen: A Cinematic History* (2014), providing a standalone history of the genre that implicitly argues for comedy's importance and unpacks the nuances of performance, narrative, and social commentary.[9] In both books, Fournier-Lanzoni considers the work of Francis Veber, but the scope of the projects inadvertently reduces his work to anecdotal or representative examples of broader trends in genre and national cinema.

In France, Veber's work has often been glossed over or even casually dismissed by scholars. Claude Beylie's *Une histoire du cinéma français* (2000) moves away from the strict narrative approach of most film histories to give an almost encyclopedic overview of French cinema, with standalone entries for various actors and directors.[10] Beylie includes an entry for Veber that highlights his popular success and the attention he has garnered from Hollywood.[11] This entry is fleeting and somewhat flippant, but Veber is included. The appearance of Veber reads like Beylie checking off boxes as he attempts to be as inclusive as possible; a brief detour from the book's broader project of handling genre films (*les policiers*, comedies) alongside auteurist art cinema and global Francophone film culture (Québec, Africa). René Prédal, on the other hand, trades in Beylie's descriptive approach for a fiercely evaluative assessment of Veber. Writing in 1984, Prédal discusses Veber alongside other writer-turned-directors Jean-Paul Rappeneau, Michel Audiard, and Jean-Charles Tacchela, only finding value in the directorial output of the latter.[12] When discussing the early '80s career turn of Gérard Depardieu, Prédal facetiously refers to Veber as an "immortal writer-director" following a screed where he laments actors being too stupid to judge the quality of their projects and collaborators.[13] For Prédal, Depardieu's decision to work with Veber on *La chèvre* and subsequent comedies is a tragic fall from grace after his previous collaborations with Marguerite Duras or Maurice Pialat. Prédal sees the pairing of Depardieu and Pierre Richard—the duo would make three films together for Veber—as "purely mathematical" economic calculations, seeing Veber and popular comedy as the best example of the dominance of commerce over art within 1980s French cinema.[14] Prédal's venom for Veber may easily be chalked up to broader critical sentiments toward comedy.

Fournier-Lanzoni makes the case that only two "pure" comedies have been awarded the César for Best Film and, therefore, the genre is looked down upon by both critics and the French film industry despite it being their "financial backbone."[15] Of course, this is not a uniquely French phenomenon. The César Awards were inaugurated in 1976 and in the same timeframe only one comedy has won the Academy Award for Best Picture (Woody Allen's *Annie Hall* in 1977).[16] The stark divide in scholarship, however, may be more indicative of the difference between perspectives on the importance of comedy in France and the U.S. As Fournier-Lanzoni writes, ". . . scholarly work on French comedies (non-silent, that is) is close to non-existent, except for rare works dealing mainly with particular auteurs such as Jacques Tati or Sacha Guitry."[17] Furthering his point later on, he states that, "French cinema, too often restricted to the work of a few 'masters' such as Truffaut or Renoir, sits uneasily between French literature and film studies, and it seems imperative to bridge this gap by turning some of the concerns and methods of current film studies toward comedy and popular culture."[18] Fournier-Lanzoni's history of French film comedy is an important first step, but more work needs to be done to bridge the gap.

ReFocus: The Films of Francis Veber strives to add detail and complexities to the above works, placing Veber in conversation with a broader history of both French and American cinema while providing concentrated analysis of his films. Although he is a major cinematic figure with wide name recognition, a book-length analysis of Veber has yet to be published. The scholarly neglect of his directorial career is at once confounding and predictable. Few directors have played such a prominent role in shaping the cinematic identity of France over the past forty years, yet his chosen genre of comedy has relegated his work to the margins of film studies. Veber's 2010 memoir *Que ça reste entre nous* (the title translates to "It stays between us") remains the only book-length publication dedicated to his career.[19] Lacking analysis and scholarly context, *Que ça reste entre nous* is yet to be published in translation, limiting its readership to French speakers. What I hope to accomplish in the following pages is to provide a long overdue academic treatment of Veber's career that also gives English speakers increased exposure to a writer-director who has had a pronounced impact on French cinema and shaped British and American consumption of French culture as well. Placing his career in a framework of high/low art debates and the contours of popular cinema in France, issues of taste, genre, canon, authorship, and cultural specificity will be major points of emphasis.

Veber serves as an ideal vessel for exploring the use of comedy to make social commentary and the interplay between globalization and cultural specificity due to both his commitment to working within the genre (all twelve of his directorial credits are comedies, as are the vast majority of his screenplays) and a unique career split between France and the U.S. Veber uses comedy to critique class and privilege, often through the prism of François Perrin/Pignon, a bumbling but good-hearted recurring character in his films. The political dimensions of Veber's films are central to how his work is read within France, where his films remain popular decades after their initial release. The cultural specificity of his work has led to an awkward global translation, as Hollywood studios often remake his films rather than distributing subtitled or dubbed versions of the originals. The nature of French comedy, steeped in cynicism and absurdity, is often incompatible with the tastes of an American audience, yet the success of Veber in France has provided Hollywood with the hope that his scenarios (and later his directorial approach) could be molded to fit American tastes. A central figure in a national cinema that has fought to remain significant and independent in the face of Hollywood's encroachment, Veber alternately speaks to the viability of comedies made for a domestic French audience and the pull of money and recognition provided by American studios. Regardless of Veber's sojourn in Hollywood and the large body of American adaptations of his screenplays, he is undoubtedly French through self-definition, cultural sensibilities, and reputation. Still, he is critically underexplored relative to the reach of his work.

The idea for this book coincided with conversations and conflicts in teaching a French Cinema course for undergraduates. In looking to craft a syllabus that gave students a rigorous understanding of a national cinema without falling into the familiar traps of exclusivity, I wanted to balance the greatest hits of auteurist filmmaking with popular genre films rarely seen outside of France, much less explored in the context of an American university classroom. Veber's films became a useful entry point for addressing comedy, domestic box office, and the international ambitions of French screen artists and studios. Pointing to the past, the success of his films and their continued place in the national imagination recall mainstays like *La grande vadrouille* and *Les tontons flingueurs* (1963, Georges Lautner). At the same time, his career foregrounds massive domestic hits like *Bienvenue chez les Ch'tis* (2008, Dany Boon) and *Qu'est-ce qu'on a fait au Bon Dieu* (2014, Philippe de Chauveron) both in finding financial success at home in the face of competition from big budget imports, and in the inability to fully translate humor and social context to a global audience. Ultimately, using Veber in the course became part of a much broader conversation about the ways in which national cinemas get defined, reduced, and dismissed within academia.

As an undergraduate I took a global survey of film history that, in essence, encapsulated the recurring tensions of studying national cinemas from an American perspective. The course was taught by a respected scholar deeply invested in the auteurist debates that had shaped his entry into the discipline during the 1960s and 1970s. Along with formal analysis and contemplation of stylistic hallmarks came an embedded evaluation of films and filmmakers, mimicking Andrew Sarris's preoccupation with lists and hierarchies. The sense of argumentation and declarations about value at the heart of this brand of auteurist film studies was invigorating to me as a student, but it also showed glaring weaknesses when evaluating work located outside of the established critical canon. One comment remains seared into my mind and informs the way I think about and teach national cinemas. In addressing South Asian cinema this professor said, "India makes more films per year than any other country in the world, but aside from Satyajit Ray they're all terrible, so you don't have to worry about them." That was the entirety of the semester's discussion of Indian cinema. Apparently, from this professor's vantage point at least, Ray's films embody the sophistication and aesthetic richness of European art cinema while the thousands upon thousands of other films made in India are low-budget, formulaic genre trash. In a single sentence the massive body of Bollywood films, to say nothing of the linguistic, cultural, and aesthetic complexities of regional Indian production, had been firmly dismissed. That a national cinema as exciting and complicated as India's could be so easily misrepresented by an otherwise thoughtful scholar made me question the viability of our approach to understanding and defining global film culture.

Keep in mind that this was in the early 2000s, right on the cusp of important works by Tejaswini Ganti, Ranjani Mazumdar, and others who have created a subsequent flood of scholarship on Indian cinema that has either put an end to such thinking or at least exposed it as outmoded and uninformed. This wave of scholarship has not only redressed past omissions by filling in gaps, but has also challenged the criteria for critical investigation by opening up film studies to genres, regions, and modes of production once deemed unworthy of inquiry. I am not presumptuous enough to think that this book will cause the sort of sea change in academic inquiry that followed the work of Ganti and Mazumdar, but I do hope to play a small role in expanding the parameters of scholarship on French genre cinema. Francis Veber's career is long overdue for analysis and it is time that his films, and screen comedy as a whole, are taken seriously.

It is important to clarify what this book is and is not. Biographical details will be interwoven into the analysis, but this is not a long-form biography of Francis Veber. Nor is it a comprehensive guide to every screenplay he has written or his frustrations working with various directors, although his experiences working solely as a screenwriter will appear when relevant. While there will be contextual information to help situate my readings of individual films, this book is not a history of the French film industry, comedy as a genre, or French popular culture in the aftermath of the student protests of May 1968. Instead, this book is organized around textual analyses of each of Veber's twelve directorial credits. A comparative analysis of American remakes will be included to examine the nature of transnational adaptation and Veber's ongoing frustration with Hollywood in contrast to his self-contained model of writing and directing his own films. In the case of *L'emmerdeur*, Veber's directorial effort will be placed in conversation with its cinematic predecessors. But rather than opening *in medias res* with Veber's 1976 film *Le jouet*—a film he made when he was 39 years old, and more than a decade into his career as a writer—a brief overview of his background will help to situate the chapters that follow.

VEBER BECOMES A WRITER

Francis Veber was born on July 28, 1937 in the affluent Paris suburb of Neuilly to a Jewish father and an Armenian mother.[20] Shaped by World War II and the Nazi occupation of Paris, Veber's earliest memories of his father consist of a depressed man in pajamas living in hiding lest he should be caught and sent to a death camp.[21] This developmental understanding of identity would eventually transform into a connection between persecution and humor that informs Veber's writing and worldview. As the second sentence of his memoir states, "Deux génocides, deux murs des lamentations dans le sang, tout pour faire un comique" ("Two genocides, two walls of lamentations in the blood, all make a comic").[22] More than a defense mechanism, the interconnectedness of humor and such intense pain suggests that Veber fully understands comedy's potential to be political, serious, and resistant. His films ruminate over deep emotional pain and alienation, but manage to read as cheerful and optimistic. Being able to compartmentalize pain, expressing it in the subtext while crafting commercially viable material, is just one of the ways in which his sophistication as a writer is evident. It would be difficult to overestimate the impact for Veber of having key years of his childhood development take place during World War II. If the pain of the Holocaust would manifest into a defensive impulse for humor and a fondness for outsider characters, the aftermath of the war can equally be seen in his future work. Marshall Plan aid and the U.S. military presence in the 1950s and 1960s brought American money, soldiers, and culture to France, leaving a legacy of simultaneous goodwill, suspicion, and resentment toward Americans. Of course, Veber had to become a writer first before finding a way to use his experience and surroundings to craft a career's work.

The ability and inclination to write did not happen by accident. Both of Veber's parents were writers, as were his grandfather, uncle, and great-uncle.[23] It was an intellectual household where politics were passionately discussed and a stream of visitors livened the conversation. It was also a household where he saw the struggles and financial uncertainties of writing as a profession. Francis describes himself during his school years as a weakling who struggled in math, gravitating toward languages and philosophy instead.[24] Despite his inclination toward the humanities, Veber chose to pursue the sciences after *lycée* and studied to become a surgeon, devoting four years toward learning science and medicine at the Bercy Institute in Paris before realizing that a life as a doctor was not for him.[25] Veber then joined the army, and it was there that he became a writer, working as a journalist for the military magazine *Bled* while stationed in Algeria.[26] Veber reviled the "imbecilic machismo" of officers and, instead, found camaraderie with other likeminded army journalists who shared his anti-military sentiments.[27] One of his fellow journalists was army photographer Just Jaeckin, the future film director who would become best known for making the transformative softcore hits *Emmanuelle* (1974) and *Histoire d'O* (1975). As Veber remembers, "he seemed to be the least complicated of us all, and . . . without a doubt the most happy."[28] The same could probably be said for Jaeckin as a director in the anxiety-riddled French film industry of the 1970s.

Upon leaving the army Veber wrote for the magazine *Lui*, describing it as a sort of French answer to *Playboy*.[29] It was there that he met his wife Françoise; they first worked together on an interview with the legendary actor Jean Gabin.[30] Eventually shifting to Radio Luxembourg, Veber never regarded the time he spent as a journalist during his late twenties as anything resembling his life's calling.[31] As he would remember four decades later, "I was a very bad journalist."[32] Perhaps this was because he was simultaneously working as a journalist and planning to write for other mediums and formats, co-writing a musical comedy for the radio and publishing short stories in the mid-1960s before moving into television and theatre by the end of the decade.[33] He was credited as a writer on the swinging television detective series *Agence Intérim* in 1969, and staged his first play at the Théâtre Édouard VII the year before. The play, *L'enlèvement*, was a modest success, running for six months.[34] Rather than exceptional pieces of writing, his work on television and for the stage between 1968 and 1969 serve as the nexus to his cinematic career. While writing for *Agence Intérim* he met the comic actor Pierre Richard, another future collaborator in film director Édouard Molinaro, and, through Molinaro, Gaumont producer Alain Poiré.[35] *L'enlèvement*, on the other hand, made the transition into the realm of movies more explicit when it was adapted into a feature film as *Appelez-moi Mathilde* (1969, Pierre Mondy, *Call Me Mathilde*).

A transnational co-production between the French company Mondex and Columbia Pictures, *Appelez-moi Mathilde* revolves around the abduction of a wealthy woman (Jacqueline Maillan) by a gang of fumbling criminals. Curiously, it is the only major work of Veber's career organized around a central female character. Its stage origins are abundantly clear as the vast majority of the action takes place within a single confined space, a country barn that serves as a hideout for the criminals. The plot touches on Cold War paranoia and class divisions, but Veber's play largely serves as a venue for broad comedy consisting of ethnic caricatures—Chinese, Spanish, and rural American stereotypes are all present—and slapstick sound effects to accompany physical gags. Veber's subsequent penchant for dark humor and fixation on suicide appear in *Appelez-moi Mathilde*, as does the character name François, which would eventually transform into his recurring François Perrin/Pignon character. Veber wrote the screenplay alongside director Pierre Mondy and while the film laid the groundwork for his subsequent projects, it was far from the big break that made everything else possible. "It was not very good," Veber would recall in a 1981 interview with Christian Salé, "and I had to wait three years before I was able to work again."[36] Not sitting by idly until film opportunities presented themselves, Veber staged his own play *Le contrat* in 1969 (later to be adapted for screen and retitled *L'emmerdeur*) and wrote the French stage adaptation of British playwright Alan Ayckbourn's *How the Other Half Loves*, which was staged in Paris as *Du côté de chez l'autre* in 1971.

If waiting three years for another screen credit was painful, the payoff was certainly worthwhile. *Le grand blond avec une chaussure noire* (1972, Yves Robert, *The Tall Blond Man with One Black Shoe*) became a major box office success, selling 3.4 million tickets in France.[37] It garnered interest outside of France as well, making Veber an in-demand screenwriter. Starring Pierre Richard as François Perrin, an innocent concert violinist unwittingly caught in the middle of an espionage power play, the comedy is premised on misunderstandings and double entendre.[38] Perrin is picked at random to serve as a red herring for police surveillance when coming down an airport escalator at Orly, wearing mismatched shoes (hence the film's title) and carrying a violin case. Thought to be a master spy, this common man stumbles his way through a series of close calls and projections on the part of those spying on him to create the false impression of intrigue, mastery, and malevolence. One example comes when Perrin talks to a fellow musician on the phone about a concert in Munich where he "butchered Prokofiev," which is then taken by the secret police to suggest he is an assassin who was hired to kill a high-ranking Soviet official. The film's commentary on Cold War paranoia is far more developed and focused than in *Appelez-moi Mathilde*, but it is also a didactic address of the growing surveillance state and threats to privacy. In case the audience misses the point of the narrative, the film ends with text on the screen showing a passage from Article 9 of France's penal code ("Chacun a le droit au respect de sa vie privée" or "Everyone has the right to respect for his or her private life").

The incompetent criminals and hit men that populate *Le grand blond avec une chaussure noire* bring to mind both the gallows humor and fixation on gangster tropes of comedies like *Les tontons flingueurs*, but there are distinct elements that reflect Veber's style and sensibilities. Yet the film does not belong to Veber, either within the traditional conditions of film authorship residing with the director or his memory of the project. "I didn't like the director," Veber would say about Yves Robert three decades later.[39] "It's bad to say bad things about someone who's dead," he explains with a mischievous humor, "but at the same time I don't risk anything now."[40] When Gaumont asked for a sequel, however, Veber agreed to continue his association with Robert and share writing credit with the director. *Le retour du grand blond*

(1974, *The Return of the Tall Blond Man*) moves away from political commentary to satirize James Bond films and repeats gags from the initial film, this time having Perrin's foot fall into a bucket of red paint at the airport to mirror the mismatched shoe from two years earlier. This element of the sequel partly explains the title change when *Le grand blond avec une chaussure noire* was remade by Twentieth Century Fox as *The Man with One Red Shoe* (1985, Stan Dragoti).

In the immediate aftermath of his success with *Le grand blond*, Veber was constantly working. His 1971 stage play *Le contrat* was adapted to the screen in 1973 as *L'emmerdeur* by Édouard Molinaro, beginning a long line of collaborations between Veber and the director that include the dramatic comedy about labor negotiations *Le téléphone rose* (1975), their screen adaptation of Jean Poiret's play *La cage aux folles* (1978), and the sequel *La cage aux folles II* (1980). Veber liked Molinaro personally, but the professional frustrations he had with Yves Robert were just as pronounced with Molinaro. From Veber's standpoint, Molinaro required a finished screenplay to begin working and was unable to shape the material beyond what was already there on the page.[41] Veber would also write the screenplay for the detective film *Adieu Poulet* (1975, Pierre Granier-Deferre, *The French Detective*) starring Lino Ventura, and declined screen credit for the Jean-Paul Belmondo spy spoof *Le magnifique* (1973, Philippe de Broca, *The Man from Acapulco*). Unhappy with the latter, Veber would remark that denying the use of his name is "the only recourse left to a writer when the film adaptation is bad."[42]

Refusing to have his name appear in the credits, much less feeling that it was his only form of agency as a screenwriter, speaks to his growing frustrations. Veber claims to have written eighteen screenplays before *Le jouet* in 1976, all of them earmarked for other directors and only some of them realized on screen.[43] More importantly, he found the collaborative relationship between writers and directors untenable. "I didn't have any close relationships with directors," Veber explains. "It's why I started directing myself."[44] Reflecting on the solitary practice of writing and his growing displeasure at handing his creations off to someone else, he says, "I was always frustrated by what the directors were doing with my movies. Not saying that I would have done better, you know, but I would be closer to my music. The music I have in my mind when I'm writing."[45] After reading Veber's screenplay for *Le jouet* his friend Claude Berri, a film director, urged him to take the plunge and start directing his own material. As Veber recalls, he took Berri's advice to heart "and my life changed completely."[46]

NOTES

1. François Truffaut's *L'homme qui aimait les femmes* (1977) was remade as *The Man Who Loved Women* (1983, Blake Edwards) by Columbia as a vehicle for Burt Reynolds. Jean-Luc Godard's *À bout de souffle* (1960) received a more artistically ambitious, albeit misguided, Hollywood treatment with *Breathless* (1983, Jim McBride) starring Richard Gere.
2. Andrew Sarris, *The American Cinema: Directors and Directions, 1929–1968*.
3. Ibid. p. 166.
4. John Patterson, "Billy Wilder, Still Less Than Meets the Eye." *The Guardian*, June 8, 2012.
5. Alan Williams, *Republic of Images: A History of French Filmmaking*, p. 4.
6. Ibid.
7. Alistair Fox et al. (eds.), *A Companion to Contemporary French Cinema*; Roy Armes, *French Cinema*.
8. Rémi Fournier-Lanzoni, *French Cinema: From Its Beginnings to the Present*.
9. Rémi Fournier-Lanzoni, *French Comedy on Screen: A Cinematic History*.
10. Claude Beylie, *Une histoire du cinéma français*.
11. Ibid. p. 510.
12. René Prédal, *Le Cinéma français contemporain*, p. 68.
13. Ibid. p. 187.
14. Ibid. p. 193.
15. Fournier-Lanzoni, *French Comedy*, p. 1.
16. The two comedies to win the César for Best Film actually happened in consecutive years with *Les ripoux* (1984, Claude Zidi) and *Trois hommes et un couffin* (1985, Coline Serreau).
17. Fournier-Lanzoni, *French Comedy*, p. 3.
18. Ibid. p. 13.
19. Francis Veber, *Que ça reste entre nous*.
20. Veber, *Que ça reste entre nous*, p. 7.
21. *A Conversation with Francis Veber* (DVD), The Writers Guild of America, 2009.
22. Veber, *Que ça reste entre nous*, p. 7.
23. Ibid. pp. 7–8.
24. Ibid. pp. 26–33.
25. Ibid. p. 47.
26. Ibid. p. 55.
27. Ibid. p. 54.
28. Ibid. pp. 56–7.
29. Ibid. p. 58.
30. Ibid. pp. 58–9.
31. Ibid. p. 61.
32. *A Conversation with Francis Veber*.
33. Veber, *Que ça reste entre nous*, pp. 58–9.
34. Ibid. p. 93.
35. Ibid. pp. 79–81.
36. Christian Salé, *Les scénaristes au travail*, p. 110.
37. Fournier-Lanzoni, *French Comedy*, p. 171.
38. Apologies to French friends for using the English corruption *double entendre* instead of *double sens*. Désolé!
39. *A Conversation with Francis Veber*.

40. Ibid.

41. Ibid.

42. Salé, *Les scénaristes au travail*, p. 4. Veber states, *"C'est le seul recours pour un auteur qui n'est pas d'accord avec le film tire de son scenario."*

43. *A Conversation with Francis Veber.*

44. Ibid.

45. Ibid.

46. Ibid.

CHAPTER 2

Toy Story: *Le jouet* (1976)

In 1964 Francis Veber was sent out to write a piece about toys for the army publication *Bled*.[1] Taking photographs at a product showcase, Veber came across a boy around ten years old who was not interested in any of the toys on display. Instead, the boy was staring directly at him. Not knowing anything about the boy or the reason for his gaze, Veber's mind filled in the blanks by imagining that the child was the son of a millionaire who, if he wanted to, could point to the journalist and have his father purchase him. It was a thought that filled Veber with fear, premised only from a child's stare and an odd indifference to being surrounded by toys. "The child didn't buy me," Veber recalls, "but the subject of *Le jouet* was born."[2]

That this passing moment resonated with Veber so powerfully, staying with him for more than a decade before he used it as the foundation of a screenplay, suggests more than a writer's need to cultivate personal experiences to craft stories. The lasting impression from this moment at the toy showcase signifies a profound sense of injustice bound to class division that reflects the political landscape of the years in which *Le jouet* was in creative gestation. The May 1968 demonstrations are the most visible manifestation of broader disaffection with de Gaulle, contemporary capitalism, and the power dynamics of daily life in France. The protests were also a venue for self-examination that can be seen in films, novels, plays, and music produced in France both before and after May '68. The concerns over modern capitalism's role in limiting critical thought and the diminished avenues for dissent permeate the era's rhetoric, with both the press and the arts as key institutions vulnerable to corporate power and state control. France in the late 1960s was alternately without progress and progressing too fast, lacking effective redress of poverty, sexism, racism, and educational failures while reshaping the country into a simulacrum of the United States in its architecture, infrastructure, and consumer culture. Didactic examples like *2 ou 3 choses que je sais d'elle . . .* (1967, Jean-Luc Godard, *2 or 3 Things I Know About Her . . .*) crystallize the combative nature of auteur directors toward the atmosphere of modern France. From the film's opening shot, capturing the construction of a highway overpass, to the final frame of consumer products systematically arranged on a grass lawn, Godard's commentary continually intersects with the political and social influence of the United States. The landscape of Paris, particularly its suburban fringes, was being transformed to look like America while its people were urged to act and think like Americans.

More than the commentaries of a handful of *nouvelle vague* filmmakers in the limited milieu of 1968, Alison Smith argues in *French Cinema in the 1970s: Echoes of May* that the demonstrations of that year caused a cultural revolution, changing what mainstream audiences saw in the years to follow.[3] Relaxed censorship and an altered mass consciousness brought with them films that carried on the legacy of May '68 well into the following decade through formal experimentation, leftist political commentary, and the boom in softcore pornography.[4] As the title of her book suggests, the 1970s were defined by the protests of the 1960s and its films were constantly grappling with the ideas and conflicts central to the uprising.

Smith outlines three themes that are prominent in the discourse of post-May '68 French cinema. First, "the possibility of destruction of hierarchical structures of society and of certain redistribution of power towards the base."[5] This, of course, is not limited to state power but also encompasses corporations and cultural institutions. Second, Smith points to "the famous desire for *prise de parole* on the part of those for whom others 'spoke,' articulated mischievously by one of the Sorbonne graffiti: '*Je ne sais pas quoi dire, mais j'ai envie de le dire.*'"[6] The sentiment of the graffiti (translated: "I don't know what to say, but I want to say it") within the context of filmmakers and the movie industry equates to a call for expanded access to the materials and means for using cinema as a medium for free expression. Third, Smith points to 1970s French cinema's recurring "notion that 'everything is political,' that the economic system and structures of power relations extend to cultural and sexual life and are to be combated there as well as in the workplace."[7] The idea that "everything is political" extends beyond the auteurist works at the heart of Smith's analysis (those of Godard, Chris Marker, William Klein, and Alain Tanner) and, instead, suggests a need for close readings of a wide spectrum of films from the era.

Comedy would play a central role in capturing the mood of France in the 1970s. As Fournier-Lanzoni observes, French comedies of the decade "appeared as a much more transparent medium since its thematic content translated not only the state of mind of an eventful era but also, uniquely, the physical and emotional background of contemporary society."[8] As *Le grand blond avec une chaussure noire* illustrates, the satirizing of Cold War paranoia and the growing surveillance state is strengthened through the visceral connection to a character's victimization, using Pierre Richard's performance as a physical embodiment of an entire nation being unknowingly spied upon and used as pawns. Despite the film's overt political commentary, Veber's relationship to the wave of protest that changed France is not particularly strong. His films show an interest in class struggle and the dispossessed, but as Veber acknowledges in his memoir, he completely missed the May '68 protests.[9] Instead, he was holed up in isolation writing the play *L'enlèvement*. Nevertheless, his body of work functions as a window into the changing national political tenor throughout the years. Each of his films uses a contemporary setting, never delving into period piece reflection or speculative visions of the future. His films are of their time and, as such, channel the key issues and conflicts surrounding the eras in which they were made.

Reading Veber as a political filmmaker follows both Smith's argument that for French cinema in the aftermath of May '68 "everything is political" and Fournier-Lazoni's claims about the unique position of comedy to make social commentary, but it deviates from broader historical overviews of Europe in the 1970s. As Tony Judt argues in *Postwar: A History of Europe Since 1945*, the ideological concerns and political activism of the 1960s were lost in the 1970s as unemployment and the aging of student protesters replaced communal concerns with self-interest.[10] Judt's observation is not another hand-wringing critique of the Me Generation's vapid narcissism, but rather an appreciation of the seriousness of the economic climate. For a generation of young people entering adulthood who grew up enjoying the growth and prosperity of the postwar "miracle" years, the economic downturn of the 1970s, defined by job insecurity, inflation, and stagflation, was particularly distressing. Rather than seeing the broadly defined goals of the 1960s and the more localized concerns of the 1970s as mutually exclusive, French cinema in the aftermath of the May events suggest the melding of the two. This mix of revolutionary rhetoric from the 1960s and the very personal concerns of the 1970s are the contextual backbone of *Le jouet*. The film and its central character simultaneously seek to speak truth to power and argue that everyone should be afforded the opportunity to make a living.

LE FILM

After writing both *Le grand blond avec une chaussure noire* and *Le retour du grand blond*, the connection between Veber and the comedic actor Pierre Richard had been firmly established both professionally and within the public imagination.

Figure 2.1 François Perrin (Pierre Richard) expresses his solidarity with a subjugated Sioux chief (Paul Horn).

In fact, when Gaumont suggested a sequel to *Le grand blond* it was director Yves Robert who took convincing, not Veber or Richard.[11] Curiously, considering Richard and Veber's decade-long professional connection, the actor refers to Yves Robert as the possessive figure when describing *Le grand blond*, not the writer, highlighting deeply held assumptions about film authorship.[12] Veber has stated that his writing is not only done in isolation, but that he crafts stories without thinking about the particulars of the film adaptation.[13] If Veber's claims are to be believed, the story and the characters exist on the page free from the needs of a studio or the sensibilities of possible collaborators. Obviously, this was not the case with *Le retour du grand blond* and it does not reflect his propensity as a director to write characters with particular actors in mind. For *Le jouet*, as a case in point, the screenplay was envisioned and executed for Pierre Richard.[14]

Three years Veber's senior, Richard was born in 1934 and followed in his family's theatrical footsteps, making his way to television and film through the success of earlier performances in music halls and cabaret theatre. Fournier-Lanzoni connects Richard to the burlesque elements at the heart of Jacques Tati, Charles Chaplin, and Max Linder's screen personas and physical comedy.[15] Like them, Richard is a director as well as an actor, working behind the camera on seven films, starring in all of them, and contributing to the screenplays. Nevertheless, he has never been granted the same status as an auteur performer.[16] Richard does not see himself as a continuation of Tati, but instead envisions his comedy in the mode of American performers like Danny Kaye, Jerry Lewis, and the Marx Brothers.[17] His success in the early 1970s came amid the deaths of French comedic icons Bourvil (who died in 1970) and Fernandel (who passed in 1971) and the end of Tati's presence on the screen (his last theatrically released film, *Trafic*, came in 1971), allowing Richard to fill the void as France's premier comedic actor.[18] Richard's performances are physical and chaotic, but underpinned by human frailty. Often oblivious to the surrounding world, Richard's characters have a tendency to leave a wake of destruction in their path. *Le jouet* is a rare instance where his impact on the world around him is calculated and controlled. It is also a rare instance of restraint in a Richard performance, coming after a contentious start to shooting with Veber having to disabuse the actor of his clownish tendencies.[19]

Contradicting Veber's claim that a conversation with Claude Berri prompted him to step behind the camera and direct his own screenplay, Richard assumes credit for the decision by recalling his own urging being the key factor in Veber taking on dual roles with *Le jouet*. Reading the screenplay, Richard says that he found the material to be profoundly original and impossible to fully realize by another director, so he recalls telling Veber, "You're never satisfied with the directors of the films you write." Remembering making a direct plea, Richard claims to have followed up this observation by telling Veber, "Do it yourself."[20] Regardless of whether the suggestion came from Berri or Richard, the decision to direct *Le jouet* himself placed Veber in an unfamiliar role of having to conceptualize performance, cinematography, and *mise en scène* as well as narrative and dialogue. Upon the suggestion that he direct, Veber remembers protesting that he didn't "know anything" about filmmaking, but Berri reassured him by saying, "It's not important. We're going to choose a good technical advisor and everything will go well."[21] This sense that commitment to the material could supersede technical knowledge and directing experience not only freed Veber to step behind the camera for *Le jouet*, but informs the stripped-down aesthetics of his body of work as a director.

Having been most closely linked to Yves Robert and Édouard Molinaro as collaborators, Veber's visual style is much closer to Robert. Long takes and traditional editing between characters in medium shots and close-ups replace the frenetic handheld camera of Molinaro's films, showing that although Veber did not personally like Robert, he did appreciate his approach to directing comedy in a manner that foregrounds performance and dialogue. While the camera placements are conventional, Veber's approach on set was to workshop each scene in the moment. As Richard explains, it was as if Veber needed the "whirring of the cameras" to start conceptualizing and refining performance, turning the film set into a theatrical stage through constant blocking, notes on inflection, and repetition that typically reached upwards of thirty takes.[22] His penchant for multiple takes did not follow an improvisational approach, but rather exhibited a playwright's perfection in communicating dialogue and tone. Veber's directorial approach is to shape performances rather than have performances reshape his writing.

The story of *Le jouet* revolves around an out-of-work journalist named François Perrin (Pierre Richard) and the levels of degradation inherent in modern corporate culture. Having been out of work for over a year, Perrin interviews for a position at *France Hebdo*, a weekly magazine owned by billionaire Pierre Rambal-Cochet (Michel Bouquet). Bearded at the beginning of the film, Perrin is asked by the interviewer to shave in order to conform to the corporate expectations. It is a small indignity that presages more to come. Having been hired, Perrin observes the cruelties and arbitrary nature of labor under Rambal-Cochet, with one of his colleagues at the magazine fired for having sweaty hands when greeting his billionaire boss. Perrin reports on a meeting of business executives led by Rambal-Cochet before being asked to write a story about the season's newest toys, requiring a visit to a department store also owned by Rambal-Cochet. Inside the store, Perrin is spotted by Eric (Fabrice Greco), the billionaire's young son. Eric has been sent by his father to choose anything in the store he wants, flanked by seven mid-level executives. In an act of defiance, Eric points his finger at Perrin and says simply, "Ça." After briefly trying to reason with the child, the executive in charge (Michel Aumont) gives in to the child's demand and negotiates with Perrin to come home with the child as his personal toy. Fearing that he will lose his job, Perrin agrees. Entering the Rambal-Cochet mansion packed in a wooden crate, Perrin is asked to serve as a personal plaything for a spoiled and mean-spirited child, going so far as to adopt the name Julien at the child's request. The journalist shows resentment and defiance toward Eric, but develops a level of empathy over time as he understands that the child has been emotionally neglected by his father, with material gifts meant to substitute for parental love. Together, Perrin and Eric vent their frustrations by making their own self-published newspaper (named "Le jouet"), serving as investigative reporters to expose the numerous personal and professional misdeeds of Eric's father. The arrangement ends, and Eric runs away to be with Perrin rather than return to boarding school. The final scene of the film shows the billionaire picking up his son in a limousine and explaining to Eric that Perrin is "nothing." Eric opens the door to the car and runs back to Perrin on the sidewalk, leaping into his arms. Perrin looks back at Rambal-Cochet with one arm extended as if to ask, "What can I say? The child chooses me." Ending in a freeze frame, the shot is a physical exclamation left for the spectator to ponder as the credits roll.

The choice of the common man over vicious affluence is the culmination of a commentary on wealth and corporate culture that is embedded throughout, beginning with the opening shot of *Le jouet*. Mounted on a rooftop to capture an image of the Eiffel Tower from the distance of a few blocks, the camera pans right to find a slim white pennant flag flapping in the wind with a black hexagonal logo and the letters "FH." Tilting down to show the side of the four-story building, the camera finds a figure walking into the large entrance. On the surface this appears to be a simple establishing shot, unambiguously placing the setting as Paris while using the FH logo to announce that the building is the headquarters of *France Hebdo* with the central character walking inside the front door. This is a function of the shot, of course, but there is also symbolic value to the simple pan. Shifting the image from the Eiffel Tower to an old building that is now the headquarters of a corporate holding, branded with a flag on top, there is the suggestion that national identity is being replaced by corporate identity. The image is just one instance where Veber displays an understanding of visual language that complements his dialogue, using symbols and motifs to reinforce the story's themes. Veber has expressed an admiration of Orson Welles and his use of *mise en scène* to convey meaning, and *Le jouet* displays Veber's most ambitious use of symbolic visuals.[23]

The axis of the film's conflict, both external and internal, comes in the interview scene. Sitting down with body language expressing the anxiety and awkwardness of the job applicant, Perrin is caught off guard by the first question. After lighting a cigarette, *France Hebdo*'s editor-in-chief, Blénac (Jacques François) dryly asks Perrin, "Do you have much affection for your beard?" Perrin is confused, leading Blénac to clarify by saying, "I advise you to shave it off. Mr. Rambal-Cochet doesn't like beards." Perrin attempts both humor and tentative resolve by responding, "Maybe a good journalist can carry off a beard." Blénac admonishes him, explaining that the magazine's culture is completely under the control of Rambal-Cochet, and Veber uses a hard cut to clean-shaven Perrin riding in a *France Hedbo* car on his first day at work to emphasize his capitulation. The brevity of the interview has comedic effect, but its arbitrary nature gives voice to the sense of frustration in Perrin's later admission that he had been out of work for seventeen months by showing that all he had to do was show up at *France Hebdo*. There are no questions about his background or qualifications, nor is there a discussion of what type of work he will be doing for the magazine. Only his facial hair is discussed.

The demand is part of a power play, reinforced by the symbols of power on Blénac's desk, from his gold cigarette case to his ridiculously large lighter. Blénac's insistence that Perrin shave his beard not only touches on the arbitrary power plays in corporate culture, but also speaks to the continued resistance to countercultural fashion by elder power figures. Pierre Richard's distinctive blond locks are even more untamed here than in other films, creating an impression along with the beard that Perrin is either an eccentric or a radical despite wearing a suit. His willingness to compromise his appearance for the sake of expediency is understandable given his joblessness, but this small indignity will be followed by others. It is not the first compromise for Perrin, however. Before being called in to speak with Blénac, Perrin sits on a couch in the waiting area looking over back issues of the magazine he hopes to join as a writer. He flips through the pages quickly, looking for something of interest, only to be disappointed with the content. For Perrin, simply finding himself at this office is an indignity, working for an uninspiring weekly magazine owned by a vast conglomerate. As he soon finds out, his fears are well founded as the corporate control of the magazine interferes with his ability to work as a legitimate journalist.

Perrin's first assignment is to cover a business banquet for Rambal-Cochet managers and executives being held outside of one of his factories. The long shot establishing the setting recalls images from Ozu, Antonioni, and Godard showing the stark lifelessness of postwar industrial landscapes. Men in suits standing around a long table, showing moneyed traditions tied to the past forming an awkward alliance with modernism, with the shot serving as a gag in and of itself, echoing the absurdist imagery of Fellini, Buñuel, and Tati. The composition of the establishing shot is compelling, but ultimately an afterthought to a gag that dominates the scene. Seated at three long tables, the guests are served their meals while they wait for Rambal-Cochet to arrive. When the billionaire finally arrives he seats himself at the head of the long center table, his chair a meter away from the edge. Rather than adjusting his chair to get closer to the table, he pulls the table closer, leaving the rest of the guests to scramble to match their plates and drinks to the altered place settings. Fearful of the man's power, no one questions the move or readjusts the table. Here, the desire of one supersedes the needs of many. Seated at the table, Perrin is disgusted but fails to act, his silence coming in the service of self-interest. His character—which would transform into François Pignon in subsequent films—is an innocent in many respects, but also complicit. At their best, Veber's films blur the lines between right and wrong to transcend being simple morality tales. Veber has expressed his admiration for Frank Capra, but his films depart from Capra's sincerity and straightforward object lessons.[24] The premise of purchasing a man to be a child's plaything is not an uncomplicated transaction with one party in the right while the other is being wronged. This moves away from Pierre Richard's belief that audiences identify with his performances because he symbolizes the oppressed, victimized, and innocent.[25] In Le jouet he represents all three, but he also slips into their converse roles, becoming at times an oppressor, victimizer, and guilty.

Perrin shows complicity in how power is conceptualized and enacted. Before being spotted in the department store by Eric, Perrin and his photographer are given a tour of the toy section. Pointing out toys manufactured in Japan, Italy, England, and the U.S., the store's saleswoman stops upon what she calls "an authentic American Indian." It is a living, breathing man of Sioux heritage brought to France (and then the department store) from the Dakotas. He is wearing a feathered headdress and standing still enough to be confused for one of the store's mannequins. Continuing, the manager states that, "there are only a few left in stock." If this is a joke about the extermination of indigenous people in the Americas, it is in poor taste. If it is a genuine statement about the man being for sale, it is just as bad. The photographer points out that it is the same Sioux man who had protested against the U.S. government a few months earlier. That action, presumably, led to his subjugation. Perrin laughs nervously and approaches the man, making a peace sign before shaking his hand and doing his best to communicate. Speaking slowly and mixing French with his limited English, Perrin says, "Américain mauvais, bad! Indien good, bon! I am with you." The handshake lingers and Perrin struggles to break free of the embrace, making it clear that his show of solidarity has limitations. Once Eric stumbles upon Perrin and the executive explains that the child wants him to serve as his personal toy, there is a moment of frustration and confusion. Perrin paces in the store, glancing at the Sioux man standing across the aisle, and instinctively pleads to the executive, "He doesn't want the Indian?" The show of solidarity just moments earlier, linking the leftist journalist to a broader global struggle against oppression, disappears as his instinct for self-preservation takes over. When presented with the possibility of being subjugated, Perrin attempts to assert his white privilege. The American Indian, he assumes, would be more amenable to subjugation. In this moment, despite his statements to the contrary, Perrin abandons his progressive worldview. It is a role reversal gag, but the joke has serious ramifications.

The film is preoccupied with role-playing and the fluidity of outward identity. From Perrin assuming the name of Julien to the multiple iterations of dress-up and playacting, Eric and his friend-for-hire make a habit of escaping from their reality through costume and performance. Unlike childish masquerading, there are consequences to these performances. When the two drive around inside the mansion in a go-kart, Eric forces Perrin to pretend to be a traffic cop and humiliate one of the butlers. Hesitant to perform as a policeman, Perrin soon relishes the role, taking it a step beyond Eric's imagined scenario by arresting the child and locking him inside of a cupboard. Perrin finds freedom in performing a character to combat the child's cruelty, using the role-play scenario as a tool of defiance. At the same time, there is a sense that Perrin loses himself momentarily and relishes the power, albeit impermanent. Perrin plays another role, forced to wear a cowboy costume for horse riding lessons and, later, during a garden party for rich and influential friends of Rambal-Cochet. On the way to the riding lesson, Perrin fully understands the implications of outward appearance when he steps out of the car in the middle of Paris, intent on leaving behind Rambal-Cochet and Eric for good, only to find himself outside of the same department store from earlier and face to face with the Sioux man. From professing to be "with" him when they met to wearing the clothes of his oppressor, Perrin's transformation is complete.

Yet the Western wear can also be used to counteract power, providing Perrin with plausible deniability to get revenge as he and Eric ruin the garden party under the guise of playing. Coinciding with a union protest that is kept safely at bay behind the gates of the estate, Perrin's use of destructive performance is far more effectual than traditional protest.

The most developed role-play scenario in the film surrounds Perrin and Eric pretending to be journalists. By starting an underground newspaper that will speak truth to power, Perrin reverses his first compromise of the film in agreeing to write for an apolitical corporate mouthpiece like *France Hebdo*. With Eric as the editor and Perrin as lead reporter, the duo publish an exposé of the scandalous personal life and business practices of Rambal-Cochet. Eric is given an object lesson when he witnesses his father walk into a country home and buy the house on the spot, forcing a family sitting at their dinner table to leave immediately once their price has been met. Told in flashback, the scene disrupts the narrative, but his sharing the story with Perrin indicates that the act of reporting has raised his consciousness. Whereas Rambal-Cochet wants his son to understand that everyone has a price and that wealth comes with great power, his son begins to understand that a free press provides a way to counteract such abuses of power.

For Veber, Perrin's reclamation of his journalistic integrity is more significant than a compromised character finding vindication. It functions along the lines of a common trope found in Hollywood musicals where a central character is a dancer, musician, or show person fighting against conformity with their art. The musical, therefore, argues for the value of musical people. In *Le jouet*, Veber uses a protagonist who is a journalist and romanticizes the act of writing to profess the value of his own profession. Using details from his own life, including an aside from one of the journalists about covering the Festival de Cannes, reinforces the idea that Perrin is a stand-in for Veber, or at least for the portion of his life spent at *Bled*, *Lui*, and Radio Luxembourg.

The makeshift newspaper and the observations of Eric and Perrin tell only part of the story. The narrative explores spaces that neither character inhabits, underscoring both the abuses of power and the grotesque nature of compliance born out of self-interest. Following the release of the paper, which Perrin and Eric distribute to both the staff working at the mansion and colleagues at *France Hebdo*, Rambal-Cochet calls the editor Blénac into his office to upbraid him over the embarrassment. Asserting his power, Rambal-Cochet sits impassively behind his desk and demands that Blénac take his clothes off immediately. After a moment's hesitation and a repeated demand Blénac concedes and slowly drops his pants. Sizing him up, Rambal-Cochet asks, "Who is the monster? Me for asking you to drop your pants or you for agreeing to show your ass?" It is a poignant question that does not redeem the billionaire, but allows him to make a valid point about culpability. This falls in line with the film's overall commentary, which is not just about the evils of wealth and power, but also the compromises made out of self-interest and fear that allow systemic abuses to remain unchallenged.

Perrin voices the same question that Rambal-Cochet expresses in earlier dialogue. Talking to a governess who lives in fear working for the billionaire and suffers from awful treatment on the part of Eric, Perrin asks, "Why do you stay? Are governesses unemployed?" Aware that she needs work, he also tries to communicate to her that she has agency. At the same time, he is unaware that the question more directly implicates his own choices. Disturbingly, his agreeing to become Eric's personal toy is not tied to a specific promise or contract. When the department store manager discusses the proposal there is no mention of money, only vague allusions and assumptions about job stability. Perrin does not agree to degrade himself in order to advance his financial situation. He does so simply to maintain his already meager status. Eric pushes his father's offer to extremes when he is told that he can choose anything he likes from the store, but this is only made possible by the manager's fear of intervening in a situation he knows is wrong. His fear that he will experience the wrath of his superior speaks to the propulsive inhumanity of power. Rambal-Cochet has never ordered the purchase or humiliation of Perrin, but his power is such, even in absentia, that underlings will discount their own better judgment and moral compass in the vague pursuit of pleasing their boss. To use a heavy-handed and extreme example, it recalls historian Ian Kershaw's concept of "working toward the Führer" in that fear and self-interest can have disastrous momentum that have nothing to do with the explicit instructions of a leadership figure.[26] By questioning the governess without also interrogating his own refusal to exert agency, Perrin stumbles upon the unspoken nature of the apparatus of labor that keeps the rich in power. This is all very heady subtext for a popular comedy, but Veber would acknowledge that *Le jouet* was envisioned as a departure from the "common comedies" he had written in the past, crafting a much more serious film instead.[27]

LE REMAKE

The primary response of audiences in France and abroad was not to the political underpinnings of *Le jouet*, but to the comedy. Veber's inventive gags and Richard's physicality combine for a film that is at once situated within the social milieu of France and universal in its appeal. The film played throughout Europe and even received a limited theatrical run in the U.S. in 1979 under the English title *The Toy*. Coming on the heels of the surprise box office success of *La cage aux folles*, which had opened in the U.S. in April of 1979 and grossed an astounding $20.4 million in North America, distributors hoped to

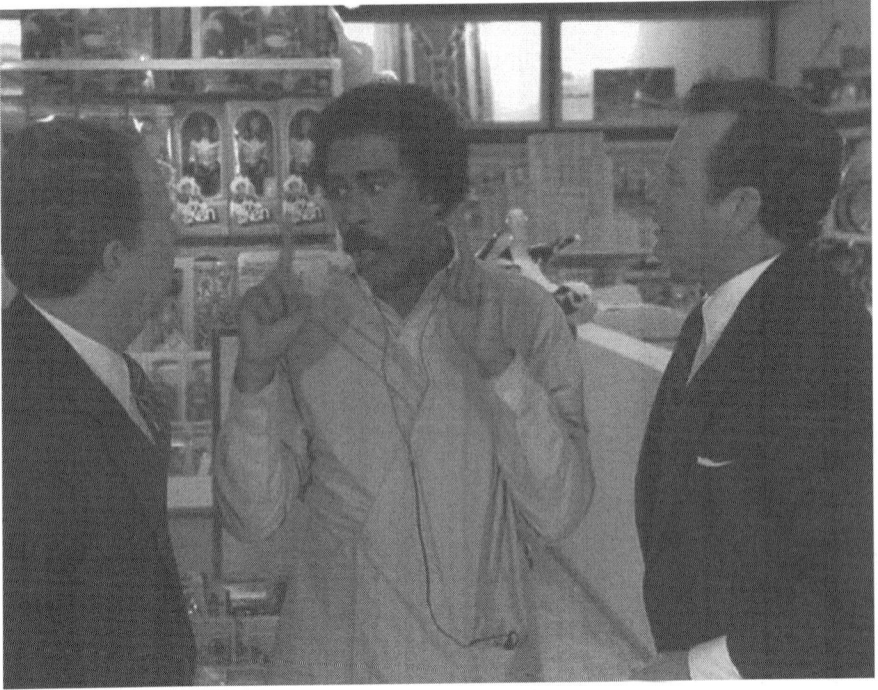

Figure 2.2 Jack Brown (Richard Pryor) is purchased by white executives (Ned Beatty and Don Hood) with the rebel flag lurking in the background.

mine Veber's back catalog for another crossover hit.[28] Interest overseas did not stop there for Veber, as Billy Wilder optioned *L'emmerdeur* and adapted it as *Buddy Buddy* in 1981. Paramount signed Veber to write the screenplay for the English-language comedy *Partners* (1982, James Burrows), and *Le jouet* was optioned by Columbia and adapted as *The Toy* (1982, Richard Donner). The first of his directorial efforts to be remade in Hollywood—four more would follow over the years—*The Toy* challenges notions that there is universality in comedic gags and is a cautionary tale in adaptation, at least on an artistic level. Donner's adaptation would make $47.1 million at the domestic box office, the fourteenth highest grossing film of 1982, laying the groundwork for future Hollywood remakes of Veber's film regardless of negative critical response.[29]

The enthusiastic response at the box office to *The Toy* was primarily due to public fascination with its star, Richard Pryor. A little over two years removed from his near-death experience at his Northridge home, where Pryor lit himself on fire and suffered severe burns across his body, the notoriety surrounding the incident lifted Pryor's public profile and for a few years turned him into Hollywood's biggest box-office draw. *The Toy* followed *Stir Crazy* (1980, Sidney Poitier), *Bustin' Loose* (1981, Oz Scott), *Some Kind of Hero* (1982, Michael Pressman), and the standup concert film *Richard Pryor:*

Live on the Sunset Strip (1982, Joe Layton) as post-Northridge releases that all over-performed at the box office.[30] On paper, *The Toy* made sense. Pryor's star was in ascendance, but the studio needed a readymade screenplay that would allow them to bypass time spent in development. Veber's film had been a modest success in France with 1.25 million tickets sold, but Pryor could be slotted into Richard's role, repeating his physical gags for an American audience largely unaware of the original text.[31] In terms of short-term financial success, Columbia made the right decision. As far as respecting Veber's material, tastefully transferring the narrative to an American setting, and providing a worthwhile venue for Pryor's talents, *The Toy* is a confounding undertaking.

As would be the case with almost all of Hollywood's adaptations of Veber's work (the lone exception being 2010's *Dinner for Schmucks*), *The Toy* is remarkably faithful to the structure and details of the source material. The narrative arc remains unchanged and numerous gags are repeated with such proximity that it would not come as a surprise if Donner or his cinematographer Lázló Kovács used screenshots from *Le jouet* for framing and decorating their shots. Not that fidelity is the mark of a successful adaptation (in fact, I will be arguing the opposite in the following chapters), but modifications to crucial details in Veber's original film account for the most troubling aspects of *The Toy*. In casting Pryor and changing the setting from Paris to Baton Rouge, Louisiana, *The Toy* reframes the central conflict along racial and geographic lines, creating a neo-slavery narrative. Whereas François Perrin performs the duty as Eric's toy as an assumed extension of his employment as *France Hebdo*, Pryor's Jack Brown is purchased outright.

The transaction, framed in a medium shot with Jack at the center of the frame and an executive on each side of him, takes place in the toy section of a department store. Directly over Jack's shoulder at the center of the frame is a Confederate flag (perhaps a piece of *Dukes of Hazzard* merchandise?). As the executives shower Jack with cash, he says, "I can't be bought. No. This was settled in the Civil War. You can't have slaves." Two seconds later, Brown concedes and proves that he can indeed be bought. The dialogue shows that Donner and screenwriter Carol Sobieski are aware of the altered political subtext by casting Pryor and setting the film in the American South, but Jack's fleeting protest and the muted commentary elsewhere in the film makes the slavery analogy subtext rather than text. The union protest outside of the garden party is replaced by an anti-KKK demonstration, but by and large *Le jouet*'s indictment of corrupting power, corporate culture, and self-interest is translated into a mélange of platitudes about love and friendship in *The Toy*. Underneath all of this is a cavalcade of debilitating racist tropes and the use of Pryor as a checklist for historical stereotypes of African Americans in Hollywood films. An out-of-work journalist, Jack does not get hired at a magazine like François Perrin. Instead, he accepts a job for the same company working as a domestic servant and, later, a janitor. Emasculated by wearing a French maid's outfit and adopting the expressive frightened posture of archetypal coon performers from the past like Mantan Moreland, Pryor's image throughout the film is a throwback to the relationship between comedic intent and the black body on screen being rooted in humiliation and victimization. Moreover, Pryor's performance is broad and clownish, completely departing from the restraint shown by Pierre Richard in *Le jouet*. Unfortunately, poor performances in films unworthy of his talents would be the rule, not the exception, of Pryor's long sojourn in Hollywood.

The ending of *Le jouet*, with Eric running away to choose Perrin over his father, is reversed into a saccharine sweet conclusion with Jack giving a heartfelt speech to the boy about his father's deep love for him. Dampening Veber's critique of wealth and power, the billionaire in *The Toy*, Jackie Gleason's U.S. Bates, is ultimately redeemable. Donner's film has no semblance of political purpose, replacing the critiques of Veber's original with asides and allusions that fail to cohere. Eric's governess is reimagined as a nymphomaniac lusting after Jack, and also a closet Nazi who watches Hitler speeches when alone in her bedroom. The cold, calculating, and intelligent young wife of Rambal-Cochet becomes an empty-headed blonde trophy wife with prominent cleavage. Even the use of comic characters in the *mise en scène* is altered enough to change meaning, as Jack and Eric wear Spiderman pajamas in *The Toy*, an empty signifier, whereas the enormous cutouts of Marvel characters and the prominent placement of Captain America in early shots of Eric in *Le jouet* reinforce a broader commentary about the Americanization of French culture. Sobieski's script changes the tone of the comedy, departing from Veber's crafted dialogue with clumsy earnestness and juvenile wordplay. For example, the formal greeting from servants and staff of "Monsieur Eric" in Veber's film becomes the recurring pun "Master Bates" in the remake.

There is nothing inherently wrong with transforming the meaning of source material and the decision to use *Le jouet*'s premise to explore race could have made for a compelling film, but the rushed nature of the project, hoping to capitalize on Pryor's newfound drawing power at the box office, never allowed it to be fully realized as a workable social commentary. In comparison to Veber's film, *The Toy* both underscores the difficulty in adapting comedy for a new set of cultural sensibilities and makes the whiteness of Veber's œuvre strikingly apparent. France has a long tradition of race-based satires and comedies dealing with African immigration, yet Veber's films largely avoid direct discussions of identity politics despite his own self-identification as being Jewish and Armenian.[32] What *The Toy* suggests, however, is not that Veber's source material is bereft of racial commentary. The project of adaptation reveals that commentaries on identity are embedded within the broader themes of his plots and characters. Unlike Jewish writers who use novels to directly explore their ethnic identity via Jewish characters—Philip Roth's *Portnoy's Complaint* (1969) and Saul Bellow's *Herzog* (1964) come to mind—Veber's body of work may reflect the approach of Bernard Malamud's *The Natural* (1954), where the outsider Gentile character of Roy Hobbs can be read as an allegory of the Jewish experience in America. Veber's development of François Perrin into the recurring character of François Pignon in the years following the release of *Le jouet* invites such symbolic examination.

NOTES

1. Being an army publication, the title of the magazine *Bled* strikes an English speaker as jarringly brutal. In France the term "bled," which is borrowed from Arabic, refers to a village or an isolated location akin to the American pejoratives boondocks or backwater. The term can also be used as a non-pejorative for home by someone living outside of their native country.
2. Veber, *Que ça reste entre nous*, p. 48. «*L'enfant ne m'a pas acheté, mais le sujet du Jouet était né.*»
3. Alison Smith, *French Cinema in the 1970s: The Echoes of May*, pp. 2–3.
4. Ibid.
5. Ibid. p. 11.
6. Ibid. p. 12.
7. Ibid.
8. Fournier-Lanzoni, *French Comedy*, p. 121.
9. Veber, *Que ça reste entre nous*, p. 95.
10. Tony Judt, *Postwar: A History of Europe Since 1945*, p. 478.
11. Pierre Richard with Jérémie Imbert, *Je sais rien, mais je dirait tout*, p. 143.
12. Ibid. p. 136.
13. *A Conversation with Francis Veber*.
14. Richard, *Je sais rien, mais je dirait tout*, p. 178.
15. Fournier-Lanzoni, *French Comedy*, pp. 110–17, 168.
16. Richard's seven directorial credits are *Le distrait* (1970, *Distracted*), *Les malheurs d'Alfred* (1972, *The Troubles of Alfred*), *Je sais rien, mais je dirai tout* (1973, *I Don't Know Much, But I'll Say Everything*), *Je suis timide . . . mais je me soigne* (1978, *I'm Shy, But I'll Heal*), *C'est pas moi, c'est lui* (1980, *It's Not Me, It's Him*), *On peut toujours rêver* (1991, *One Can Always Dream*), and *Droit dans le mur* (1997, *Straight into the Wall*).
17. Fournier-Lanzoni, *French Comedy*, p. 168.
18. Ibid.
19. Veber, *Que ça reste entre nous*, pp. 175–6.
20. Richard, *Je sais rien, mais je dirait tout*, p. 179.
21. Veber, *Que ça reste entre nous*, p. 168.
22. Richard, *Je sais rien, mais je dirait tout*, pp. 233–4.
23. Salé, *Les scénaristes au travail*, p. 118.
24. Ibid. p. 122.
25. Richard, *Je sais rien, mais je dirait tout*, pp. 230–1.
26. Ian Kershaw, *Hitler, 1936–1945: Nemesis*.
27. Salé, *Les scénaristes au travail*, p. 113.

28. *Box Office Mojo*, <http://www.boxofficemojo.com/movies/?id=lacageauxfolles.htm> (accessed January 5, 2019).

29. *Box Office Mojo*, <http://www.boxofficemojo.com/movies/?id=toy.htm> (accessed January 5, 2019).

30. Although Oz Scott is credited on the film, the majority of *Bustin' Loose* was directed by Michael Schultz.

31. *JP's Box-Office*, <http://www.jpbox-office.com/fichfilm.php?id=8119> (accessed January 5, 2019). Veber inflates the number slightly to 1.4 million in his memoir (Veber, *Que ça reste entre nous*, p. 176).

32. Fournier-Lanzoni, *French Comedy*, pp. 127–38.

CHAPTER 3

Mexican Holiday: *La chèvre* (1981)

The five-year gap between *Le jouet* and Veber's second directorial effort is anything but an indication that he was idle during that period of time. To the contrary, he continued in his previous mode of writing screenplays for other directors and enjoyed his greatest success to date with *La cage aux folles* in 1978. The following year Veber would write two films built around the recurring character named François Perrin. Based on a story concept by Alain Godard, *Coup de tête* (1979, Jean-Jacques Annaud) imagines Perrin (Patrick Deware) as a hotheaded football player who seeks revenge against rival players from his club after he is falsely accused of rape and imprisoned. Not a particularly joyful premise, *Coup de tête* would be one of the most positive experiences of Veber's career, citing Jean-Jacques Annaud years later as his favorite of all the directors he had worked with as a screenwriter.[1] Like Veber, Annaud would transition into the role of a transnational director in the 1980s, making multinational co-productions for a global audience like *Quest for Fire* (1981), *The Name of the Rose* (1986), and *The Bear* (1988).

The other screenplay from that year, *Cause toujours . . . tu m'intéresses!* (1979, Édouard Molinaro), again imagines Perrin as a journalist. Working for RTL (Radio Télé Luxembourg), there is a return to the Perrin character being used as a stand-in for Veber, or for the life of a writer at the very least. Like *Le jouet*, Perrin in *Cause toujours . . . tu m'intéresses!* is a frustrated journalist longing to do something more substantial, going so far as to pass himself off as a great writer when he meets a stranger. The division between writing as unfulfilling labor and a worthy profession marks much of Veber's career, but if the screenplay is meant to be a reflexive commentary on his own displeasure with his marginalized status in the film industry, the promotion of the film is not a piece of supporting evidence. Above a mixed media image of the lead

actors, the names at the top of the poster for *Cause toujours . . . tu m'intéresses!*
appear in bold capital letters: "GIRARDOT MARIELLE MOLINARO
VEBER," crediting the writer and using his name to sell the picture alongside
the film's stars Annie Girardot and Jean-Pierre Marielle as well as the director
Édouard Molinaro.

As the poster suggests, Veber had become much more than an anonymous
screenwriter by the start of the 1980s. The successes of *Le grand blond avec
une chaussure noire*, *La cage aux folles*, and his directorial debut *Le jouet* gave
him name recognition and situated Veber as a key voice in France's national
cinema. Nowhere is this more evident than in his participation in *Sunday Lovers*
(1980, *Les séducteurs*), a multinational comedic anthology with four separate
stories made alternately in Italy, England, France, and the U.S. The Italian
segment, "Armando's Notebook," is directed by Dino Risi and co-written by
Age and Scarpelli (Agenore Incrocci and Furio Scarpelli), a famous writing
duo who had been mainstays in Italy since their first screen credit in 1949.
The British story, "An Englishman's Home," is directed by Bryan Forbes
and written by Leslie Bricusse, a composer and sometimes screenwriter who
enjoyed major successes with his song contributions to James Bond films and
Willie Wonka and the Chocolate Factory (1971, Mel Stuart). The American
sequence, "Skippy," is written and directed by Gene Wilder, still enjoying his
peak stardom. Veber's contribution, "The French Method," again attached to
Molinaro as the director, indicates that by the start of the 1980s the duo had
become as synonymous with French comedy as Age and Scarpelli were with
Italian cinema or Gene Wilder had become with the genre in Hollywood.

Building on his growing reputation and having shown the ability to direct
with *Le jouet*, Veber signed what he refers to as a "blank contract" with Gaumont
in 1981, allowing him to choose his own projects and serve as both writer and
director.[2] This newfound freedom, backed by studio financing, could have
been an invitation for Veber to dramatically depart from the stylistic and
genre categories that had been representative of his work up until that point,
but one of the defining characteristics of his career is showing practicality in
creative expression. Remarking on the ability of certain American filmmakers
to balance artistic ambition with commercial considerations, Veber points out
the self-defeating nature of certain French auteurs, creating a national cinema
where "there is a total divorce between the 'success of esteem' and the cinema
of consumption."[3] Although he rejects the notion that he writes for a certain
public, Veber also acknowledges the need for his material to connect with an
audience. Testing his finished screenplays by reading them to friends, Veber
makes a practice out of vetting his material in hopes of predicting audience
response.[4] He may write in isolation, allowing the narrative to take shape
without the specifics of the final filmed product in mind, but his primary goal
is to connect with an audience. Still, without the fears or filters of another

director realizing his screenplays, the opportunity to make personal and politi-cal statements must have been apparent to Veber, as were the risks and respon-sibilities. On-demand projects like *Le retour du grand blond* and adaptations of preexisting work like *La cage aux folles* lack the same pressure that he would take on as a full-time writer and director. If *Le jouet* was a departure from his work as a screenwriter for hire in the 1970s, *La chèvre* would mark Veber's assumption of total control over his work in the 1980s.

LE FILM

The production history of *La chèvre* supports Veber's claims that he writes the majority of his screenplays without considering casting or production specifics. If he had known the difficulties of casting compatible lead actors and completing a film on location in Mexico, *La chèvre* would never have been written. Conceived as a buddy comedy with a *clown blanc* and a physically imposing straight man, the humor is built around polarities and repetition.[5] Veber's initial idea for the pairing was to cast Jacques Villeret as the clownish François Perrin and Lino Ventura as the hard-nosed Campana.[6] The Italian-born Ventura had moved to France in his youth, came to acting after a suc-cessful run as a professional wrestler, and worked his way into leading roles by largely playing tough gangsters and detectives. On top of his well-established screen persona, Ventura had starred in three films written by Veber, playing a

Figure 3.1 Campana (Gérard Depardieu) looks on as Perrin (Pierre Richard) sinks into quicksand in one of *La chèvre*'s many nods to pulp adventure tropes.

hit man in *L'emmerdeur* (1973), a police commissioner in *Adieu poulet* (1975), and a morally compromised businessman in "The French Method" segment of *Sunday Lovers*. Ventura agreed to do *La chèvre*, but for reasons that were never made clear to Veber, he refused to work with Villeret.[7] Choosing to find another comic lead rather than lose Ventura, Veber's reluctant second choice was Pierre Richard.[8] On the cusp of shooting, however, Ventura made contract demands that could not be met by Gaumont and he dropped out.[9] From a film that he had envisioned as a pairing of Lino Ventura and Jacques Villeret, Veber was left with Pierre Richard and a vacant co-star position right before they were set to leave for Mexico to begin shooting *La chèvre*.

In 1981, if the recollections of the principals are to be believed, Gérard Depardieu seemed to be one of the least likely candidates to replace Lino Ventura in a buddy comedy opposite Pierre Richard. A year removed from winning the César for Best Actor in *Le dernier métro* (1980, François Truffaut, *The Last Metro*), Depardieu had become France's premier dramatic actor and a sort of European corollary to a new generation of film stars in America—a connection that was solidified by his casting opposite Robert De Niro in *1900* (1976, Bernardo Bertolucci). Depardieu had made a few comedies, but his reputation remained closely aligned with serious dramatic roles. His break-through performance in *Les valseuses* (1974, Bertrand Blier, *Going Places*) comes in a film that is ostensibly a comedy, but of such a dark nature that it is difficult to consider it alongside traditional genre offerings. When *Les valseuses* was released in the U.S., for example, it was marketed as an art film, playing up critical analyses that read the story of marauding French youth as a commentary on a collective moral decay that followed May '68.[10]

Regardless of his reputation or the way his films were sold, Depardieu had made traditional comedies like *Inspecteur la Bavure* (1980, Claude Zidi, *Inspector Blunder*), playing a gangster opposite Coluche's fumbling detective. Produced by Claude Berri just a year before *La chèvre*, the memories of Veber and Pierre Richard must be taken with a grain of salt when they characterize the casting of Depardieu as a wholly unorthodox and unexpected choice for a comedy. As was the case with Veber's decision to direct *Le jouet*, there is a discrepancy between his memory and the claims of Richard about where the idea to cast Depardieu originated. According to Richard, it was his idea to cast Depardieu and Veber came around to the idea almost immediately, convinced by his past work with Bertrand Blier that he could handle comedy.[11] Conversely, Veber recalls the suggestion coming from his agent Jean-Louis Livi and having reservations because he thought of Depardieu in the same vein as a young Marlon Brando.[12] Hosting a dinner with Depardieu and Richard before making a final decision, Veber recalls that he and producer Alain Poiré saw that the actors had instant chemistry and headed to Mexico shortly thereafter, revised cast in tow. Veber's comments on the film in his memoir are almost exclusively comprised of colorful anecdotes about the misadventures on set in Mexico, ranging from Depardieu's drunkenness and Richard's sexual conquests to the difficulty of shooting in the jungle with an inexperienced Mexican crew and a Mormon polygamist stuntman in a gorilla costume.[13] The intrigues of shooting aside, the final film is fascinating in its own right.

The film opens in Puerto Vallarta, Mexico, where Marie (Corryne Charbit), the clumsy and unlucky daughter of powerful CEO Alexandre Bens (Michel Robin), is on vacation alone. After being mugged and left unconscious on the street, Marie is kidnapped by a local criminal and goes missing without a trace. Weeks later, with all options exhausted, Bens is pitched a crazy idea by one of his executives: to use a company employee, François Perrin (Pierre Richard) to find her. Perrin, as uncannily prone to disaster as Marie, is hired to follow in her footsteps to accidentally track her down. Assigning tough private detective Campana (Gérard Depardieu) to accompany Perrin and lead the investigation, the pair fly to Puerto Vallarta. To Campana's chagrin, he must play along and keep Perrin under the false impression of being in charge. In a way, neither are in charge, as their search is guided by happenstance that could pass for divine intervention. Perrin and Campana are at odds once they start working together, largely because the serious private investigator is the victim of the destruction that is left in Perrin's wake. From misadventures in travel to close calls with Mexican gangs and cops, the pair form a grudging respect for each other and stumble upon Marie deep in the Mexican jungle, in a Catholic mission hospital bed next to an injured Perrin. The two fall in love with each other at first sight, presumably to enjoy a shared life of disaster and misfortune together. After standing together on a wooden pier that collapses and transforms into an impromptu raft, the final freeze frame shows them holding hands as they float down river.

In what had already been established as a trademark of Veber's writing, humor is found in repetition and the compounding of gags, building momentum through physical comedy and slightly modified reiterations of previous scenes.[14] In search of money stolen from Perrin, Campana forces his way into an underworld hangout by knocking on the door, grabbing the guard through the small opening of a peephole window by his nostrils, refusing to let go until he opens the door. Pulling the guard toward him, Campana head-butts him, moves into the bar, head-butts the bartender, kicks the door to a back room completely off its hinges, and pulls a gun on the collection of gangsters sitting around a poker table, giving a backhand slap to one for good measure. Having secured the stolen money and driven away, Perrin points out that one of the men at the table was Arbal (Jorge Luke), the man suspected of kidnapping Marie. They return immediately, and the sequence plays out in exactly the same order: nostril grab, head-butts, pushing the back door off its hinges, a pulled gun, and a backhand slap to one of the poker players. This time they leave with Arbal. This doubling of action is a staple of Veber's comedy, as changed context, expectation, and character responses give the excesses of repeated gags both a sense of inevitability and audacity.

Stylistically, *La chèvre* has an almost television aesthetic, with very basic set-ups and a lack of visual coherence between exteriors and interiors. Rudimentary tools, such as a low-angle set-up for the introduction of Depardieu to emphasize his physical stature, are employed, but by and large the compositions of Veber and cinematographer Alex Phillips are rushed afterthoughts to dialogue and performance. Yet the opening sequence reinforces the film's thematic drive. Whereas the first shot of *Le jouet* has concise and emblematic *mise en scène*, the opening shots of *La chèvre* appear to do little more than establish the film's Mexican resort setting, following a man parasailing over the water and hotels of Puerto Vallarta captured in a series of helicopter shots. There is a cutaway to a single shot of a hotel entrance as a taxi arrives to drop Marie off, followed by a series of crosscuts between the man on the parasail, Marie on the phone, and her father on the other end of the call in his Paris office. Marie, distracted by the man on the parasail, falls off the balcony and drops a few stories into an elastic awning that breaks her fall. Her father is crying out for her over the phone while the man in the parasail looks on in an awkward close-up, the last time he is shown in the film. Veber spends a lot of screen time on a character with no lines and only a tangential purpose of distracting Marie into the first of her many misfortunes, but the sequence attempts to convey an impending collision that is more than coincidence. The parasail, like Perrin's uncanny bad luck, has a destination and predetermined purpose. It is a clumsy sequence in its conception, but Veber's intent is clear. More successful are sequences with Perrin that allow Richard's performance to convey meaning.

The sequence where Perrin unknowingly auditions for Bens is a good example of Veber's ability to design visual gags with meaning and Richard's unique skill in delivering a performance to realize the scene. Meyer (André Valardy), the executive pitching the idea to Bens, goes into a boardroom with a large round table and breaks a leg from one of the nineteen chairs, placing it back where it was. Inviting Perrin into the room, Meyer and Bens ask him to sit down wherever he likes. Almost sitting in the closest chair, Perrin reconsiders at the last moment and hesitantly circles the table, trying to make the right decision and not offend the company's upper brass. Smiling at Bens and Meyers, Perrin shrugs his shoulders and finally chooses a seat at random, falling through the very one that had been damaged. Campana tries a similar experiment, unscrewing one of two saltshakers at an airport restaurant to see which one Perrin will choose. More striking than the decisions and ensuing calamity are Perrin's reactions. Empting the saltshaker onto his breakfast, he does not miss a beat, scraping the salt away with his fork, eating his meal, and then casually commenting to Campana that the breakfast was "too salty."

The common man, through Veber's use of the François Perrin character, normalizes hardship and misfortune as a part of the human condition. There is bleakness in Perrin, but also resilience. Simultaneously, his innocence is complicated by pride, stupidity, and selfishness. Late for a flight at the airport, Perrin assures Campana that everything will be fine and walks away. Moments later, the departure board marks all the flights as delayed, seemingly a benefit of Perrin's supernatural bad luck. The truth, as Perrin shamelessly explains, is that he called in a bomb threat. Alternately sympathetic and sinister, Perrin is imaged more as a force of nature than an everyman who is a stand-in for the audience. His belief in luck and supernatural forces shaping events runs counter to the sense that, perhaps, his misfortune is karmic justice. Placing the superstitious Perrin opposite the evidence-based belief system of Campana, the buddy comedy is shaped as a conflict between faith and logic. Carolyn Durham sees conflicts in *La chèvre* as "the contrast between the rational and the capricious," in a larger French tradition of reason, scientific method, and Cartesian logic.[15] By placing the action outside of France and into the untamed landscapes of Mexico, *La chèvre* suggests a primal set of forces that challenge the intellectual orthodoxy of modern Europe.

Once in Mexico, their search follows a reverse trajectory of development and civility. Beginning in high-end resorts, Campana and Perrin descend into nightclubs, brothels, gambling houses, the desert, an abusive prison, and finally the jungle. Mexico is exotic and dangerous, alternately idealized for its physical beauty and demonized for its lawlessness. The moment Marie walks out of the resort hotel she is knocked unconscious by two local men on a motorcycle and immediately picked up and kidnapped by an unrelated gangster who is driving by on the street. Scammed out of his money by a prostitute, Perrin's faith in people is his undoing, whereas the cynical Campana overpowers Mexican gangsters with brute force and head-butts that carry almost superhuman strength. At the same time, Mexico's lack of development is idealized and mythologized. The wooden flute compositions that Vladimir Cosma uses as a motif for every appearance of Marie's kidnapper Arbal express an exotic Latin American spirit akin to Eric Serra's "La Raya" score for the Peruvian sequence in *Le Grand Bleu* (1988, Luc Besson, *The Big Blue*). There is also a scene with an indigenous man in glasses that recalls Veber's use of the Sioux man in *Le jouet*, while the lingering camera on a mural in the Acapulco airport hints at the artistic and political dimensions of Mexico that are often overlooked by vacationing Europeans and Americans.[16] These glimpses of respect and fascination for Mexico are complicated by a pervading sense of neocolonial ownership and superiority throughout the film, manifested in both the characters and the choices Veber makes in regard to language.

In the imagined Mexico of *La chèvre*, the French investigators either enjoy or expect a mastery over this foreign country. Aside from one prostitute, every character in the film speaks French with ease and there is never a moment of linguistic negotiation that defines international travel. This choice can be written off as a narrative device so often used by Hollywood, where the audience is asked to suspend their disbelief for the ease of dialogue and avoidance of subtitles. Yet, imposing French on a region whose language has already been shaped by other colonial and imperial powers is grating in its ahistorical conception of a culture that *La chèvre* feigns to respect. Veber had previously used Latin America as a setting in *Le retour du grand blond*, with a significant portion of the film shot on location in Rio de Janeiro. In that film there is a similar sense of mastery, notably in a scene where the blond man is reading *Le Monde* while getting his shoes shined by a local man who speaks fluent French. Largely, though, the film fixates on the outer trappings of Brazilian culture and limits its conflicts to characters from France rather than intercultural oppositions. *La chèvre* departs from this strategy and locates conflict firmly in the divisions between French visitors and the people, land, and institutions of Mexico. Nowhere is this made more explicit than in the prison scene where Perrin and Campana are unjustly arrested and thrown into an arcane and abusive Mexican prison. Banging on the jail cell door, Perrin exclaims, "Open up! We're French!" as if their first world status makes them immune to imprisonment. Recalling the protest in *Le jouet* where Perrin tries to offer the sale of the Sioux man in his place, the fact that in *La chèvre* Perrin and Campana are sharing the cell with a falsely imprisoned and equally abused Mexican brings the arrogance and privilege of "Open up! We're French!" into sharp relief.

The film benefits from the built-in production value of the Mexican locations, creating a visual texture that the film's cinematographer Alex Phillips would replicate later in the decade in the same role on *Born in East L.A.* (1987, Cheech Marin), but crafting a realistic vision of the country is not a primary concern of *La chèvre*. The depictions of Mexico in *La chèvre* recall the sort of explorative fantasies embodied by Karl May's novels and Hergé's *Tintin* comics, but abandon the premise of realism and the practice of research. Instead, Veber crafts a fantastical Mexico that matches his own preconceptions of the country with a grab bag of exotic elements that have no actual connection to the region his characters inhabit. Lost in the jungle, Perrin and Campana are having a quiet talk expressing a growing mutual respect when, suddenly, a silverback gorilla jumps out, grabs Perrin, and takes him away. The random jolt of the moment quickly turns into confusion (and then laughter based on one's sensibilities) upon the realization that gorillas are not native to Mexico or anywhere else in Latin America. The same holds true for Campana and Perrin's encounter with a king cobra moments later. This addition of African and Asian species into the jungles of Mexico is certainly inaccurate, but it also gives *La chèvre* a nostalgic aesthetic that brings to mind pulp fiction and B movies from decades earlier. The film even has Perrin getting stuck in quicksand, a well-worn adventure trope that was quickly being phased out of movie existence following its peak popularity in the 1960s.[17]

Rather than geographical ignorance or a lack of research, there is personal meaning to be found in the imagined Mexico of *La chèvre*. For Veber, this recycling of adventure tropes can be read as an homage to his own parents, specifically his mother. While his father Pierre-Gilles Veber was a journalist and screenwriter, his mother Catherine published hundreds of pulp novels under the pseudonym Georgette Paul.[18] Cranking out work fast and being paid pennies per page, the speed and low expectations of this work brought about absurd literary inventions that would stay with her son well into adulthood. Recalling a conversation between his parents while they were writing at home when he was a child, Francis remembers his mother asking across the room, "Gilles? Are there crocodiles in the Mississippi?"[19] After an annoyed response from his father, Catherine decided that there would be crocodiles in the Mississippi River, if only in the imagined world of her pulp novel.[20] The unintended humor of his mother's misconceptions about North American reptiles transforms into a series of conscious incongruities in *La chèvre*, creating a whimsical version of Mexico where everyone speaks fluent French, gorillas and cobras roam free, and uncanny bad luck can be harnessed to solve mysteries.

The farcical spirit of the film, and the chemistry between Depardieu and Richard, struck a nerve with French audiences. The film sold seven million tickets at the domestic box office, five times as many paid admissions as *Le jouet*.[21] *La chèvre* managed to beat out Hollywood competition to become the number one film in France for 1981, gaining more admissions than Disney's *The Fox and the Hound* (1981, Ted Berman, Richard Rich and Art Stevens, *Rox et Rouky*) and *Raiders of the Lost Ark* (1981, Steven Spielberg, *Les aventuriers de l'arche perdue*), which finished second and third respectively at the French box office that year. Its success in the face of an influx of big budget Hollywood releases made *La chèvre* both a resistant anomaly and a rational counterpoint to the panic within France about the state of its art and culture in the 1980s.

In July of 1982, France's Minister of Culture Jack Lang made a now infamous speech at a UNESCO conference in which he denounced the cultural influence of the U.S., calling for "a real crusade against . . . the financial and intellectual imperialism that no longer grabs territory, or rarely, but grabs consciousness, ways of thinking, and ways of living."[22] The speech was part of Lang's attempt to insulate the French film industry from what he called "a certain invasion, a certain influx of images produced elsewhere" through government financing of domestic productions and quotas for exhibitors to assure that French films would not be marginalized at home and swallowed up by the global appetite of and for Hollywood, as was becoming the case in other European countries.[23] That Lang delivered this speech in Mexico City, of all places, apparently failed to strike him as ironic. Here was Lang, only months after the release of *La chèvre*, decrying the "invasion of images produced elsewhere" in a nation that was the setting for his country's most successful film. Lang may have conceptualized cultural imperialism in terms of trade and finance when he made his comments at UNESCO, but *La chèvre* is a prime example that America does not have a monopoly on art and entertainment tinged with colonial sensibilities.

LE REMAKE

La chèvre, like *Le jouet* before it, eventually received a modest North American theatrical release, but it came in 1985 following the U.S. release of *Les compères* in 1984. The English-language poster for *La chèvre* confuses their order of production, reading at the top, "They're back! The comedy team behind *Comperes*." Perhaps "comedy team" refers to the buddy partnering of

Figure 3.2 Pierre Richard's performance in *La chèvre* (above) being painstakingly recreated by Martin Short in *Pure Luck* (below).

Depardieu and Richard as well as Veber (and possibly producer Alain Poiré), but it certainly does not convey that *La chèvre* was their first outing. Neither film garnered anywhere near the interest that accompanied *La cage aux folles*, but their success in France made them all candidates for Hollywood adaptations. It took a decade for *La chèvre* to materialize as an American remake, but it became one of the most faithful Hollywood adaptations of a Veber original. Perhaps this was because Veber himself took part in the production, serving as an executive producer.

The U.S. theatrical run of *La chèvre* came with a title that was first literally translated on the poster as "The Goat" under the French title and, later, retitled as *Knock on Wood* for home video release. The remake follows this lead by literalizing the central theme of the movie even further by naming the film *Pure Luck* (1991). Directed by Australian Nadia Tass, the work of adapting Veber's screenplay fell to the writing partners Timothy Harris and Herschel Weingrod, a successful pair responsible for the original screenplays to *Trading Places* (1983, John Landis), *Twins* (1988, Ivan Reitman), and *Kindergarten Cop* (1990, Ivan Reitman). For all of the creative invention and financial success of those films, the writing partners' only previous adaptation credit was the critically reviled Richard Pryor vehicle *Brewster's Millions* (1985, Walter Hill).[24] The box office magic of Pryor was wearing off by 1985, but *Brewster's Millions* was still a modest hit, which may have obscured Harris and Weingrod's difficulties in writing the adaptation.[25] Far from transforming the material into something removed from Veber's original, the screenplay for *Pure Luck* makes only a few cosmetic changes, while the imprint of Tass and cinematographer David Parker is even less evident, as a large number of scenes, gags, locations, and camera set-ups are explicitly duplicated from *La chèvre*. The remake goes so far as to retain head-butting as the preferred form of violence, transposing a European staple of aggression onto an American character.

This is not to suggest that *Pure Luck* and *La chèvre* are identical films with an interchangeable set of social and political contexts. The investigating team now being American, the gravity around issues including a shared border and identity politics between the U.S. and Mexico supersedes anything facing Perrin or Campana in terms of subtext. Proximity makes Veber's fanciful and exotic vision of Mexico untenable for an American remake. The cobra and gorilla are missing in the remake, replaced by a snake indigenous to the region and a cliffhanging sequence to substitute for the random scare of a rogue simian. The heightened awareness of the Mexican setting is made clear when Eugene (Martin Short), the renamed François Perrin character, is offered the job of investigating the disappearance of the CEO's daughter south of the border. "Mexico?" Eugene incredulously asks, "But I don't even speak Spanish!" In an instant *Pure Luck* puts forth an understanding of cultural displacement that is all too often absent in *La chèvre*. Campanella (Danny

Glover), the renamed Campana character, is bilingual and is asked to join Eugene because he can serve as both a leading detective and translator. His use of Spanish rarely comes into play, of course, as *Pure Luck* is like most Hollywood films in that English is omnipresent even when illogical to the setting; but the fact that linguistic difference is mentioned at all shows a very different negotiation with Mexico than Veber's original.

Another striking alteration in the remake comes in the casting of Glover and Short as unwitting partners. Short, who had starred in Veber's own *Three Fugitives* two years prior, may have been a logical choice as a Hollywood version of Pierre Richard. Still, his background in improv and sketch comedy is an inexact match for the talents of Pierre Richard, making him an awkward fit for Veber's material. Glover, on the other hand, deviates from the physical matching of Nick Nolte to Gérard Depardieu in *Three Fugitives*. Creating a racial binary by casting a prominent African American actor, Campanella's blackness goes unmentioned within the film, but race nevertheless changes the narrative's dynamics and would become an overdetermined aspect of *Pure Luck*'s marketing campaign. Referencing Glover's role in *Lethal Weapon* (1987, Richard Donner), the trailer borrows from the action film's iconography and uses a voice-over narration to make the connection unmistakable. "To find her they'll need the best team in the business," the trailer's narrator explains as a white outline of two men appears over a black screen. "He has the experience," it continues, now filling in the outline with a photograph of Glover. "But his regular partner," it continues, stopping for a beat, "wasn't available." With a white "X" placed over the second outlined face, clearly modeled after Glover's *Lethal Weapon* co-star Mel Gibson, the image cuts to Martin Short walking into a glass door and the narrator saying, "So they found someone even more lethal—to himself."

In situating *Pure Luck* as a spoof of *Lethal Weapon*, the trailer not only mischaracterizes the film, but also places it firmly in the tradition of the biracial buddy films that dominated black representation in the 1980s. Referring to it as a Hollywood "formula," Ed Guerrero remarks that the black buddy character is used by studios as a strategy "by which the industry contains and controls the black filmic image and conforms it to white expectations."[26] The variations on the black buddy trope in *Lethal Weapon* notwithstanding, the reference to the film in the casting of Glover and the explicit reference in the trailer places blackness at the center of *Pure Luck* despite the fact that it goes unmentioned within the film itself. This is not to say that the film completely adheres to colorblind casting in Glover assuming Depardieu's role. The seemingly minor alteration of Campana to Campanella ties Glover's character to a specific historical reference, alluding to baseball legend Roy Campanella. A catcher for the Brooklyn Dodgers from 1948 to 1957, Campanella was the first black teammate to join Jackie Robinson in the majors, serving as a collective symbol alongside a wave of former Negro League players who transformed the sport and broader conceptions of race in America during the 1950s.

Tying Glover to an athletic icon of the Civil Rights era while simultaneously embodying the neoliberal traits of both colorblind casting and the black buddy trope, the film is unsurprisingly hesitant to morally complicate Campanella. Whereas Depardieu's hulking, brutish Campana is alternately annoyed and antagonistic, Glover's Campanella is relatively controlled and well-meaning. Repeating a scene from *La chèvre*, Campana tricks Eugene into approaching a woman and insinuating that she is a prostitute, which gets Eugene slapped. Glover's expression at the end of this scene conveys immediate regret over the prank as opposed to Depardieu's triumphant grin. In *Pure Luck*, the straight man is stripped of any personality, rendering him as a passive story element rather than a counterpoint to the clown. Changes and restraint rooted in identity politics also influenced casting of the Arbal character, now renamed Frank Grimes (Scott Wilson), as a white American surviving on the criminal margins in Mexico. Rather than have the kidnapper be Mexican, *Pure Luck* avoids possible backlash about ethnic stereotyping by coding the threat onto a white body, a Hollywood device that came to prominence concurrently with the "new racism" of the Thatcher and Reagan era.[27] The conscious decision to avoid negative representations of the Latino character is underlined when Jorge Luke, the actor who played Arbal in *La chèvre*, appears in *Pure Luck* as a pilot rather than reprising his role as the narrative's central criminal.

Acknowledging the film's shortcomings, Veber was also likely displeased with the identity-based political considerations of the remake (or, in the parlance of the 1990s, "political correctness"). The tension between Veber's comedic sensibilities and changing social mores relating to representation will be explored further in discussions around his 2001 film *Le placard*, but the subtle deviations from the source material in *Pure Luck* are far from isolated to concerns over race and ethnicity. The remake upends the thematic foundation of forces beyond human explanation by using a research psychologist to pitch Eugene's bad luck as a scientific phenomenon, not a borderline spiritual gift. The comedy plays it safe one minute and goes too far the next. Perrin calling in a bomb threat in the airport is replaced by a serendipitously delayed flight so as not to overly complicate Eugene by associating him with a terrorist threat. At the same time, facial prosthetics and a fat suit are used on Short for a scene where Eugene has an allergic reaction to a bee sting, taking a gag from *La chèvre* and ruining it through visual overkill.[28] The final image of the film, with Eugene and the lost daughter (Sheila Kelley) floating down river on the broken segment of the wooden pier, is a process shot with the couple heading toward a waterfall and their impending doom. It is a step too far, but indicative of Hollywood's disdain for subtlety.

Trying to explain why the French original works and the American remake does not, especially since they are nearly identical on so many levels, goes beyond the normal realm of film studies. The subtleties of performance and cumulative mood are hard to pinpoint, whereas differences—or, in this case, similarities—in aesthetics and narrative can be more easily isolated, explained, and analyzed. The idea of adapting successful material for a new audience is understandable, ranging from the speed of remaking Hollywood films in the pre-television era to the phenomenon of "le remake." *La chèvre* struck a nerve for French audiences in 1981 and, in many ways, still works comedically despite its dated political underpinnings. *Pure Luck*, on the other hand, was mercilessly panned by critics and underperformed at the box office.[29]

NOTES

1. *A Conversation with Francis Veber.*
2. Salé, *Les scénaristes au travail*, p. 111.
3. Ibid. p. 113.
4. *A Conversation with Francis Veber.*
5. Veber, *Que ça reste entre nous*, p. 185.
6. Ibid. pp. 185–6.
7. Ibid. p. 186.
8. Ibid.
9. Ibid. p. 187.
10. Paul Chutkow, *Depardieu: A Biography*, p. 189.
11. Richard, *Je sais rien, mais je dirait tout*, pp. 229–30.
12. Veber, *Que ça reste entre nous*, pp. 187–91.
13. Ibid. pp. 191–208.
14. Fournier-Lanzoni, *French Comedy*, p. 172.
15. Carolyn A. Durham, *Double Takes: Culture and Gender in French Films and Their American Remakes*, p. 192.
16. The mural recalls the style of Diego Rivera, although there is no evidence that he is the artist. Rivera did spend a considerable amount of time in Acapulco during the 1950s as part of an "artists' haven," likely influencing whoever eventually painted the airport mural.
17. Daniel Engber, "Terra Firma: The Rise and Fall of Quicksand." *Slate*, August 23, 2010. <http://www.slate.com/articles/health_and_science/science/2010/08/terra_infirma.html> (accessed January 5, 2019).
18. Veber, *Que ça reste entre nous*, p. 16.
19. Ibid. pp. 16–17.
20. Ibid. p. 17.
21. *JP's Box-Office*, <http://www.jpbox-office.com/fichfilm.php?id=7229> (accessed January 5, 2019).
22. Samuel G. Freedman, "French Minister Cites U.S. Cultural Influence." *New York Times*, November 16, 1984.
23. Mazdon, Lucy, *Encore Hollywood: Remaking French Cinema*, pp. 6–7.
24. George Barr McCutcheon's 1906 novel *Brewster's Millions* was first adapted as a stage play, but became a staple for film remakes. Eight film versions have been made in the U.S.

(1914, 1921, 1926, 1935, 1945, 1961, and 1985), four in India (1954, 1985, 1988, 1997), and, most recently, one in Brazil (2016).

25. The film grossed $40.8 million at the North American box office. *Box Office Mojo*, <http://www.boxofficemojo.com/movies/?id=brewstersmillions.htm> (accessed January 5, 2019).

26. Ed Guerrero, *Framing Blackness: The African American Image in Film*, p. 127.

27. Martin Barker, *The New Racism: Conservatives and the Ideology of the Tribe*.

28. The choice to use a fat suit and facial prosthetics did have an unintended benefit, as the scene inspired Short to use the same makeup process in developing his caustically funny and long-running Jiminy Glick character.

29. The film made $22.6 million at the domestic box office, but cost $17 million to make. *Box Office Mojo*, <http://www.boxofficemojo.com/movies/?id=pureluck.htm> (accessed January 5, 2019).

CHAPTER 4

The Road to Fatherhood:
Les compères (1983)

The box office success of *La chèvre* and the pairing of Gérard Depardieu and Pierre Richard as a viable comedy team made the quasi-sequel *Les compères* inevitable. A creature of comfort who uses the same character names film after film, employs a recurring set of actors, and returns to similar scenarios and gags, Veber was never going to cash in on *La chèvre* by leveraging Gaumont to make an offbeat passion project. Instead, practicality and personal style combine in *Les compères* to probe the possibilities and expose the limitations of his comedy, returning to formula and structure much in the way that Douglas Sirk's melodramas in the 1950s work as a coherent unit and Howard Hawks's late career Westerns rehash similar narratives. Returning to the buddy comedy, *Les compères* solidifies an investment in the narrative device that would dominate the rest of his career. Of the ten films he would direct after *La chèvre*, eight of them can be classified as buddy comedies.

Rémi Fournier-Lanzoni points to *Le corniaud* (1965, Gérard Oury, *The Sucker*) as an early example of the "comic double act" that would gain prominence in French comedies in subsequent years.[1] The teaming of Bourvil and Louis de Funès in *Le corniaud* was followed by the unprecedented success of *La grande vadrouille* the next year, but the possibilities of the pair making more films together ended with Bourvil's death in 1970. Veber's pairing of Depardieu and Richard reenergized the buddy comedy, premising conflict and humor on an unlikely friendship among opposites. The pairing evokes a long line of American comedy duos in the strict division between the straight man and the clown. In the mode of Stan Laurel and Oliver Hardy, Bud Abbott and Lou Costello, Bob Hope and Bing Crosby, and Jerry Lewis and Dean Martin, the teaming of Gérard Depardieu and Pierre Richard is defined by physical and temperamental polarities. The separation between the performers is aided by Depardieu's reputation as a dramatic actor, much in the same way that fame as a singer helped reinforce the straight man roles of Bing Crosby (and to a lesser extent Dean Martin).[2]

The aura surrounding Depardieu when placed within the confines of the buddy comedy does much more than support a sense of seriousness for his straight man characters. His very inclusion in a popular comedy can challenge critics and spectators, prompting questions about the nature of a specific project and film art in general that would not be at the forefront if, say, Lino Ventura had starred in *La chèvre* and *Les compères*. Depardieu biographer Paul Chutkow reflects a common impulse to romanticize and laud non-commercial filmmaking as a higher art form when writing about the actor. Speaking of Depardieu's films with Marguerite Duras, Chutkow writes, "This was a cinema as *le septième art*," as if to suggest that any subsequent commercial films would be unworthy of his presence.[3] The implication by Chutkow reflects in tone if not substance the explicit hand-wringing of Réné Prédal, lambasting Depardieu's choice to work with people like Veber.

This division between high art and commercial genre cinema has thank-fully been complicated by scholars like Ginette Vincendeau, whose work on French film stars appreciates the fluidity of Depardieu rather than vilifying his appearance in popular genre films as heresy against cinema as an art form.[4] As Vincendeau explains, "In French comedy, stars establish and per-petuate a closeness with their audience, and signs of social identity, despite the common critical charge that mainstream French comedy is escapist."[5] Describing Depardieu as "the axiom of French cinema," Vincendeau opens up his entire body of work to analysis by understanding that his importance is located in critical reputation *and* his ability to move easily across genres.[6] For audiences at home and especially abroad, Depardieu has served as a symbol of France. More specifically, his performance of a masculinity that is alternately brutish and sensitive is tied to his age and era. Vincendeau refers to this defining trait of Depardieu's star persona as the "suffering macho."[7] Depardieu embodies a generation informed by the May 1968 protests and the frustrations of the 1970s, with his performances, particularly in the first two decades of his career, closely linked to collective anxieties, sorrows, and memory. Having met Depardieu only weeks before shooting began on *La chèvre*, Veber departed from his usual model of writing characters without concern for the specifics of production when he sat down to write the follow-up, *Les compères*. He knew that the film would reunite Depardieu with Pierre Richard and composed the story accordingly. Unlike their first film together, the screenplay for *Les compères* is infused with the signifiers of Depardieu's screen persona.

Figure 4.1 François Pignon (Pierre Richard) as an absentminded and suicidal writer in *Les compères*.

LE FILM

Opening with a shot of two denim-clad teenagers hitchhiking along a tree-lined French highway, the plot of *Les compères* revolves around the search for one of the runaways. When sixteen-year-old Tristan (Stéphane Biery) leaves with his unsavory new girlfriend, his parents report him missing but receive little help from the police. Desperate, his mother Christine (Anny Duperey) decides to contact an ex-lover, Jean Lucas (Gérard Depardieu), who is now an investigative journalist. Rather than ask for help, Christine tells Lucas that he is Tristan's father. Rebuffed by Lucas, she tries the same scheme again with François Pignon (Pierre Richard), another former lover who is a failed poet and prone to suicide attempts. Pignon's acceptance of the news and agreement to help coincides with a change of heart by Lucas, leading them both on separate paths to find the boy. They eventually connect on a joined search, each working under the assumption that one of them is the father. Locating Tristan in Nice, Lucas and Pignon have to pry him away from a pack of teenage delinquents who congregate around arcades, roller-skating rinks, and rock concerts. Along the way, they develop a fondness for the boy and each hope that they are his real father. Meanwhile, two mafia hit men trail Lucas to stop him from writing an exposé, leading to danger on two fronts: the mafia and rogue teens. Saving Tristan by killing the mafia hit men, Lucas breaks a story that leads to the arrest of a leading underworld kingpin and Pignon recovers from a gunshot wound. Reconciling with his real father (Michel Aumont) over the phone before returning home, Tristan agrees to tell Lucas and Pignon the truth. Instead, Tristan tells both of them separately that they are his father, swearing them each to secrecy in order not to hurt the other. Overcome with joy, both Lucas and Pignon walk arm in arm with the teenager they believe to be their son, leading Tristan to quip "C'est comme la fête des pères" ("It's like Father's Day"). In standard Veber fashion, the film ends with a freeze frame of the three central characters.

Marking the first use of the François Pignon character name in a directorial effort, replacing the previously omnipresent François Perrin, the subtext of the film rests on the age of the son and the supposed freewheeling pasts of Christine, Lucas, and Pignon. Tristan being sixteen places his birth in 1967, making the liberal sexual partnering and distant memories more than an indication of the characters' past youthful exuberance. Instead, it places them at the center of the revolutionary spirit of the times, with their romances a manifestation of the era's challenge to social norms. Christine's suggestion to Lucas and Pignon that they may be fathers sets the narrative in motion, but it also causes them to reflect on the past and reevaluate the present. Lucas's careerism and unapologetic materialism are at odds with the countercultural values of the late 1960s, while Pignon's inability to function in a changing world suggests the melancholy of a former radical whose idealism was never realized. Christine's domesticity and choice of an outwardly bland, unfeeling, but financially successful husband shows that she has traded in her liberated past for a safe and conservative present. The reflective nature of Les compères, although packaged as a popular buddy comedy, explores the same issues as its contemporary American hit The Big Chill (1983, Lawrence Kasdan). Far more direct and pensive, The Big Chill is structured around baby boomers coming to terms with adulthood and either a vanished idealism or the toll of continued commitment to the values of the late 1960s. Stripping away the gags and genre manipulations, the central characters in Les compères are asking the very same questions about their lives as they reach the cusp of turning forty. Tristan, then, initiates numerous levels of reflection for Lucas and Pignon simultaneously. He is a reminder of being young, and a possible byproduct of their past.

Tristan is also, as a supposed recipient of the genetic makeup of one of them, a window into Lucas and Pignon's differing conceptions of masculinity. Both project their own traits onto Tristan and alternate between identification and renunciation. Particularly for Lucas, who defines himself through physical toughness and unsentimental sexuality, the perceived shortcomings of Tristan read as an indictment of his own masculinity. Lucas fits the model of the "comic loubard" that Vincendeau uses to describe the screen persona (and often off-screen persona as well) of Depardieu.[8] An updated version of the violent and unsophisticated character he played in *Les valseuses* (1974), in the 1980s Depardieu retained the central traits of the character despite his age or the profession of his characters. In *Les compères*, as is the case in *La chèvre*, his character may be clean-cut and professional, but he has the ability to tap into his past and unleash his violent, brutish true self. Looking at Tristan, Lucas seems to be wondering how it could be possible for him to be the father of a boy who cannot fight and breaks down emotionally over a girl. His conflation of violence and masculinity are so pronounced that when Tristan considers backing down from a fight with the youth gang leader who has stolen his girlfriend, Lucas suggests that by refusing to fight he may become gay.

For Pignon, these are the very traits that seem to confirm that he is the father, as the boy is a reflection of his own sensitivities and frailties. Pignon's unhinged emotions and penchant for crying embarrass and frustrate Lucas, but eventually the two alternate their acts of physical bravery and nurturing to each embody less rigid expressions of masculinity. The changes in Lucas and Pignon stem from fatherhood. The need to care for a son allows Lucas to let his guard down and show sensitivity, while Pignon's desire to protect his offspring throws him wholeheartedly into the face of physical danger. Tristan, his arm broken in a fight, needs help tying his shoes, and it is Lucas who steps into the role of father, having a moment of clarity that is later reinforced when he cuts Tristan's steak at dinner, realizing the years he may have wasted where he should have been raising a child. Upon Tristan's individual revelations about his "real" father, Pignon is overjoyed but does not cry, whereas Lucas tears up and struggles to compose himself, completing their shared move toward a balanced masculinity.

The polarities of Lucas and Pignon fit the parameters of the buddy comedy and also provide a narrative logic for the repetition of gags at the core of Veber's comedy. Acts of violence are doubled and reversed, most elaborately with Lucas attacking the father of Tristan's girlfriend with a phone, only to have the father use the same phone to assault Pignon moments later. Veber even uses the hit men to repeat violence, throwing an arcade owner through a window shortly after Lucas had thrown the man through another window. The first act of repetition comes when Christine meets with Lucas in a restaurant to tell him that he is the father of her missing son. She shows him a photo of Tristan and tries to override his cynicism by saying "il y a quelque chose, non?" ("There is something there, no?") When meeting with Pignon in a café—with Veber using identical shots and editing approach from the previous sequence—she shows him the photo and repeats "il y a quelque chose, non?" to Pignon when his smile turns into an expression of doubt. *Les compères* deviates from the traditional multiple father story where there is genuine uncertainty about paternity. Christine knows all along that her husband is the true father, and uses her past relationships with Lucas and Pignon to elicit their help. Her prompting of both men to see their likenesses in the photograph reinforces a broader theme of uncaring females pushing men into peril, an act that is doubled by Tristan's girlfriend.

The scenes with Christine show comedic repetition and matched shots, but the *mise en scène* is used to demonstrate difference as much as similarity between Lucas and Pignon. The elegant restaurant where Lucas meets with Christine is juxtaposed with a casual café for her meeting with Pignon. The class dynamics between the characters are punctuated again by the hotels they check into when in Nice, their varying wardrobes, and the prominent placement of Lucas's BMW throughout the film. More than a divide between the two presumptive fathers, Christine and her husband's anxieties over Tristan's disappearance are informed by class as well. Having run off with a girl whose parents are working class and unsophisticated—the father runs a flophouse hotel and the mother is a gas station attendant—there is a sense that he has renounced his privilege in order to fit in with the lower classes. In the opening shot of the teenage couple hitchhiking, there is an impression of wayward and listless youth. From rock and roll to the denim and leather fashion of the teenagers throughout the film, there is a preoccupation with juvenile delinquency that links 1983 to the iconography of the 1950s. For the group of teenagers that Tristan is attempting to join, there is a sincere sense of disaffection stemming from joblessness and a still developing overhaul of French education (namely the university system). Yet, the contrast of his affluent home in Paris with the shantytowns of Nice that are shown in *Les compères* highlights Tristan's confusing of teenage angst and rebellion for the grounded disaffection of the poor and working-class teens he is trying to befriend.

An outward marker of teenage rebellion in *Les compères* is a connection to American popular culture. Teens congregate and act like characters from American teenage movies from the late 1950s and early 1960s, replete with motorcycles, denim vests, and hangout spaces. The Video Flip (a video game arcade) and the roller-skating rink Rockers are ludicrously imagined parodies of American culture, but in Veber's translation of teenage rebellion into physical spaces he evokes the same sort of inexact simulacrum of American rock and roll that is best represented by the unequivocally French icon Johnny Hallyday. The teens perform their toughness and rebellion by assuming the outer trappings of American culture, going so far as to use a hamburger and "American" mustard to threaten Pignon. Late in the film, Tristan's father walks through his bedroom and contemplates the divide that has separated him and his son. The walls of the bedroom are plastered with posters including a vintage Cadillac, San Francisco's Golden Gate Bridge, Elvis Presley, the animated Pink Panther character, and movie posters for *Superman* (1978, Richard Donner) and *Superman II* (1980, Richard Lester). Tristan has the French poster for the first film, reading *Superman: Le Film*, but has taken a cutout picture of his own face and placed it over Christopher Reeve, figuratively willing himself to become the most American of fictional characters. This desire for American identity filtered through French context informs the generational split between Tristan and his parents while also, possibly, reflecting on Jack Lang's paranoia about cultural imperialism explored in the previous chapter.

In walking through Tristan's bedroom, there is a reminder of the liminal nature of adolescence. Tristan is old enough to leave home, have sex, and get into serious trouble, yet his room is still populated by toys and images of cartoon characters. This moment of sentimentality is in stark contrast to the recurring jokes, fears, and misunderstandings regarding Tristan's sexuality. The first scene in the film following the teenage hitchhikers has Tristan's parents at the police station to report him missing. The cynical detective asks if Tristan is on drugs and then he says to the father, "Do you ever watch your son shower?" The suggestion and ensuing beat before the detective clarifies that he is asking in case they have seen needle marks invites speculation about sexual abuse. His next question, asking if Tristan is homosexual, furthers the idea of Tristan as a sexual being, not an asexual and innocent child. Later, the tension of Lucas carrying an unconscious Tristan through a hotel lobby is matched by the boy's confusion the next morning when he wakes up to two grown men staring at him sleeping. The discomfort of moments that seem incriminating without context is part of an undercurrent of dark humor throughout *Les compères*.

Pignon is a suicidal depressive whose introduction into the narrative is accompanied by a gag that walks a fine line between humor and pathos. Sitting at his typewriter reading over his suicide letter, Pignon picks up a pistol, places it in his mouth, and is about to pull the trigger when the phone rings. Looking at the phone and pausing, Pignon picks up the phone and mumbles "Allo?" with the gun still in his mouth. Brightening with happiness when he hears Christine's voice, he continues the conversation, only removing the gun from his mouth when she asks him if he is eating. Instead, he absentmindedly places the gun at his temple as he joyfully makes plans to meet his former lover. The physical comedy in Richard's performance of the scene coincides with the agony and ecstasy of Veber's comic mantra of turning pain into laughter. In another scene, where Lucas asks Pignon to cry on demand, the depressive instead breaks into uncontrollable laughter. Pignon's laughter is mistaken for sobbing, furthering the idea that joy and pain are linked to the point of being indistinguishable from each other.

If explorations of pain and laughter coincide with Veber's philosophy on comedy, the characters themselves are surely reflections of a split sense of himself as a writer. The hardnosed journalist Lucas and the flighty failed poet Pignon represent opposite ends of the writing spectrum. One is practical, logical, and financially successful while the other is dreamy, expressive, and so professionally impotent that he wants to kill himself. Together, Lucas and Pignon contain the inner struggles of most professional artists. Trying to find a balance between practical concerns while maintaining creative fulfillment is a classic story for life in the arts, particularly within a commercially oriented medium like cinema. As such, *Les compères* follows in the footsteps of *Le jouet* by crafting a narrative that touches on a number of topics, but is structured around the life of writers.

Released in November of 1983, *Les compères* was a success at the French box office, although not quite at the same level as its predecessor *La chèvre*. Still, with 4.8 million tickets sold, *Les compères* finished fourth at the annual box office, one place ahead of the top American import from that year, *Return of the Jedi* (1983, Richard Marquand).[9] Veber traveled to the Soviet Union with Richard and Depardieu to screen the film at the Moscow Film Festival, foregrounding his growing global reputation.[10] Released in a limited theatrical run in the U.S., the film was retitled *The ComDads* as a clumsy attempt to match the double entendre of the French title. Literally translated, *compères* means accomplices, but the sounds of "co" and "pères" placed together in the word also suggest "co-fathers." *ComDads* sounds like comrades, but the title itself is both nonsensical and confusing. When Hollywood finally decided to give the film "le remake" treatment they would settle on a less ambitious title in *Father's Day* (1997, Ivan Reitman).

LE REMAKE

Following the critical and financial disappointment of *Pure Luck* in 1991, Veber returned as a viable subject for a Hollywood remake following the success of *The Birdcage* (1996, Mike Nichols). Adapting *La cage aux folles* to contemporary American political issues, the film grossed $124 million domestically and an additional $61 million overseas.[11] Again matching Robin Williams to Veber's material, Warner Bros., along with producers Joel Silver and Ivan Reitman, hoped to capitalize on the success of *The Birdcage* by placing a heavy bet on *Father's Day*. Reitman, who had previous success with the buddy formula as the director of *Twins* (1988), also had a track record of success making big-budget comedies, most notably with *Ghostbusters* (1984). He was also responsible for some high-profile flops, such as *Junior* (1994), the failed reteaming of *Twins* co-stars Danny DeVito and Arnold Schwarzenegger. Budgeting *Father's Day* at an estimated $85 million, and casting Williams alongside his friend and recurring award show and charity event comic partner Billy Crystal, the film looked to offset its bloated budget with excitement over the first big-screen pairing of the comedians.[12] Using *Les compères* as a

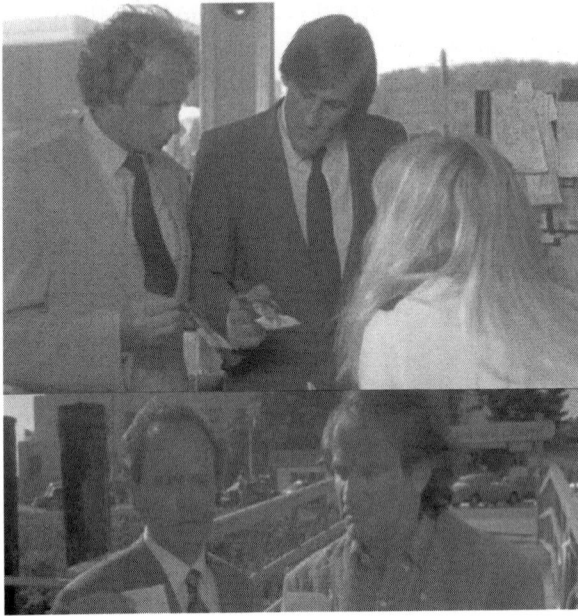

Figure 4.2 The realization of Pignon and Campana (Pierre Richard and Gérard Depardieu, above) replicated with Jack and Dale (Billy Crystal and Robin Williams, below) in *Father's Day*.

vetted buddy comedy property, the project is a prime example of Hollywood's calculated appeals to a mass audience as well as the creative miscalculations of taking such an inorganic approach to making art. Critically panned, *Father's Day* earned a meager $28.5 million at the box office; a cost-to-profit difference that easily outpaced the notorious economic disasters *Ishtar* (1987, Elaine May) and *Hudson Hawk* (1991, Michael Lehmann).[13]

Adapted by the screenwriting team of Lowell Ganz and Babaloo Mandel, Reitman and Silver looked to reliable writers with a knack for connecting with a mass audience. Ganz and Mandel were responsible for writing hits like *Splash* (1984, Ron Howard), *Parenthood* (1989, Ron Howard), and *City Slickers* (1991, Ron Underwood). The latter starred Billy Crystal, and Ganz and Mandel would subsequently write both of Crystal's forays into feature film directing, *Mr. Saturday Night* (1992) and *Forget Paris* (1995).[14] Their close working relationship with Crystal makes the screenwriters' choices in *Father's Day* all the more curious, relegating Crystal to a thankless straight man role opposite the unrestrained clownishness of Robin Williams. Crystal plays Jack Lawrence, a reinterpreted version of Depardieu's Lucas who is no longer a journalist but a high-powered Los Angeles attorney. Physically diminutive, Jack nevertheless retains Lucas's physical strength and fondness for head-butting people into unconsciousness. Crafting the character to better match Crystal, Ganz and Mandel also remove the commentaries on the writer's life in *Les compères* by turning him into a lawyer. Assuming the Pignon role, now renamed Dale Putley, Robin Williams plays a failed Berkeley playwright. Dale remains suicidal, which in retrospect has a tragic sense of foreboding.

Far more important than the changes to the characters, the altered temporality of *Father's Day* completely upends the central theme of Veber's original. The missing son Scott (Charlie Hofheimer) is seventeen, placing his birth in 1980. Still, the film attempts to trade on nostalgia for free love and the rebellious energy of the Woodstock generation. Reminiscing about their wild pasts with Scott, Jack and Dale invent an alternative vision of 1980. Mining their generational split, the men complain about contemporary music and try to convince Scott about the merits of the Rolling Stones, Jimi Hendrix, and Sly & the Family Stone. The age of Crystal and Williams would match with this investment in late 1960s counterculture, but Scott's age suggests that he is an outgrowth of a different stage in their lives. Whereas *Les compères* directly connects Lucas and Pignon to the late 1960s, causing them to reflect on adulthood and how they have matched up to the idealism of their youth, *Father's Day* is premised on actions that were a decade removed from their wild days. The difference between a child conceived in 1967 Paris and Southern California in 1980 could not be more striking. *Les compères* revolves around a child born on the cusp of a leftist revolution, while *Father's Day* places Scott's birth during the year of Ronald Reagan's election and stages his conception in the candidate's hometown of Los Angeles for good measure.[15]

The failures of *Father's Day* have less to do with altering Veber's political commentaries than they do with the excessiveness and calculation of the film as a sellable product. Key gags are repeated from the original with diminished returns due to the extreme physical and comedic differences in the lead actors, while updated dialogue strains to translate the French original for an American audience. Dale's macho shortcomings are apparent in his lack of knowledge about baseball and, being 1997, there is a compulsory O. J. Simpson Bronco chase joke. The most Hollywood of all the changes in the film is its sentimentality over the sanctity of the family. Whereas Tristan's father is aloof and resentful in *Les compères*, the mafia subplot is replaced by a parallel narrative in *Father's Day* where Scott's real father (Bruce Greenwood) heads out on the road to find his son. Reuniting the family, Jack and Dale are told the same lie by Scott that Tristan tells to Lucas and Pignon, but this time they both know that they are not the father. Instead, Jack finds the motivation to start a family with his long-suffering wife (Julia Louis-Dreyfus). Dale takes off in Jack's red convertible Jaguar and picks up a stranded motorist (Mary McCormack) who also happens to be an attractive blonde intrigued by his awkward charm. The two drive off into the sunset on the Pacific Coast Highway as the credits roll.

In addition to broad performances, unfunny dialogue, and narrative clichés, the overall stiffness of the film is furthered by the financial largesse and corporate concerns of Warner Bros. being apparent throughout. From the opening credit song, written and performed for the film by Paul McCartney, to a cameo appearance by Mel Gibson, there is a sense that the studio felt it could create a hit movie simply by throwing money at the project. At the same time, the prominence of the pop-rock band Sugar Ray speaks to how laughably out of touch the film is with youth culture and the transparent manipulations of corporate synergy. Imaging the band as edgy punks with an underground following of tough teenagers, Sugar Ray and its lead singer Mark McGrath take up an inordinate amount of screen time. On one hand, setting action at their concerts shows a ludicrous reimagining of alternative music fans in the 1990s, blending a hodgepodge of rough-kid stereotypes ranging from Goths to the type of store-bought movie punks from the 1980s in leather, dyed mohawks, spikes, and piercings. As laughable as it is to connect a radio-friendly band like Sugar Ray to a dangerous subculture that is threatening to steal Scott away from his family, the band's appearance and imagined following in *Father's Day* was designed to boost album sales, not contribute to the narrative of the film. Signed to Atlantic Records, a subsidiary of the Warner Music Group and part of the Time Warner media conglomerate, the film division at Warner Bros. helped promote the band in advance of the release of their mainstream breakthrough album *Floored* (1997).[16] That a band like Sugar Ray could be deemed as dangerous and debauched in *Father's Day* may be the most faithful aspect of the translation, mirroring Veber's detachment from French youth culture in *Les compères*.

Taken collectively, *The Toy*, *Pure Luck*, and *Father's Day* all support Veber's distaste for Hollywood remakes of his films. "I had seven movies remade here," Veber would say to a Los Angeles audience a year before the release of the eighth, *Dinner for Schmucks*, "and most of them were pieces of shit."[17] It is safe to say that *Father's Day* is not the implied exception in Veber's statement. The safe distance of being uninvolved in most of these adaptations frees Veber to make such honest assessments, of course, but at the same time he recognizes the difficulty of making something funny again for a new audience. "Comedy is something so mysterious," he would say, capturing in a single sentence the struggles of creation, the impossibilities of adaptation, and the limitations of critical and textual analysis to explain humor.[18] Like most comedy writers, Veber has internalized the struggle of creation and grown immune to critical and scholarly analysis of his work. With his next two films, *Les fugitifs* and *Three Fugitives*, he would step into the dual role of creating an original work for a French audience and then adapting it for Hollywood.

NOTES

1. Fournier-Lanzoni, *French Comedy*, p. 104.
2. Aside from his 1953 hit "That's Amore," Martin's commercial success as a singer came after he and Jerry Lewis had parted ways professionally.
3. Chutkow, *Depardieu*, p. 178. Depardieu made four films with Duras: *Nathalie Granger* (1972), *La femme du Gange* (1974, *Woman of the Ganges*), *Le camion* (1977, *The Lorry*), and *Baxter, Vera Baxter* (1977).
4. Ginette Vincendeau, *Stars and Stardom in French Cinema*.
5. Ibid. pp. 218–19.
6. Ibid.
7. Ibid. p. 223.
8. Ibid. p. 219.
9. *JP's Box-Office*, <http://www.jpbox-office.com/fichfilm.php?id=6817> (accessed January 5, 2019).
10. Veber, *Que ça reste entre nous*, p. 218.
11. *Box Office Mojo*, <http://www.boxofficemojo.com/movies/?page=intl&id=birdcage. htm> (accessed January 5, 2019).
12. *IMDB*, <http://www.imdb.com/title/tto1119109/> (accessed January 5, 2019).
13. *Box Office Mojo*, <http://www.boxofficemojo.com/movies/?id=fathersday.htm> (accessed January 5, 2019).
14. Crystal would also direct the baseball feature *61** (2001) for HBO, but *Mr. Saturday Night* and *Forget Paris* remain his only two theatrically released films as a director.
15. Reagan's primary residence from 1957 until he entered the White House in 1981 was located in the Pacific Palisades neighborhood of Los Angeles.
16. *Floored* would eventually be certified double platinum, with sales largely due to the hit single "Fly."
17. *A Conversation with Francis Veber*.
18. Ibid.

CHAPTER 5

The Great Escape:
Les fugitifs (1986)

Julian Schnabel's 1996 biopic *Basquiat*, made as a personal reflection on his late friend and rival painter Jean-Michel Basquiat, asks probing questions about the intersections of artistic expression and financial success. Using the classic biopic figure of the longtime friend whose stability serves as a moral barometer for the changing subject, Schnabel deploys the composite character Benny Dalmau (Benicio Del Toro) to function as a running commentary on Basquiat's ambitions and frustrations.[1] Talking with a pre-celebrity Jean-Michel (Jeffrey Wright) while playing basketball, Benny responds to his friend's question about the pathway to fame by saying:

> "First, you're gonna have to dress right, you know? Then you're gonna have to hang out with famous people, you know? Make friends with the right blond people. Go to the right parties. Yeah, socialite. Then, you gotta do your work all the time when you're not doing that. But I'm talking about the same kind of work, the same style, so people can recognize it and don't get confused, you know? Then once you're famous— airborne, you know?—you gotta keep doing it in the same way. Even after it's boring. Unless you want people to really get mad at you, which they will anyway."

The cynicism of the dialogue regarding success, creation, and public expectations can be applied to artists working in any medium, but Benny's words seem particularly apt in explaining elements of the crossroads Francis Veber found himself facing in 1986. This is not to suggest that Pierre Richard was one of the "right blond people" or that Veber's success came through socializing, but there is a pervading sense that the momentum of success was both exhilarating and frustrating for Veber. Having used the buddy comedy formula to gain independence as a writer-director, leaving behind his screenwriter-for-hire past, he must have felt the need to go back to the well one more time, which in many ways he does with *Les fugitifs*. Referring to the film in his memoir as the "last of the Depardieu-Richard trilogy," Veber's understanding of *La chèvre*, *Les compères*, and *Les fugitifs* as a unified whole speaks to him finding his own personal style as a filmmaker and replicating himself to meet public demand.[2]

Of course, the films are not a literal trilogy. Although Veber makes a habit of reusing character names from film to film, all three narratives are independent of each other. Still, in Veber's conception and their public consumption, *Les compères* and *Les fugitifs* read as quasi-sequels to *La chèvre*. The fact that the ordering can be reversed, as is shown in the U.S. release poster for *La chèvre* selling it as a follow-up to *Les compères*, only furthers the idea that the films can be read as interchangeable companion pieces despite having independent narratives. Yet there are differences in tone and visual aesthetics between *Les fugitifs* and the previous two films with Depardieu and Richard that suggest Veber's boredom with the formula and an ambition to do more as a director than simply facilitate the screen stardom of his leads, especially Richard. Veber stated in 1981 that writers must be mindful of money, but that it was never a prime motivator for him.[3] Explaining that he could have done better for himself financially in the 1970s had he demanded a percentage of the gross for his screenplays, Veber frames his ambitions as purely artistic while also recognizing missed opportunities.[4] *Les fugitifs* and its immediate aftermath can paradoxically be viewed as an assertion of his artistic principles and acquiescence to the monetary motivators of the movie business.

The viability of French comedy in the years separating *Les compères* and *Les fugitifs* was certainly not in question. The action-comedy hybrids *Marche à l'ombre* (1984, Michel Blanc) and *Les ripoux* (1984, Claude Zidi, *My New Partner*) finished in first and second place at the annual box office, selling 6.1 million and 5.8 million tickets respectively.[5] The following year's biggest hit, *Trois hommes et un couffin* (1985, Coline Serreau, *Three Men and a Cradle*), sold an astounding 10.2 million tickets in France.[6] Fournier-Lanzoni writes of the genre in the 1970s and 1980s, "French comedies addressed the desire to 'deconstruct' the daily realities of the French people and were characterized by an unprecedented liberalist wave bringing modernity, relevance, and truth in their representation of the spirit of the times."[7] As such, comedies that found a way to tap into shared anxieties and topical issues tended to find success, starkly moving away from the genre's avoidance of real-life situations prior to 1968.[8] More than a series of gags, *Les fugitifs* and *Les compères* bookend Serreau's *Trois hommes et un couffin* to explore ideas surrounding masculinity and the French family in crisis in the 1980s. The stylistic approach of *Les fugitifs*, however, would depart from both Serreau's comedy and Veber's previous film.

LE FILM

If Pierre Richard's recollections of the shoot are any indication, Veber's approach to directing took a serious turn on *Les fugitifs*. Taking his penchant for multiple takes to extremes, Veber demanded eighty takes on the first day of shooting with the actor Jean Carmet, who plays a retired veterinarian bordering on dementia.[9] The desire to work through the scene with the camera rolling and arrive at the most perfect take possible paid off for Carmet, earning him a César nomination for supporting actor, but Richard also suggests that it left Carmet traumatized and unsure of how to deal with Veber.[10] In another memory, Richard recalls a moment on set where Depardieu suggested an alteration to the script, feeling that a slight change in dialogue would benefit the scene. Reflecting on the suggestion for only six seconds, Veber responded that if they changed the line it would upend a plot element on page 63 of the screenplay.[11] Veber's ability to have immediate and precise recall, down to exact the page number, indicates the intensity he brought to the making of the film. The long incubation period for the film, separated by three years from *Les compères* without any other writing projects, was by far his longest gap between projects since he staged his first play, *L'enlèvement*, in 1968. From the departures in visual design and tonal shifts apparent in the finished film to

Figure 5.1 Jean Lucas (Gérard Depardieu) walks out of prison in *Les fugitifs*.

Veber's intensity on set, *Les fugitifs* is a starkly different buddy comedy than the previous two installments in the "trilogy."

Released from prison, convicted bank robber Jean Lucas (Depardieu) sets out to go straight despite the doubts and open hostility of police superintendent Duroc (Maurice Barrier). Determined to catch Lucas when he returns to his old ways, Duroc watches from outside a bank as Lucas enters to cash a check. While opening an account, Lucas is taken hostage by François Pignon (Richard), a bumbling amateur criminal. Assuming that Lucas is the bank robber and Pignon is the hostage, Duroc and the police surrounding the bank, sparking Lucas to escape with Pignon. Lucas is accidentally shot in the leg, tying his fate to Pignon's after they outrun the cops and the ex-convict has to rely on the disaster-prone stranger for medical attention. Enlisting the help of a retired veterinarian friend to remove the bullet (during which process Lucas is literally treated like a dog), Pignon explains the motivation for the bank robbery. He is jobless and the death of his wife has traumatized their young daughter, leaving her unable (or unwilling) to speak. Initially cold and dismissive of Pignon's plight, Lucas becomes emotionally invested in helping after he meets the daughter, Jeanne (Anaïs Bret). When Jeanne is placed in a state-run orphanage Lucas and Pignon work together to get her back, breaking into the orphanage and taking her in the middle of the night. Breaking her silence, Jeanne talks to Lucas. On the run, Lucas helps Pignon and his daughter make it to the Italian border, posing as a father while Jeanne and Pignon dress in drag to fool the police. At the last minute, Lucas decides to go with them to Italy as part of a reformed nuclear family. For the first time as a director, Veber chooses not to use a freeze frame and instead ends the film with a long shot of the trio walking toward the Alps to cross the border. Lucas is placed in the middle, holding Jeanne's hand on one side and taking Pignon's arm on the other. It is a remarkably optimistic ending to a dark film.

The first shot of a prison hallway foregrounds a darker mood and stronger sense of despair than Veber's previous films. An exposed brick wall to the left of the frame and steel bars at the end of the hallway contrast with an antiseptic white wall with solid doors and elaborate modern handles to create a tension between old and new, retrofitting an old prison with new designs to connect past and contemporary punishment. Walking through the prison with a guard upon his release, Lucas leaves one entrapment for another: moving from cell to barred hallway to barred stairwell, and finally past the windowed guard stand at the center of the panopticon prison and down another barred hallway, to enter a new series of enclosures. Lucas enters the center room from one hallway and exits through another, but there are numerous other hallways connected to this center spoke of monitoring and control. Instead of a single establishing shot of the prison and another medium shot showing Lucas exiting, which would convey the necessary narrative information, Veber spends an inordinate amount of time and energy on the opening sequence. The labyrinthine prison corridors, shown in thirteen shots over the span of three minutes to open the film, establish a claustrophobic and frustrating tone that informs the tensions that run throughout *Les fugitifs*. Michel Foucault, connecting the "observatory" prison model exemplified by the panopticon design to broader state and social control, remarks on the French origins of a system of discipline and surveillance that has become normalized outside the prison context.[12] The prison is a real space connected to the world of the character, but it is also a symbol for something broader. When compared to the cartoonish Mexican prison of *La chèvre*, the realistic setting, elaborate camera movements (for Veber, at least), and expressive framing convey a seriousness and artistic intent that separates *Les fugitifs* from any of Veber's previous films.

Both the François Pignon and Jean Lucas character names are reused from *Les compères*, and the duo retain some outward markers of oppositional masculinity, but they are dramatically altered in terms of tone. The hostage reversal connects the criminal and the common man, showing their plights as interchangeable and, therefore, stemming from the same cause. The entire film reads as a meditation on a broader malaise defined by restrained individualism and the failed promise of a social welfare state under then president François Mitterand. The threat of the government taking away Pignon's daughter and the pressures of Duroc rooting for Lucas's failure place both characters at odds with the state. Moreover, both are left behind in the current economic climate. Using the Italian border as a resolution, solving all of Lucas and Pignon's problems, underlines that their troubles are directly tied to France. Throughout the film the antagonists are symbols of the state, ranging from Duroc and his fellow policemen to the child services workers who take Jeanne.

Discontent and hopelessness run deeper than government policy and heartless bureaucracies. The sense that the country is changing pervades the film, as does the lack of economic opportunity. Exterior shots during the bank robbery juxtapose old and new. Shoppers and peddlers at *des brocantes* (an outdoor street market with antiques) are forced out to make way for the police, while an aerobics class above them comes out to watch from their balcony. Privileging the young, wealthy, and modern over the old is handled exclusively through *mise en scène*, with no need for dialogue to tease out or explain meaning. When stealing a Porsche 944 from a wealthy older man calling on an attractive but much younger woman, Lucas roughly throws the man out of the car and onto the sidewalk. The moment is as much a cathartic revenge against the excesses of the bourgeoisie as it is a means of escape to further the narrative. In an alternate moment of compassion among strangers, a homeless Pignon, separated from Jeanne and Lucas, is caught stealing the castoffs from a produce stand. Rather than chase him off, the vendor calls out to Pignon, hands him a few of his best apples and tomatoes, and says, "Here. These are much better." Giving Pignon a knowing look, this act of kindness is a show of solidarity between poor and working-class people that inverts the hostility and class difference of the carjacking sequence.

The sentimentality of the grocer, however, is a rare break from the resentments that run through the film. Approached by two young punks in an abandoned warehouse, Lucas turns the tables by sticking them up and demanding their clothes. Although the punks share some characteristics with the wayward youth in *Les compères* (namely the 1980s filmic stereotype of the oversized beat box being held over the shoulder), the pair that threaten Lucas in *Les fugitifs* appear to be far more dangerous and destitute than the cartoonish delinquents in Tristan's orbit from the earlier film. Similarly, a scene in which Lucas sends Pignon to meet with one of his former underworld acquaintances to try to score forged passports marks both a changing France and perceived threats from "others." Told to meet Lucas's connection Labib (Jean Benguigui) at Café du Rond-Point, Pignon walks into a loud room filled exclusively with men, most of them of African and Middle Eastern origin. The perceived threat of difference is realized as Pignon is threatened and assaulted by three men in the club. Later, Lucas returns to set things right and retrieve their forged passports by driving a van through the café and firing a shot just past Labib's head as a warning. Between wayward punks and an influx of criminal immigrants, threats abound for the white male leads in *Les fugitifs*. For good measure, Lucas and Pignon watch in hiding as Jeanne is approached by a possible pedophile offering her candy. Danger is everywhere in the France of *Les fugitifs*.

Carolyn Durham is especially perceptive in her analysis of the film and its remake in unpacking the crises of family and masculinity that Veber constructs with Lucas and Pignon. Durham makes a compelling case for the homoerotic subtext of the film and the devaluing of femininity, particularly in light of the film ending with Lucas assuming the father role and Pignon dressed as a woman to perform as his wife.[13] As is the case in *La chèvre* and *Les compères*, the difference in physical stature between Depardieu and Richard helps to reinforce gendered norms. Moreover, a scene with Lucas lying unconscious on a warehouse floor and Jeanne walking over to him and curling up into his arms uses Depardieu's physical size to envelop the child. The difference in the size of their bodies is striking, referencing Depardieu's brutish screen persona while softening its hard edges. Jeanne, as Durham points out, appears to be suffering more from the lack of an acceptable father than the literal lack of a mother, as the introduction of Lucas and his commitment to her erases the trauma of her mother's death.[14] The reconstituted family at the end of the film promises to function without a female parent. It also remains intact without disrupting expectations of heterosexuality between Pignon and Lucas.

With its themes of prison, crime, joblessness, homelessness, death, separated families, and sundry other fears and anxieties, it is easy to forget that *Les fugitifs* is a comedy. The presentation of gags in the film is part of the tonal shift from Veber's previous work rather than a counterpoint to a pervasive seriousness. The most notable physical gag of the film comes during the bank robbery. Pignon, wearing pantyhose over his head to hide his identity, uses his teeth to remove the pin from a hand grenade and inadvertently splits open the nylon stocking, exposing his entire face. There is a moment of embarrassment and recognition, then a continuation of the robbery. The gag follows in the tradition of Richard's physical comedy, but it is fleeting and altered by the narrative and aesthetic context of the film. This Pignon is not the same type of idiot as prior iterations of the character. He may not be a capable criminal, but he lacks the almost mystical aura of incompetence shown in previous films. Rather than being akin to Jerry Lewis or Jacques Tati, Richard's performance is more subdued throughout *Les fugitifs* and his gags fall within the realm of realistic possibility. Unlike Perrin in *La chèvre* and *La grand blond avec une chaussure noire* or Pignon in *Les compères*, this Pignon is certainly not accustomed to his bad luck, resigned to his incompetence, or defined by a distorted self-confidence. This is a restrained Pierre Richard that is most reflective of his performance in *Le jouet*.

The subdued gags written for Pignon coincide with others that vacillate between the ridiculous and disturbing. Entering the orphanage in the middle of the night to take back Jeanne, Lucas and Pignon step into a large room with rows of beds filled with sleeping children. Quietly moving over to pick up Jeanne and stepping out of the room, Lucas hands the child to Pignon. Only, this girl is Asian. The pause as the girl looks up at the two men, processing the situation while they do the same, is meant to induce laughter, but it is a cheap laugh premised on the clumsy foregrounding of difference that recalls the more tasteless aspects of *La chèvre*. The moment of processing passed, the child screams, which crescendos a few minutes later when Lucas returns the child to the bed and the entire room of children scream as well, collectively convinced that he is there to abduct them. It is a humor predicated on fear and trauma. Later, forcing an inebriated doctor (Michel Blanc) to care for a comatose Jeanne, the intended humor of the drunk shtick is offset by the gravity of the situation. Devoid of the conscious breaks from realism that are at the heart of *La chèvre* and *Les compères*, laughing as a drunk doctor tends to a small child who appears to be dying would be an unnatural response.

From tone and performance to visual style and music, *Les fugitifs* marks a departure for Veber. Not only is it more realistic and muted in its comedy, the film often seems like the work of a different director. Gone is the slapdash television aesthetic, replaced by the moody cinematography of Luciano Tovoli, working with Veber for the first time. Tovoli's contributions to the mood and meaning of *The Passenger* (1975, Michelangelo Antonioni) and *Suspiria* (1977, Dario Argento) might have made him seem an unlikely candidate to shoot the third film in the supposed Depardieu-Richard trilogy. Vladimir Cosma's score is unrecognizable in comparison to his work on Veber's three previous films, using a bluesy slide guitar and emotive traditional scoring in place of the repetitive folk arrangements that had set the light comedic mood of those earlier films. Overall, the film feels more like an action film than a Veber comedy. As Fournier-Lanzoni explains, French comedies can often "be described as a hybrid art form," which is apparent in a number of Veber's screenwriting credits from the 1970s that use the model of the *film policier* as a venue for comedy.[15] *Les fugitifs* certainly adheres to this sense of hybridity, but its connection to the previous pairings of Depardieu and Richard make the seriousness and darkness especially pronounced.

Although it was a box office success, the film would mark the last collaboration between Veber and Richard. Seeing himself and Depardieu as the French Laurel and Hardy, Richard wanted to continue making films in the same mold with Veber. Instead, he was left to wonder about the reasons behind the conclusion of their partnership and a growing personal distance over the years.[16] Chalking the decision up to the simple fact that Richard was getting too old to play the Pignon character, Veber addresses the ending of his partnership with Richard in his memoir as taking place under less than stellar terms. Feeling that Richard had an expectation that they would keep working together, Veber expresses disappointment that Richard had stopped writing and directing from 1976 to 1986, instead becoming professionally reliant on Veber's projects.[17] Coupled with Fournier-Lanzoni's critique of Richard that, "The pseudo revolutionary aspect of his character which was his trademark during the 1970s gradually disappeared to give way to a more conformist character in the following decade," there is a sense that Veber realized that the collaboration had run its course, as had Richard's time as a viable screen artist.[18]

The response to the release of *Les fugitifs* was enthusiastic, albeit not as overwhelming as the box office returns for *La chèvre*. It was not known at the time that the film would be Richard and Depardieu's final pairing. Finishing sixth at the annual French box office in 1986, with 4.4 million tickets sold, *Les fugitifs* was the top grossing comedy of the year. Unlike Veber's previous films, however, it was not picked up for distribution in the U.S. The reasons for this had nothing to do with the perceived marketability of the film with the type of American audiences who frequented foreign and art house films. Instead, it was intentionally held back so as not to undermine the enthusiasm for its impending Hollywood remake. As Durham points out, the rise of French remakes in Hollywood brought along with it a strategy, particularly on the part of Touchstone Pictures, of blocking American distribution of the films they planned to remake.[19] Veber did not know *Les fugitifs* would be remade in Hollywood until after the film had been released, and he certainly did not know that he would be the director tasked with translating the film for an American audience. Still, the groundwork for his eventual transition had been laid the previous summer.

Veber credits his friend Claude Berri with changing his life in 1976 by urging him to direct his own screenplays. In 1985, he says, his life changed for a second time when Gilles Jacob invited him to serve on the jury at Cannes, leading to his eventual move to Hollywood.[20] Returning to the place where he had worked as a journalist in the 1960s covering the festival as an outsider for Radio Luxembourg, Veber was now a successful figure and peer of serious filmmakers such as the president of that year's jury, Miloš Forman. Recalling deliberations where he was arguing against the idea of awarding Jean-Luc Godard's *Détective* (1985), the debates in the jury room mirror the ongoing tensions surrounding Veber's critical status.[21] Rather than automatically lauding Godard or other canon auteurs, Veber's concept of good cinema connected concept with execution, performance, and audience connection, all of which he found lacking in *Détective*. Eventually the jury awarded the Palme d'Or to *Otac na sluzbenom putu* (1985, Emir Kusturica, *When Father Was Away on Business*). But Veber's time at Cannes was not life-changing because he had a voice to resist the excesses of cinephilia. Instead, the energy of the festival presented a new array of opportunities for networking, and it was meeting the newly hired Disney executive Jeffrey Katzenberg, who professed admiration for his work, that eventually led Veber to move to Hollywood.[22]

The timing could not have seemed better. *Les fugitifs* illustrates Veber's creative restlessness, trying to craft a new visual and tonal approach to filmmaking within the formulaic guidelines of a Depardieu-Richard buddy comedy. A move to Hollywood would present new challenges and possibilities. Equally important to Veber's creative concerns, the poor health of the French film industry must have also informed his decision to go to California following *Les fugitifs*. Marked by instability, French cinema in the second half of the 1980s was in many ways a realization of the fears and combative philosophy of France's Minister of Culture Jack Lang. Pushing against Lang's strategy of *avances des recettes*, the influx of Hollywood films and the adoption of American aesthetics by French filmmakers coincided with an increased reliance on the star system and genre movies to pre-sell films and offset risk in an otherwise fickle era.[23] Pierre Richard and Gérard Depardieu were certainly key figures of the built-in star approach to selling domestic films in France, whereas the rise of Luc Besson and the turn toward large-scale international co-productions by Jean-Jacques Annaud suggested an Americanization of French auteur cinema.

The same year Veber made *Les fugitifs* saw the release of Claude Berri's *Jean de Florette* (1986) and *Manon des Sources* (1986, *Manon of the Spring*), which finished one and two at the French box office for 1986.[24] Berri's films briefly suggested a realization of Lang's "heritage film" strategy that would wed government financing of high culture with public tastes.[25] A few years later in 1989, however, box office returns would show the dominance of American films, the limited popularity of heritage films, and an overall downturn in filmgoing throughout France. The top nine films at the French box office in 1989 were made by Hollywood studios, while the tenth film was the Italian-language French-Italy coproduction *Cinema Paradiso* (1989, Giuseppe Tornatore).[26] The highest grossing French film of that year, *Trop belle pour toi* (1989, Bertrand Blier, *Too Beautiful for You*) sold just over two million tickets, a total for a top annual domestic film in France that had not been as low since the immediate postwar years.[27] The decline of the French industry was swift, as overall movie attendance in France dropped from 200 million in 1982 to half of that by 1990.[28] For Veber in the late 1980s, as was the case for Lucas and Pignon at the end of *Les fugitifs*, it was clearly time to leave France.

NOTES

1. George F. Custen, *Bio/Pics: How Hollywood Constructed Public History*, pp. 69–71.
2. Veber, *Que ça reste entre nous*, p. 222.
3. Salé, *Les scénaristes au travail*, p. 121.
4. Ibid.
5. *JP's Box-Office*, <http://www.jpbox-office.com/charts_france.php?filtre=datefr&infla=0&variable=1984> (accessed January 5, 2019).
6. *JP's Box-Office*, <http://www.jpbox-office.com/charts_france.php?filtre=datefr&infla=0&variable=1985> (accessed January 5, 2019).
7. Fournier-Lanzoni, *French Comedy*, p. 121.
8. Ibid.
9. Richard, *Je sais rien, mais je dirait tout*, p. 234.
10. Ibid.
11. Ibid. p. 235.
12. Michel Foucault, *Discipline and Punish: The Birth of the Prison*, pp. 170–7.
13. Durham, *Double Takes*, pp. 185–6.
14. Ibid. p. 186.
15. Fournier-Lanzoni, *French Comedy*, p. 1.
16. Richard, *Je sais rien, mais je dirait tout*, p. 238.
17. Veber, *Que ça reste entre nous*, pp. 224–5.
18. Fournier-Lanzoni, *French Comedy*, pp. 168–9.
19. Durham, *Double Takes*, p. 9.
20. Veber, *Que ça reste entre nous*, p. 228.
21. Ibid. pp. 228–9.
22. Ibid. p. 229.
23. Fournier-Lanzoni, *French Comedy*, p. 124.
24. *JP's Box-Office*, <http://www.jpbox-office.com/charts_france.php?filtre=datefr&infla=0&variable=1986> (accessed January 5, 2019).
25. Russel Cousins, "Jean de Florette." In Phil Powrie (ed.), *The Cinema of France*, p. 185.

26. *JP's Box-Office*, <http://www.jpbox-office.com/charts_france.php?filtre=datefr&infla=0 &variable=1989> (accessed January 5, 2019).

27. *JP's Box-Office*, <http://www.jpbox-office.com/charts_france.php?filtre=datefr&infla=0 &variable=1989> (accessed January 5, 2019).

28. Fournier-Lanzoni, *French Comedy*, p. 124.

CHAPTER 6

Francis Goes to Hollywood: *Three Fugitives* (1989)

The trend of Hollywood remaking French comedies did not start with Francis Veber, but as Carolyn Durham writes, "Veber virtually incarnates the remake phenomenon entirely on his own."[1] While a large number of French filmmakers and writers have had their work adapted by Hollywood and some have also come to Los Angeles to work, Veber's career is particularly symbolic of the phenomenon of "le remake" because it represents so many different elements of transnational adaptation. His French screenplays and directorial efforts have been optioned by Hollywood studios and turned into English-language movies without his direct input, as has been the case with *The Toy*, *The Man with One Red Shoe*, *Buddy Buddy* and more. He has also worked on the other side of the process by adapting French films for an American audience, co-writing the screenplay for Gérard Depardieu's English-language comedy *My Father the Hero* (1994, Steve Miner), a remake of *Mon père, ce héros* (1991, Gérard Lauzier) which also stars Depardieu. Even without these films, Durham's statement would still hold true if only accounting for Veber's role in making and remaking *Les fugitifs* as *Three Fugitives*.

Veber moved to California following the release of *Les fugitifs* with the intention of returning to his role as a screenwriter, now working with American directors and writing in English. After a few abandoned projects, though, Veber had the feeling that he should return to directing.[2] This inclination was reinforced by the urging of Disney executive Jeffrey Katzenberg, who had not only brought Veber to California but had also optioned the rights to *Les fugitifs* and wanted Veber to take on the remake as well.[3] Katzenberg was especially interested in adapting another popular French comedy after Touchstone's success with *Three Men and a Baby* (1987, Leonard Nimoy), a remake of Coline Serrau's *Trois hommes et un couffin* from two years earlier. A massive hit that outpaced Hollywood imports and domestic competition in France, Serreau's film looked like a good investment for Touchstone. Released in the U.S., the French original made a decent $2 million at the box office in limited release by the distributor Samuel Goldwyn, which Touchstone hoped would not eat into the remake's profits. The fears turned out to be unwarranted when *Three Men and a Baby* grossed $167 million, becoming the number one film at the North American box office for 1987.[4] Katzenberg had previously enjoyed success remaking French comedies at Touchstone, with *Down and Out in Beverly Hills* (1986, Paul Mazursky) earning an impressive $62 million at the box office, but differences in the level of success and mode of production between the two films are stark.[5] Whereas *Three Men and a Baby* quickly adapted a contemporary French comedy, *Down and Out in Beverly Hills* is a remake of *Boudu sauvé des eaux* (1932, Jean Renoir, *Boudu Saved from Drowning*) and more reflective of Mazursky's cinephilia than a calculated attempt to cash in a hot foreign property.[6] From the standpoint of a studio executive's logic, the $100 million difference in their box office performance clearly signaled which path to take on future remakes.

Hollywood's inclination toward remaking French films was not new, but certainly saw a dramatic increase in the 1980s. As Lucy Mazdon points out, there were nineteen studio remakes of French films between 1930 and 1950, only six between 1950 and 1980, and then a boom in production that largely focused on French comedies.[7] In addition to remakes of Veber's screenplays and *Three Men and a Baby*, a number of relatively contemporary French comedies were the subject of Hollywood adaptations, including: *The Man Who Loved Women* (1983, Blake Edwards) from *L'homme qui aimait les femmes* (1977, François Truffaut); *The Woman in Red* (1984, Gene Wilder) from *Un éléphant ça trompe énormément* (1976, Yves Robert); *Blame it on Rio* (1984, Stanley Donen) from *Un moment d'égarement* (1977, Claude Berri); *Happy New Year* (1987, John G. Avildsen) from *La bonne année* (1973, Claude Lelouch); and *Cousins* (1989, Joel Schumacher) from *Cousin cousine* (1975, Jean-Charles Tacchella).

The push toward remaking comedies, as opposed to stateside distribution of the originals or pulling from a wider array of French film genres, reflects the peculiarities of American distribution strategies and the growing aversion to risk on the part of studios as they came under the control of conglomerates in the blockbuster era. The refusal, or at least reluctance, of American distributors to release dubbed movies has limited the release of foreign genre films to audiences receptive to subtitles and, in turn, inadvertently recontextualized popular French comedies as art films.[8] Corporate and conglomerate ownership of studios in the 1980s, on the other hand, led to risk-averse investments that favored sequels, knock-offs, and remakes over unproven projects.[9] The choice of French comedies as opposed to other genres reflects this conservatism in that these were commercially successful films abroad, making them supposedly vetted properties.[10] In many ways this is a self-perpetuating method of selection, as Hollywood imports displace other popular genres around the globe (namely action-based genres), leaving comedy as the most resistant, and therefore popular, form of national cinema production due to the cultural specificity of humor. Hollywood's rationale for remaking French comedies, then, is informed by a decontextualized financial logic that uses a false one-to-one equivalence of box office success at home and abroad, ignoring the cultural idiosyncrasies of humor. A number of modest commercial successes and the massive box office haul of *Three Men and a Baby*, however, have validated this approach, at least from a financial perspective.

Artistically, the remake phenomenon is far more complicated and fraught with pitfalls than the simple formula used by Hollywood studio executives where French success equals American success. The renaming of the French originals, as Durham points out, are littered with unnecessary changes (as is the case with *Three Fugitives*) and impossibilities in translation that reflect the incompatibility of the broader project as an American text.[11] For example, the embedded meaning in the masculine-feminine doubling of Tacchella's *Cousin cousine* is completely lost in Schumacher's *Cousins*, whereas the attempt at translating Yves Robert's *Un éléphant ça trompe énormément*, a title borrowed from a popular French children's song, is avoided entirely with Wilder's unimaginative *The Woman in Red*. More than the titling of remakes, Mazdon explains that French originals are typically more "verbose" and dialogue-heavy than their Hollywood remakes, shifting the focus from language and meaning in French versions to straightforward descriptive dialogue and an emphasis on physical gags in their American counterparts.[12] The impossibility of faithfully adapting verbose humor into another language, of course, accounts for the foregrounding of physical comedy, but that does not necessarily forgive the shortcomings of Hollywood remakes.

Durham notes that critical responses to *Three Men and a Baby* were almost universally concerned with the impact of the changed cultural context from the French original to the American remake.[13] Often consisting of a critical default setting that favors the original text, the idea of cultural specificity can be complicated and expanded to do more than argue for an "authentic" text. Debates surrounding the cross-cultural remake also provide a framework for an argument about the continued need for national genre cinemas in the face of Hollywood's cannibalization of global screens and the universalist sensibilities of international art and festival filmmaking practices. Rather than good/bad or authentic/inauthentic binaries, comparative analyses of French comedies and their Hollywood remakes highlight differences in cultural sensibilities. Comparative readings often share a tendency to overvalue French originals and dismiss remakes out of hand, but evaluative hindsight is less compelling than a thorough unpacking of the texts and subtexts themselves.

THE FILM . . . ET LE REMAKE

Francis Veber was not the first French filmmaker that Jeffrey Katzenberg approached to remake one of their own films. Touchstone had originally hired Coline Serreau to direct *Three Men and a Baby*, but replaced her with Leonard Nimoy before shooting began.[14] The idea of replacing Serrau with Nimoy was curious, seeing that his only previous credits as a film director were *Star Trek III: The Search for Spock* (1984) and *Star Trek IV: The Voyage Home* (1986), neither of which obviously relate in style or substance to the domestic comedy of *Trois hommes et un couffin*. The American version of the film, which is used as a pop culture example by Susan Faludi in her book *Backlash: The Undeclared War against Women*, contains subtle changes that Faludi sees as emblematic of national anxieties over feminism, reinforced by Touchstone's decision to replace Serreau with a male director.[15] For Veber, of course, gender did not come into play, but his hesitation about agreeing to take on his own project almost caused Touchstone to find a replacement.[16]

The idea of Veber remaking his own film had plenty of precedents: other directors who had previously done this included Alfred Hitchcock, John Ford, Howard Hawks, Frank Capra, Yasujirō Ozu, Oscar Micheaux, and Veber's fellow French filmmaker Roger Vadim, who remade *Et Dieu . . . créa la femme* (1956) in America three decades later as *And God Created Woman* (1988). The vast majority of preceding remakes assigned to the original director departed from Veber's work on *Les fugitifs* in that they had longer gaps between production and, often, a technological impetus for revisiting the material. Ozu's *Floating Weeds* (1959), for example, departs from *A Story of Floating Weeds* (1934) in that it has synchronous sound, color cinematography, and a dramatically altered context in that the narrative is repositioned from prewar to postwar Japan. The linguistic translation for a lucrative American audience is the prime motivator for such a quick turnaround in remaking *Les fugitifs*, which explains Veber's lack of enthusiasm for the project. In subsequent years, however, the practice of foreign filmmakers returning to direct English-language remakes of their own films would become almost standard, including the likes of George Sluizer (*The Vanishing*, 1993), Ole Bornedal (*Nightwatch*, 1997), Jean-Marie Poiré (*Just Visiting*, 2001), Takashi Shimizu (*The Grudge*, 2004), and Michael Haneke (*Funny Games*, 2007).[17] For Veber, though, the opportunity to make a film on a Hollywood scale and explore a new set of creative possibilities was offset by Touchstone casting the leads in the remake without his guidance or consultation.[18] Rather than being allowed to explore the possibilities of his screenplay through casting choices, Veber was assigned Nick Nolte as a physical doppelganger for Gérard Depardieu and Martin Short as the American—make that Canadian—equivalent to Pierre Richard.

Figure 6.1 *Les fugitifs* (above) as a Hollywood repetition in *Three Fugitives* (below), replacing Pierre Richard and Gérard Depardieu with Martin Short and Nick Nolte.

Reflecting on directing a remake of *Les fugitifs*, Veber says of *Three Fugitives* that "its existence is an aberration."[19] His memories are colored with regret over the project, which may have been reinforced by the critical response to the film upon its release. The general suspicion of the project is crystalized by Durham, who states: "Veber is the first French filmmaker hired to remake his own original film; indeed, he reportedly agreed to direct *Three Fugitives* (1988) [sic] before he had even begun to shoot *Les Fugitifs* (1986)."[20] Of course, it takes Durham shaving a year off of the actual release date of *Three Fugitives* for Veber to beat Roger Vadim's *And God Created Woman* to the punch. More importantly, Durham's conspiratorial suggestion about Veber signing with Touchstone to direct the remake before shooting began on *Les fugitifs* contradicts Veber's own timeline of his move to Hollywood. The claim is even more curious in that the "report" she cites (a 1989 Vincent Canby article from the *New York Times*) does not even hint at Veber striking a secret advanced deal with Touchstone in 1986 or earlier.[21] Regardless, the implication of Durham's claim may be more important than its accuracy. Veber making a nearly shot-for-shot remake of his own film is antithetical to film as an art form, encapsulating in a single project the cynicism and crassness of Hollywood's remake strategy. *Three Fugitives* is the repackaging of a product rather than a creative reinterpretation of the original. Even so, the subtle and not-so-subtle departures from the original speak volumes about the cross-cultural differences in political context, performance traditions, and the creative feasibility of remakes in general. Being Veber's first directorial outing working with unoriginal material, the film would seem to provide a unique opportunity for isolating elements of his filmmaking approach. In some ways it does, but *Three Fugitives* also demonstrates creative exhaustion and an awkward attempt at bridging the gap between French and American humor.

The story and gags remain largely intact from *Les fugitifs*, with changes to setting and, obviously, language. As Durham states, the changes are almost entirely "essentially linguistic," confined to the sort of unavoidable changes that come with making the film in America.[22] Bordeaux is replaced by Tacoma, Washington, although neither film makes much of an effort to comment on or make explicit their specific settings. The border that the titular fugitives cross at the end of the film shifts from Italy to Canada. Nolte's character, like Depardieu's, is named Lucas, while the very French character name François Pignon becomes Ned Perry and Jeanne becomes Meg. None of these are groundbreaking changes, although each of them modifies subtext. The most glaring difference comes in the ending. Whereas *Les fugitifs* ends on a hopeful note, with Lucas walking arm in arm with Pignon and Jeanne over the Alps and into a new future together as a reformed family, *Three Fugitives* adds an additional scene once the trio have crossed over the Canadian border. Lucas drives Ned and Meg to the nearest town, gives Ned a handful of cash, and plans on heading back stateside to continue his life on the straight and narrow path. Taking off his drag costume, Ned turns to Meg and says, "This is Canada, baby, so you can call me daddy again," making it abundantly clear in action and words that his compromised masculinity has been repaired. Heading into a bank to change over his American bills to Canadian dollars, Ned is taken hostage by a bank robber and cops race to the scene, repeating the robbery scenario from the beginning of the film. Lucas, standing across the street with Meg watching as the cops surround the bank, turns to her and says, "Maybe I ought to stay with you guys a little longer." They smile at each other and the film ends with a freeze frame of the two happy fugitives. Ned is out of frame, presumably with a gun still pointed at his head.

The altered ending is bizarre, speaking to an American tendency for embellishing jokes that Veber would later complain about. "Try to make it richer," is a common suggestion he received from studios regarding jokes, with Veber calling this approach to adapting comedy "the beginning of trouble."[23] Doubling the scenario of the bank robbery gone wrong, Veber returns to the predilection for repetition that he displayed more clearly in

La chèvre and *Les compères*, but it is markedly subdued in *Les fugitifs*. Rather than Lucas choosing to stay with Pignon and Jeanne, circumstance forces the restored family to stay together and, as Durham argues, allows both Lucas and Ned to remain "real" men.[24] Rather than the ideal middle ground of masculine performance proposed by the ending of *Les compères*, where Lucas softens and Pignon toughens up, both *Les fugitifs* and *Three Fugitives* essentialize masculinity. Although Ned states his manhood at the end and removes the wig and dress, Meg looks to Lucas as her true father because he exhibits the outward physical and personality markers of masculinity. Comparing both versions to another French-to-American remake, Durham explains that "Veber's two films, like Serreau's *Trois Hommes*, portray the reconstruction of the nuclear family by an all-male parental couple, which nonetheless continues to respect traditional gender roles and the conventional notions of masculinity and femininity that characterize the heterosexual norm."[25] Even so, reading Veber's original and remake as identical commentaries on gender is problematic. The altered ending attempts to counteract the homoerotic subtext both through Ned's proclamations of his masculinity and circumstances forcing the pair to stay together. Lucas and Pignon, on the other hand, commit to each other by choice and walk off in a physical embrace, with one still dressed in drag.

If the ending of *Three Fugitives* points to the thematic alterations of the remake, the opening shot clarifies the stylistic departures from Veber's work on the original. The opening shot of *Three Fugitives* exemplifies the appeal to the lowest common denominator and aversion to subtle artistic expression associated with Hollywood production of popular genre films. As opposed to the symbolically rich prison hallway that opens *Les fugitifs*, the remake starts with an exterior shot of the prison accompanied by text at the bottom of the screen reading "McNeil Island Prison. Washington State." The uninspired and perfunctory shot lacks the symbolic richness of the original and shows an inkling of contempt for its audience, assuming that they cannot deduce setting from an interior shot of a corridor with bars and jail cells. However, context matters, and the decision to shoot at McNeil as opposed to any other American prison was certainly a conscious one.

Granted access to shoot inside the still operational prison and using its actual name, the significance of the location apparently meant enough to Veber and Touchstone to bypass the far more practical approach of shooting at a closed prison. The Lincoln Heights Jail in Los Angeles, for example, closed in 1965 and subsequently became a recurring set piece for prison sequences in countless Hollywood films and television shows, including Nick Nolte's scenes opposite Eddie Murphy at the beginning of *48 Hrs.* (1982, Walter Hill).[26] Veber using the exterior of McNeil and then shooting interior shots with Nolte walking amongst the actual prison population shows a desire to convey something more than the clumsy opening shot and text description suggests. After the closing of Alcatraz in 1963, McNeil was the lone U.S. correctional facility to be accessible only by air or water, pointing toward symbolic purpose in the unique context of the prison.[27] If John Donne's claim that "no man is an island" is founded on the need for human connection, Lucas's transformation rests with him leaving a literal and figurative island and finding fulfillment and purpose in Meg and Ned rather than living in isolation. It is a broad symbol that lacks the political urgency of *Les fugitifs*, but it demonstrates that the remake is not bereft of metaphor. Lucas leaving the prison does contain one modification that is political, however, commenting on the revolving doors of the prison system, with his exit mirrored by the entrance of a new inmate wearing an orange jumpsuit.

Veber enlisted legendary cinematographer Haskell Wexler to shoot the film, and *Three Fugitives* is much more visually polished than Veber's first three directorial outings. Compared to Luciano Tovoli's work on *Les fugitifs*, however, Wexler's cinematography is uninspired and clumsy. Wexler often places the camera too close to its subject. Bodies and faces fill the frame, leaving little room for the complicated and evocative compositions that define Tovoli's approach in the original. More than diminishing the emotional texture of the original, Wexler undercuts the comedy with a formulaic approach to camera placement that fails to account for visual humor. A gag from the bank robbery scene is particularly mishandled: a bank teller throws a bag full of money to Ned, only to have it get caught on a light fixture just out of reach. After jumping for the bag in vain, Ned demands that the teller come out onto the floor and jump for it himself. Rather than the single long shot used by Tovoli to show the entire body of a much shorter bank teller come around from the counter and comically jump for a bag he could never reach, Wexler chooses a medium shot with the teller and Ned in a two shot. The camera placement obscures the teller's height, his distance from the bag, and any part of the physical comedy that is apparent in the original. There is a brief cut to a wide shot for the last few hops, but the joke is already over at that point. Instead of a single static shot, Wexler uses multiple set-ups with diminished results as Hollywood convention trumps the efficacy of a long take that leaves an editor with only one option. Elsewhere, the visual style is informed by convention and stylistic excess. The overuse of tracking shots is jarring and the duration of shots is noticeably shorter than in the original, cutting back and forth between various vantage points in a scene rather than utilizing long takes. Editing and cinematography reflect contemporary Hollywood aesthetics, but the style of the film often detracts from the physical comedy present in Veber's script.

The Hollywoodification of Veber's style extends to small additions that may not upend the narrative, but mark the film as decidedly American. The perceived need to overexplain plot elements in *Three Fugitives* results in new dialogue written for the detectives and additional scenes of them reviewing video surveillance footage from the bank robbery. New gags are included as well, such as a boy outside of the bank stealing money from an ATM while the police are preoccupied with the hostage standoff. One scene that stands out in pinpointing additions is when Ned picks up Meg from her school following the robbery. In *Les fugitifs* Pignon arrives, brings Jeanne out to the car, and they leave a moment before the police arrive. In *Three Fugitives* the close call is replaced by a car chase, with the neurotic Ned having to outrun and outmaneuver a squad car. Later, in a scene repeated from the original where Lucas drives a van through the window of a bar, the sound editor adds the Hollywood flourish of a Wilhelm scream. Although it has no impact on the narrative, one of the most glaring additions is the rampant product placement of Moosehead Beer throughout the film. Rather than an unpaid use of a small company's logo to help situate the Pacific Northwest setting, the prominent display of neon ads and the Moosehead delivery van that Lucas steals are part of the Canadian brewery's partnership with RJR Nabisco to expand their market in the late 1980s.[28] As would be the case with *Pure Luck* two years later, the remake retains a limiting closeness to the original while still managing to distract with its American excesses.

Alterations also impact the political message of the original, removing the sense of solidarity among the working class. Ned is berated by a fisherman as he sleeps in a net along a dock. Seeing him as a homeless nuisance, the fisherman shakes his head in disgust as Ned walks away. Gone is the moment of charity and empathy between Pignon and the street grocer from the original. Other changes, like the substitution of Tacoma for Bordeaux, seem superficial and expedient but are politically significant. In choosing Tacoma, an American city that is a few hours away from a foreign border, the film avoids the charged context that a Southern California setting would have carried. Having Ned and Lucas escape to Mexico would have a different connotation (and would unintentionally refer back to *La chèvre*), whereas the decision to use Canada avoids the anxieties over immigration and identity that the southern border evokes. The removal of immigration from the film extends to the ethnic makeup of the men inside the underworld bar. Unlike the Café du Rond-Point in *Les fugitifs*, populated by African and Middle Eastern immigrants, the King Salmon Bar in *Three Fugitives* is made up of black and white American tough guys. Balancing racial connotations, the film also places African Americans in positions of power, casting James Earl Jones as Detective Dugan in place of Michel Barrier's Superintendent Duroc. Dugan and his partner, though, are relatively sympathetic characters, as opposed to the spiteful Duroc. Largely, the remake is consciously apolitical in comparison to the original, sidestepping commentaries about the state, class, and identity.

The biggest differences between the original and the remake are stylistic and rooted in the performances of Nolte and Short. Veber's memoir has a lot to say about Nolte, almost all regarding his off-camera antics and prodigious alcohol consumption. Speaking of performance, Veber says, "Nolte was good at doing what he did well, while Depardieu could do anything."[29] Touchstone's casting of Nolte as Lucas was governed primarily by appearance. Nolte has the outward markers in body type and hair, but his gruffness is a far cry from Depardieu's gentle brute. Nolte lacks the vulnerability of Depardieu in the role, with an emotive performance pulling from pain and anger that is unlike the French actor's dramatic arsenal. The steely intensity that defines Nolte's career, then, may have only suited portions of *Three Fugitives*, whereas the versatility of Depardieu allowed for the alternating toughness, tenderness, and silliness required for the project as a whole. As opposed to Nolte's reimagining of Michel Simon's Boudu in *Down and Out in Beverly Hills*, Veber comparing the actor to Depardieu makes the distinctions even more prevalent due to their contemporaneity, nationalities, and body of work.

Considering that the darkness of *Les fugitifs* is lessened in the more obvious comedy of *Three Fugitives*, it is curious that Veber has little to say about Martin Short. Decent to the point of being boring, at least for the purposes of providing entertaining anecdotes for a memoir, Short's professionalism and family commitment leave him largely excised from Veber's written reflections on the film. Veber is complimentary about Short as a performer, even if "he was a little light on the charm of Richard" as a comedian.[30] Chalking up the difference to an elusive "charm," the comment hints at an obliviousness to—or at least lack of concern for—Short's background and skill set. Short's work in Toronto's improv theatre Second City in the 1970s led to his star turn on television in *SCTV* and *Saturday Night Live* in the 1980s, eventually paving the way for him to appear in the feature films *¡Three Amigos!* (1986, John Landis), *Innerspace* (1987, Joe Dante), and the romantic comedy *Cross My Heart* (1987, Armyan Bernstein).

Sketch comedy provided an ideal venue for Short's improvisational creativity and knack for character development, but his film appearances in the 1980s often stripped him of the spontaneity and structure that were essential to his performance style. Yet, Hollywood was increasingly paving the way for similar performers. The sea change in American comedy that began with the Compass Theatre and Chicago's Second City in the 1950s had come to dominate the production of Hollywood comedies by the 1980s, with its biggest stars either directly tied to improv theatre (for instance, Bill Murray, John Belushi, Dan Aykroyd, John Candy) or connected to the sensibilities of improv through sketch comedy and *Saturday Night Live* (Billy Crystal, Steve Martin, Chevy Chase, Eddie Murphy).[31] Short was a major part of this transformation, but aside from ¡*Three Amigos!* his film performances in the 1980s fail to provide a framework for him utilize his talents.

Veber's choice to shoot *Three Fugitives* as a nearly identical remake of *Les fugitifs* makes sense in theory, retaining as many possible elements from the original for a new audience. Touchstone blocking the release of *Les fugitifs* made this strategy even more logical because an American audience did not have the original as a reference point. In practice, however, Veber's approach fails to consider the comic sensibilities of both an American audience and his performers. Matching shots, editing patterns, and gags requires Short to recreate Pierre Richard's performance rather than create one of his own. Without space to transform dialogue or create new actions, Short performs broadly to make the character his own, undercutting the tone of the movie with cheeriness and slapstick gestures. If Nolte lacks Depardieu's range as an actor, Short lacks Richard's nuance, but this is more likely a result of Veber's incompatibility with American improv traditions than of Short's limitations. The playwright's exacting preoccupation with the written word is antithetical to the improv tradition, exposing the mismatch in the forced pairing of Veber and Short. More generally, it exposes the mismatch between Veber and American comedy.

The French original casts its shadow on every decision made by Veber and calls into question every aspect of the remake. For critics and scholars this often leads to a preference for the original that falls in line with conventional thinking about art, authorship, and national cinemas. Awareness of Veber's nationality and of the existence of a French original guides the response of audiences and critics toward *Three Fugitives*, as it would any film falling under the banner of "le remake." Durham states, "This belief in the specificity of French cinema resurfaces repeatedly in discussions of American remakes of French films, where it provides the most common explanation for the equally widespread opinion that the Hollywood version is always inferior to the original on which it is based."[32] Durham points out that there is an innate tendency, even in the "absence of knowledge," to prefer the original; she quotes Pauline Kael's review of *Three Fugitives*, which guesses about the French original's superiority despite the fact that Kael had not seen *Les fugitifs*.[33] The connotations of French film culture for an audience outside of France, shaped by the nearly exclusive distribution of art house and auteurist films, factors into the harsh comparisons between the remake and the original. The popular genre origins of the project complicate this assessment. *Three Fugitives*, in essence, is cut from the same cloth as Universal's Spanish-language *Drácula* (1931, George Melford). Shot simultaneously on the same set using the same script and costumes as Tod Browning's English-language *Dracula*, the Spanish version was conceived as a duplicate with only linguistic difference. Veber's recycled script and attempts at duplicating shots point to a film that is similarly conceived as a sellable product, not as art.

Hoping to avoid comparisons, Touchstone blocked the American release of *Les fugitifs*. The film screened at the Sarasota Film Festival, but otherwise American audiences were unable to see the French original in advance of *Three Fugitives*.[34] The remake grossed a respectable $40 million at the box office, paving the way for Veber to stay in the U.S. and continue working in Hollywood.[35] The film also placed Veber at the center of a much larger conversation about globalization and the Americanization of culture. Vincent Canby's 1989 *New York Times* article "Movies Lost in Translation" uses *Three Fugitives* as an example of Hollywood "swallowing up other countries' movies with a desperation unknown in the past," moving away from the inclusion of foreign talents like Jean Renoir, Max Ophüls, Billy Wilder, and Fritz Lang to absorb foreign talent, properties, and sensibilities into a homogenized American culture.[36] That *Three Fugitives* was made by Disney's Touchstone Pictures, the biggest purveyor of "les remakes," only strengthens Canby's paranoia over cultural absorption. Coinciding with the construction of Euro Disney (now Disneyland Paris) and the increasing dominance of Hollywood films at the global box office, *Three Fugitives* and other American remakes of French originals played out against a broader backdrop of anxiety over retaining cultural independence. Veber certainly appeared to be absorbed by Hollywood in the immediate aftermath of *Three Fugitives*. Instead of a continuation of the personal control and singular voice of his writer-director approach, he would stay in California to direct another writer's screenplay for the first time in his career.

NOTES

1. Durham, *Double Takes*, p. 181.
2. Veber, *Que ça reste entre nous*, p. 242.
3. Ibid.
4. *Box Office Mojo*, <http://www.boxofficemojo.com/yearly/chart/?yr=1987> (accessed January 5, 2019).
5. *Box Office Mojo*, <http://www.boxofficemojo.com/movies/?id=downandoutinbeverlyhil ls.htm> (accessed January 5, 2019).
6. Mazursky's cinephilia and love of French auteurs is displayed in full with his *Willie & Phil* (1980), a reformatting of the narrative to *Jules et Jim* (1962, François Truffaut) that begins with the titular characters meeting outside a movie theatre showing Truffaut's film.
7. Mazdon, *Encore Hollywood*, p. 13.
8. Durham, *Double Takes*, p. 9.
9. Mazdon, *Encore Hollywood*, pp. 21–3.
10. Ibid. p. 91.
11. Durham, *Double Takes*, p. 144.

12. Mazdon, *Encore Hollywood*, pp. 95–6.
13. Durham, *Double Takes*, p. 70.
14. Ibid. pp. 70–71.
15. Susan Faludi, *Backlash: The Undeclared War against Women*, pp. 146–7.
16. Veber, *Que ça reste entre nous*, p. 242.
17. Jean-Marie Poiré is credited pseudonymously as Jean-Marie Gaubert on *Just Visiting*.
18. Veber, *Que ça reste entre nous*, p. 242.
19. Ibid. p. 250.
20. Durham, *Double Takes*, p. 181.
21. Vincent Canby, "Movies Lost in Translation." *New York Times*, February 12, 1989.
22. Durham, *Double Takes*, p. 181.
23. *A Conversation with Francis Veber*.
24. Durham, *Double Takes*, p. 187.
25. Ibid. p. 185.
26. Other films with scenes shot inside of the closed Lincoln Heights Jail include *L.A. Confidential* (1997, Curtis Hanson), *The Long Goodbye* (1973, Robert Altman), *A Nightmare on Elm Street* (1984, Wes Craven), *Out of Sight* (1998, Steven Soderbergh), *Caged Heat* (1974, Jonathan Demme), and *Penitentiary* (1979, Jamaa Fanaka).
27. Jennifer Sullivan, "Doors Closing at McNeil Island Prison After 135 Years." *Seattle Times*, March 1, 2011.
28. George Lazarus, "Beer Accounts Flow at McCann." *Chicago Tribune*, January 10, 1986.
29. Veber, *Que ça reste entre nous*, p. 243.
30. Ibid. p. 245.
31. Sam Wasson, *Improv Nation: How We Made a Great American Art*.
32. Durham, *Double Takes*, p. 10.
33. Ibid. p. 182.
34. Ibid. p. 180.
35. *Box Office Mojo*, <http://www.boxofficemojo.com/movies/?id=threefugitives.htm> (accessed January 5, 2019).
36. Vincent Canby, "Movies Lost in Translation." *New York Times*, February 12, 1989.

CHAPTER 7

A Parisian in America:
Out on a Limb (1992)

In accepting an offer from Universal to make the comedy *Out on a Limb* in 1992, Veber appeared to be reinventing himself as a director. He had written all of the previous films he directed, but *Out on a Limb* uses an existing screenplay by Daniel and Joshua Goldin and tells a story that has no natural connection to Veber's body of work aside from its genre classification. Hiring a comedy director to realize a comedic screenplay may have been a logical decision for Universal, but the studio failed to consider the sensibilities or working method of Veber. The gap between the release of *Les compères* in 1983 and *Les fugitifs* in 1986 is indicative of Veber's creative process once he became a full-time writer-director. Creating his own films, the process of conceptualizing a story, writing the screenplay, and finally shooting the material meant that he could never direct one or two films per year like his sometime collaborator Édouard Molinaro. Working in isolation to begin with, Veber's began to take more time over the writing process as he moved into directing his own material, bypassing the for-hire mentality that had defined his screenwriting career in the 1970s. How then are the three-year gaps separating *Les fugitifs* and *Three Fugitives* and, again, between *Three Fugitives* and *Out on a Limb* explained? Neither of Veber's Hollywood directorial efforts required him to write new material, and the overall similarity between *Les fugitifs* and its remake suggest a less time-consuming process than seeing a project from concept to fruition.

The reason for the three-year gaps separating 1986–9 and 1989–92 was that Veber had not come to Hollywood with the primary purpose of directing American films. Following *Les fugitifs*, Veber had moved to Hollywood at the invitation of Jeffrey Katzenberg and started work from his office on the Disney lot with the intention of working primarily as a screenwriter.[1] A fresh set of opportunities and the challenges of a linguistic transition may have informed his scaling back from the all-encompassing duties of a writer-director, but Veber first approached his move to Hollywood as a venue for his writing. Reversing course six years later, Veber found himself directing someone else's screenplay. Years later he would call *Out on a Limb* a "catastrophe," and his frustrations with the film are not reflective of a single ill-conceived project. *Out on a Limb* was simply the culmination of a series of disappointments that came with the move to America, dampening Veber's initial enthusiasm about a new life in Los Angeles.

With his reputation preceding him, Veber found that his talents were in demand when he arrived in the States. The Zucker brothers approached him to work on Dale Laurer's screenplay *Ruthless People* (1986, Jim Abrahams, David Zucker, and Jerry Zucker), which he declined.[2] Instead, Veber worked on a stalled project that screenwriter Tab Murphy (no relation to Eddie) had previously attempted to craft for studio approval. Hired by Paramount to write a screenplay for Art Buchwald's story concept *A King for a Day*, Veber became the second and most decorated screenwriter to try fleshing out the story.[3] The project had been attached to Jeffrey Katzenberg before he departed Paramount for Disney in 1984, and was pitched as a vehicle for Paramount's contract star Eddie Murphy.[4] The story revolves around an African king who is in Washington, D.C. for a state visit and ends up alone and penniless in one of D.C.'s more destitute areas. Veber flew from California to meet with Murphy in New Jersey and discuss the project, but the actor abruptly cancelled the meeting the night before and the project was abandoned shortly thereafter.[5] In 1988, Murphy would claim sole story credit for David Sheffield and Barry W. Blaustein's screenplay *Coming to America* (1988, John Landis), a remarkably similar narrative about African royalty adapting to life in a poor black American neighborhood and finding love with a local woman.[6] Buchwald would later file a lawsuit against Paramount and win for damages. Veber went from working on a picture stalled in development hell to being part of a broader courtroom drama that exposed the creative pilfering of Hollywood elites and the suspect accounting practices of the studios.[7]

It was an inauspicious start to Veber's new life in California, and it would be followed by a similar run-in with Warren Beatty. Veber had been writing an English-language remake of *Les tribulations d'un Chinois en Chine* (1965, Philippe de Broca, *Up to His Ears*), the adventure comedy reworking of Jules Verne's 1879 novel starring Jean-Paul Belmondo.[8] Beatty was interested in starring in the project and had friendly meetings with Veber, but despite his admiration for Beatty as an actor and director, Veber felt he was too old for the role.[9] Flash forward to the release of *Bulworth* (1998, Warren Beatty), which had a similar plot device as Verne's novel and de Broca's film, but altered the story to an American political setting. Having written the screenplay with Jeremy Pikser, Beatty also received sole story credit for the film. No lawsuits were forthcoming, and the *Bulworth* situation lacks the same clear-cut moral dimensions as the *Coming to America* story concept, since Verne's novel was in the public domain; but Veber felt used by Beatty all the same.

The bitterness and disappointment of his misadventures with two of Hollywood's biggest movie stars pale in comparison to the impact that *Out on a Limb* would have on Veber. Not only did the film prompt his return to France, it ultimately made him question making movies altogether.[10] Reflecting on the film, Veber confesses that he agreed to direct the project out of "pure vanity" after Universal executive Tom Pollock told him that he was the only director in the world who could make the film.[11] Lacking a Veber script, *Out on a Limb* does not offer a text primed for an auteurist reading. Stylistically, the film exhibits workmanlike and nondescript direction, showing Veber to be a competent if uninspired filmmaker on this project. What the film does offer is a salient example of the fragmented authorship that can result from studio production strategies, resulting in a corporate product that appears bereft of voice. *Out on a Limb* combines disparate elements without regard to fit. Veber is just one part of a mismatched collective.

THE FILM

Written by the sibling writing partners Daniel and Joshua Goldin, *Out on a Limb* had been gestating for six years at Universal before finally being realized by Veber.[12] A native New Yorker, Joshua had earned his MFA at Columbia in 1986 and quickly found himself being courted by Hollywood.[13] He sold the screenplay *Welcome to Buzzsaw*, which he had written with his brother Daniel, to Universal, and the duo moved to Los Angeles shortly after his graduation.[14] The screenplay became one of many in Hollywood to be optioned but unproduced, and the Goldin brothers tried their best to keep busy and stay financially afloat as professional writers, but it took four years for them to receive their first screen credit. Brought in by Universal to work on the screenplay for Sam Raimi's superhero-cum-horror homage *Darkman* (1990), the Goldins were the fifth and sixth writers tasked with realizing Raimi's original story concept when they took part in composing the middle portion of the twelve total drafts of the screenplay.[15] A far cry from the solitary writing of Veber, the 'screenplay by committee' approach to *Darkman* is a Hollywood staple, and would come to define the Goldin brothers' careers as uncredited contributors and script doctors. Still, after they had spent six years working at Universal on various projects, the studio finally decided to produce *Welcome to Buzzsaw*, retitling the film *Out on a Limb*.

Told from the perspective of Marci (Courtney Peldon), a ten-year-old on the first day of school, *Out on a Limb* is framed around her regaling the class

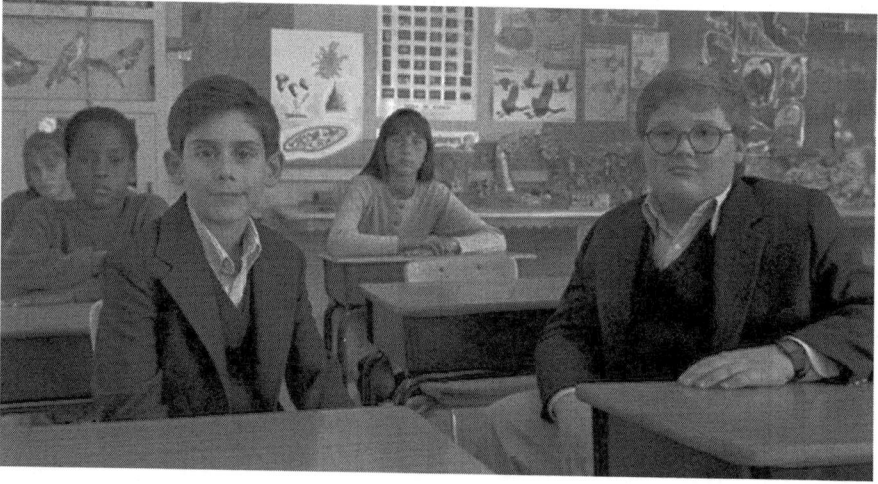

Figure 7.1 Junior versions of Gene Siskel and Roger Ebert comment on the viability of the narrative in *Out on a Limb*.

about her summer vacation. Presented in flashback and utilizing Marci's voice-over narration, she recounts her family's ordeal living in the small logging town of Buzzsaw (presumably located in Northern California). Her stepfather (Jeffrey Jones), the mayor of Buzzsaw, has an identical brother who has just been released from prison. Attempting to extort the mayor, the twin brother murders him and assumes his identity. Intent on murdering the family and emptying their savings account, the criminal brother passes himself off as the mayor in the meantime. Marci, suspicious of her stepfather even before he was murdered, calls her brother Bill (Matthew Broderick) to help get to the bottom of things. On his way to Buzzsaw, Bill is waylaid by a woman running from the cops (Sally, played by Heidi Kling). He is left naked on the road after she steals his car and demands that he strip, and is then picked up by two backwoods drunks, brothers both named Jim (John C. Reilly and Michael Monks). Three plot lines intersect as Sally tries to escape from Buzzsaw, the evil twin attempts to cash in on his dead brother's fortune, and Bill, a high-powered banker, tries to find his lost wallet and recover a phone number he needs to close a $140 million deal. Both overly complicated and underdeveloped, the story is essentially a device for slapstick chase sequences (both on foot and by car) and sophomoric physical gags. The film ends with the evil twin dying, a restored family, and the romantic pairing of Sally and Bill.

Marci's storytelling, beginning with the knowingly clichéd dialogue, "It was a dark night. Actually, it was a dark and *stormy* night," adds ambiguity to the narrative. Are these events real or imagined? Marci's story about a murder in Buzzsaw is delivered with a flair for entertainment and questioned by her teacher and classmates. Even within her own story, Marci is shown to be a media-obsessed dreamer with an overactive imagination. Clues abound within the classroom sequences and in the story itself that Marci might be making it all up. One of the first reaction shots of her classmates includes two identical twins in matching sweaters. One of the twins has a black eye. At the end of the film, after Marci has finished her story and the class bell rings, a freckled classmate in overalls approaches her to ask about "the Jims," the child's rural fashion matching his interest in the backwoods brothers. These parallels could be hackneyed excesses, but they support the notion that Marci's tale is akin to the Verbal Kint/Keyser Söze tale from *The Usual Suspects* (1995, Bryan Singer), using surrounding visuals to improvise a complex story. Did Marci have an evil stepfather with a twin, or were they characters inspired on the fly by her classmates? The constructed falseness of the entire film calls the validity of all the characters into question.

Incongruities in the story, such as Bill's alternating familiarity with and ignorance of Buzzsaw, strengthen the theory that it is all a figment of Marci's imagination, but the lack of logic and consistency may simply be due to a poorly executed screenplay by the Goldin brothers. Overall, *Out on a Limb* is an incomprehensible grab bag of references and structural conceits. Sally's introduction to the narrative—riding a stolen police motorcycle and being shot at by a pursuing cop—is a prime example of the arbitrary nature of the film. Her apparent criminality is only later explained by Marci, who points out to her confused classmates that the policeman is Sally's ex-boyfriend. The plot point is never developed or explained any further. Periodically the action returns to the classroom, where the teacher and students ask questions of Marci, interrogating the narrative and offering a running commentary on the story. Still, the film shifts tonally from one scene to the next and loses the classroom framework for large stretches of time. In some ways, cutting between the Buzzsaw story and Marci's classroom recalls the structure of *The Princess Bride* (1987, Rob Reiner); but here it is the child telling a story, and one that is supposedly true. Unlike Reiner's film, *Out on a Limb* has no identifiable moral or sense of purpose.

The structural similarities to *The Princess Bride* are just one of a number of references and echoes present throughout the film. By and large, the screenplay is a mash-up of other movies, reappropriating elements from contemporary films. Marci's obsession with horror movies points to a metatextual preoc-cupation, but *Out on a Limb* is not a knowing commentary on contemporary cinema. It is a clumsy retread of past gags, tropes, and stylistic flourishes. Being an outsider and presumably lacking familiarity with all of the references and echoes to American comedies, Veber was unable (or perhaps uninterested) in challenging the Goldin brothers' lack of originality. Taken as a whole, the film is a compendium of American comedy fro 1980 to 1992 and moments that border uncomfortably on plagiarism. If it is a pastiche of American cinema, it cannot quite commit to its indulgences.

Some references are more obvious than others. Car chases, for example, conjure up a style rather than invoke a specific film. Helped by Van Dyke Parks's banjo- and harmonica-heavy score, the rural road scenes and car crashes feel like they have been rescued from a lost Burt Reynolds film. Other elements in the film, though, are explicit rip-offs of previous texts. Stumbling upon the dead mayor, the dimwitted Jim brothers assume that he is "shit-faced" and take him out dancing, puppeteering his limp body. Propped up at a table, the corpse charms a woman who thinks his steely gaze is penetrating and mysterious. Preceded three years earlier by *Weekend at Bernie's* (1989, Ted Kotcheff), the scene is an inept attempt at replicating a joke that had already been run into the ground.[16] The Jims themselves are a rip-off of the popular sitcom *Newhart*, which featured three dimwitted backwoods siblings whose recurring introduction of "I'm Larry. This is my brother Darryl and this is my other brother Darryl," became one of the most recognizable television catchphrases of the 1980s. In another scene, the character actor Larry Hankin reprises his role as an ineffectual and disinterested cop from *Home Alone* (1990, Chris Columbus) so closely as to transcend typecasting and border on self-parody.

Casting well-known actors naturally brings in associations with their screen personas and connections to past performances, but the combination of Matthew Broderick and Jeffrey Jones as adversaries goes beyond gentle allusion. Jones's angry pursuit of Broderick is at the heart of *Ferris Bueller's Day Off* (1986, John Hughes); returning to that dynamic, the tension between Bill and his stepfather, or the twin pretending to be his stepfather, is so closely tied to their previous film that it displaces the scenario in *Out on a Limb*. Broderick's character Bill, a hotshot banker, recalls a slew of Wall Street-based films from the late 1980s—namely *Wall Street* (1987, Oliver Stone) and *The Secret of My Success* (1987, Herbert Ross)—while the eventual demise of Jones's evil twin character is clearly appropriated from *The Blues Brothers* (1980, John Landis), using a bird's eye view of his car dropping from an enormous height. Even then, the film only commits halfway to the reference, denying the humor inherent in the duration of the fall from *The Blues Brothers*, but extending it long enough to deny any semblance of realism. Having an actor play his own twin, Veber struggles with the technical aspects of doubling images of Jones during a scene where the the two brothers meet, but the actor is the lone saving grace of the film with some genuinely funny moments of misunderstanding as he pretends to be his brother during breakfast at the family house. Broderick, on the other hand, gets lost in the machinations of the story.

The narrative and marketing iconography, showing Broderick as a young urban professional out of his element in rural America, recalls the previous year's hit comedy *Doc Hollywood* (1991, Michael Caton-Jones), starring Michael J. Fox. The style of the film, however, most closely resembles Savage Steve Holland's directorial efforts *Better Off Dead* (1985), *One Crazy Summer* (1986), and *How I Got Into College* (1989). Overloaded with pop culture references and creating worlds with malleable rules, *Out on a Limb* strains to replicate Holland's playful eccentricities and departure from narrative logic. Evoking the Howard Cosell impression from *Better Off Dead*, Marci's story is challenged by two classmates who are miniature versions of film critics Gene Siskel and Roger Ebert. Critiquing her story and debating finer points with each other, the pair dress like the iconic movie critics and resemble their physical stature and mannerisms. Turning to the teacher, Marci protests, "Those guys are bothering me." The teacher responds, "Just tell your story and if it's good they won't bother you anymore." Turning around to take in the pair, seated next to each other in a junior reproduction of their television show *At the Movies*, Marci responds, "I'm not so sure." The scene, and the inclusion of the arrogant classmates, is a clumsy takedown of Siskel and Ebert as popular tastemakers. Their newspaper columns and nationally syndicated television show had an outsized influence on American cinema in the 1980s and 1990s that was ripe for interrogation, but the scene projects an anti–intellectualism that strives to forgive trite genre films like *Out on a Limb*.[17]

Of all the references and echoes, one glaring absence is anything that points to Veber's involvement. There are superficial similarities to *La chèvre* in the random inclusion of wildlife (a skunk and a grizzly bear, as opposed to the cobra and gorilla), but locating Veber through image or aesthetic is difficult at best. Bill driving his BMW down a country road may match images of Lucas and Pignon's search in the same car from *Les compères*, but to consider this a reflexive commentary is a stretch. As was the case with *Three Fugitives*, the opening shot of *Out on a Limb* trades in the symbolism of Veber's first four French films for a pedestrian establishing shot, panning down from a tree to the front entrance of Mortwill Elementary. The building is an over-the-top suburban ideal, with children playing outside on the grass and a flower-lined walkway to the front door. If this image reflects Veber's vision of America, the response at the box office to *Out on a Limb* expresses the massive divide between the director and his second home.

Veber's frustrations in making the film explain the lifeless final product. Although he had hoped to work with the young and relatively inexperienced Goldin brothers on improving their script, the young writers refused to change a word of the original screenplay.[18] According to Veber, the Goldins enlisted Broderick as an ally, making any proposed changes more difficult with the star of the film taking the writers' side. Veber felt that Broderick, unfamiliar with his French films, treated him like a first-time director, openly balking at suggestions and refusing his requests for retakes. Without his own script and unable to follow his preferred method of shooting, it is no wonder that Veber left no identifiable markers on the film.

Opening as the thirteenth highest grossing film of the weekend despite being the only widely distributed new release that week, *Out on a Limb* earned a paltry total of $1.6 million during its entire theatrical run.[19] A flop by all accounts, it was Veber's first financial failure as a director. For the Goldin brothers, the film placed them back in the margins of Hollywood's vast pool of screenwriters. In the years that followed they worked on projects that were never realized, did rewrites that were not incorporated into finished films, and served in various capacities that did not warrant screen credit.[20] The brothers were one of a ludicrous thirty-two writing teams brought in to work on Universal's expensive and overhyped summer blockbuster *The Flintstones* (1994, Brian Levant) and contributed to *Night at the Museum* (2006, Shawn Levy).[21] Veber, in the immediate aftermath of *Out on a Limb*, stayed in Hollywood for one last project.

As a favor to Gérard Depardieu, Veber worked with the American screenwriter Charlie Peters to adapt the French comedy *Mon père, ce héros* (1991, Gérard Lauzier) into *My Father the Hero* (1994, Steve Miner) for Touchstone.[22] Reprising his role from Lauzier's original, the film was a continuation of Depardieu's attempt to become a popular American star as opposed to a critical darling confined to art house imports. His first two high-profile Hollywood films, *Green Card* (1990, Peter Weir) and *1492: Conquest of Paradise* (1992, Ridley Scott), attempt in different ways to trade on Depardieu's reputation with a popular American audience. *Green Card* distills his screen persona as a fragile brute and exotic symbol of French masculinity, gearing the film toward an urbane adult audience. Playing Christopher Columbus in the quincentennial epic *1492*, Depardieu functions as a living symbol of Europe as the most celebrated actor from the continent. *My Father the Hero*, on the other hand, translates a previous performance rather than creating something new expressly for an American audience. Still, it is ironic to have Veber adapt Lauzier's script after having seen so many of his own films lost in translation. A modest financial success and critical failure, *My Father the Hero* finds Veber and Peters unable to translate the open sexuality of the French original for a reserved American audience. The film did nothing to further Depardieu's Hollywood ambitions and serves as a fitting capstone to Veber's time in Hollywood.[23]

Veber had left France in 1986. His long sojourn in America left him with a number of abandoned projects, one paint-by-numbers remake of his own film, one dispassionate directorial outing using a poor screenplay, and a turn at translating a fellow countryman's work to dubious effect. The wasted years were so disheartening that Veber not only decided to move back to France; he chose to step away from making movies altogether, for a few years at least.

Isolating himself to write something from scratch for the first time since *Les fugitifs*, Veber laid the groundwork for his creative and commercial renaissance by writing a stage play. Premiering in 1993 at the Théâtre des Variétés and directed by Pierre Mondy, *Le dîner de cons* marked his first original stage play since *Le contrat* in 1969 and eventually led to his greatest success as a filmmaker. In typical fashion, Veber's greatest comedy was born out of pain and frustration.

NOTES

1. Veber, *Que ça reste entre nous*, p. 242.
2. Ibid. pp. 233–4.
3. Aljean Harmetz, "Buchwald Sues Studio over Murphy Film Idea." *New York Times*, November 22, 1988.
4. Ibid.
5. Veber, *Que ça reste entre nous*, 234–5.
6. Sheffield and Blaustein had worked with Murphy as staff writers on *Saturday Night Live*.
7. Pierce O'Donnell and Dennis McDougal, *Fatal Subtraction: The Inside Story of Buchwald v. Paramount*.
8. Veber, *Que ça reste entre nous*, p. 236.
9. Ibid. p. 237.
10. *A Conversation with Francis Veber*.
11. Veber, *Que ça reste entre nous*, pp. 255–6.
12. Weiner, Jonah, "A Long Journey from Obscurity." *New York Times*, December 30, 2009.
13. Ibid.
14. Ibid.
15. John Kenneth Muir, *The Unseen Force: The Films of Sam Raimi*, pp. 125–40.
16. If there is such a thing as poetic justice in trampling over an existing movie, the original screenplay for *Weekend at Bernie's* was penned by Robert Klane, the writer who had adapted Veber's work four years earlier with *The Man with One Red Shoe*.
17. Premiering on PBS in 1975, *At the Movies* became a commercially syndicated program in 1982. From 1986 until 1999, the year of Gene Siskel's death, the show was named *Siskel & Ebert & the Movies*.
18. Veber, *Que ça reste entre nous*, p. 256.
19. *Box Office Mojo*, <http://www.boxofficemojo.com/movies/?id=outonalimb.htm> (accessed January 5, 2019); *Box Office Mojo*, <http://www.boxofficemojo.com/weekend/chart/?view=&yr=1992&wknd=36a&p=.htm> (accessed January 5, 2019).
20. Jonah Weiner, "A Long Journey from Obscurity." *New York Times*, December 30, 2009.
21. Ibid.
22. Chutkow, *Depardieu*, p. 33.
23. Depardieu's run as a featured star in Hollywood films would end a few years later with his performance opposite Whoopi Goldberg in *Bogus* (1996, Norman Jewison).

CHAPTER 8

Rainforest Redemption: *Le jaguar* (1996)

Veber had been a central figure in his nation's cinema, and his ten-year absence from making French-language films is a wild detour placed directly in the middle of his career. The appeal of Hollywood is understandable both financially and as a site for new creative challenges, but the lack of productivity must have been galling to Veber. Thinking in terms of statistics, between *Le grand blond avec une chaussure noire* in 1972 and *Les fugitifs* in 1986, Veber wrote twenty new screenplays either alone or with co-writers that were turned into feature films. From 1986 until the release of Gérard Oury's *Fantôme avec chauffeur* in 1996, the only new screenplays that Veber worked on and had realized were *Three Fugitives* and *My Father the Hero*, both English-language adaptations of previous films rather than original scripts. Clearly, he had been working during that span of time and returned to the theatre in 1993 with *Le dîner de cons*, but the stark downturn in productivity appears as a wasted decade that consumed the majority of Veber's fifties.

As discussed at the end of Chapter 5, the state of French cinema at the end of the 1980s was precarious at best. Taking into account a diminished domestic film audience coupled with the growing hold of Hollywood imports, Veber must have seen America as an escape valve. The France that he returned to in the mid-1990s, however, had proven fears about the calamitous future of its domestic genre film production to be unfounded. During his absence, Veber's former collaborator Yves Robert and his longtime producer Alain Poiré had scored consecutive successes with adaptations of Marcel Pagnol's novels *La gloire de mon père* (1990, *My Father's Glory*) and *Le château de ma mère* (1990, *My Mother's Castle*). Finishing second and fourth respectively at the French box office that year, the films combined to sell 10.6 million tickets in France.[1] Having taken a break from directing films since the Pierre Richard comedy

Le jumeau (1984, *The Twin*), Yves Robert's success in 1990 coincided with Veber's accepting of the *Out on a Limb* assignment.[2] Considering Veber's less than fond memories of working with Robert, his former collaborator's success in France while Veber was wasting his talents in Hollywood must have been particularly irritating in retrospect.

As successful as Robert's two Pagnol adaptations were, the runaway success of *Les visiteurs* (1993, Jean-Marie Poiré, *The Visitors*) a few years later made them pale in comparison. Selling 13.7 million tickets in France, *Les visiteurs* was the most popular film in France since the 1960s.[3] It also nearly doubled the combined entries for that year's two biggest Hollywood imports, *Aladdin* (1992, Ron Clements and John Musker) and *Jurassic Park* (1993, Steven Spielberg).[4] A comedy about medieval knights sent through time to modern France, *Les visiteurs* was the most potent example of a domestic comedy being able to out-strip the appeal of big-budget imports. Directed by Jean-Marie Poiré, son of Veber's longtime friend and producer Alain Poiré, the film's success was even more striking. Veber returned to France in the year of its release, and *Les visiteurs* surely reinforced his decision to leave Hollywood behind. Released in the U.S. by Miramax in 1996, the film made it overseas in limited release, albeit in the traditional art house repackaging applied to nearly all theatrical runs of foreign films. Unfortunately, Jean-Marie Poiré would follow in Veber's foot-steps at the end of the decade, directing the Hollywood remake of his own film with *Just Visiting* in 2001. A messy adaptation that retains the French leads from the original (Jean Reno and Christian Clavier) but transports the action to England and Chicago, the movie so frustrated Poiré that he refused to add his name to the final picture, choosing the pseudonym Jean-Marie Gaubert instead. Regardless of future missteps, Poiré's hit set the stage for a resurgence of domestically produced comedies at the French box office.

The release of *Un indien dans la ville* (1994, Hervé Palud, *Little Indian, Big City*) followed the success of *Les visiteurs* and, in many ways, foregrounds Veber's story elements in *Le jaguar* two years later. The story of a self-absorbed banker (Thierry Lhermitte) reuniting with a teenage son who has been raised by a tribe in the Amazon, *Un indien dans la ville* is a double-edged fish-out-of-water story. Placing the banker in stark contrast to the jungle setting at the beginning and end of the film, the middle act shows the son in Paris with his customs and dress juxtaposed with his urban surroundings. A hit in France, selling 7.8 million tickets, the film also fared well elsewhere, generating over $70 million at the global box office.[5] It was so successful that Disney decided to buck tradition and release a dubbed English version, in the hope of reaching a young audience; but American audiences' resistance to dubbing and the inability to use subtitles for a children's release caused it to fail at the U.S. box office in 1996. Taking a more traditional approach, Disney remade the film the following year as *Jungle 2 Jungle* (1997, John Pasquin), starring Tim Allen.

This version also stars Martin Short, performing in his third French remake following his two turns reimagining François Pignon/Perrin in *Three Fugitives* and *Pure Luck*.

If the isolated successes of *Les visiteurs* and *Un indien dans la ville* in the face of American competition looked promising in 1993 and 1994, the combined success of French comedies in 1995 made the possibility of Veber finding future success seem even more probable. Reversing the momentum of Hollywood imports, *Les trois frères* (1995, Didier Bourdon and Bernard Campan, *The Three Brothers*) and *Les anges gardiens* (1995, Jean-Marie Poiré, *Guardian Angels*) finished one and two at the French box office for the year, while *Le bonheur est dans le pré* (1995, Étienne Chatiliez, *Happiness Is in the Field*) and *Gazon maudit* (1995, Josiane Balasko, *French Twist*) took the fourth and fifth spots.[6] For Veber, his return to feature filmmaking in 1996 was perfectly timed. Reconnecting with Alain Poiré and securing financing from Gaumont, Veber set out for South America to shoot his most visually rich project to date.

LE FILM

The scale and difficulty of the production for *Le jaguar* may not have reached Werner Herzog levels, but shooting a film largely in the Amazon was nevertheless an arduous undertaking. To endeavor to make a comedy under such conditions, at the age of fifty-nine no less, is the clearest indicator of Veber's

Figure 8.1 Campana (Jean Reno) looks on as Perrin (Patrick Bruel) shares a greeting with Amazonian shaman Wanú (Harrison Lowe) in *Le jaguar*.

renewed energy and enthusiasm for making movies. Shot in France, Brazil, and Venezuela, *Le jaguar* rehashes elements of *Le retour du grand blond* and *La chèvre*, but depicts Latin America in a wholly different light. More than an exotic backdrop for European characters, the Amazon is granted respect and reverence while its indigenous cultures and belief systems serve as moral guidelines for the film. Providing evidence of Veber's changing perspective and a newfound interest in environmental politics, *Le jaguar* inverts the jungle adventures of *La chèvre* to craft a didactic story about caring for the planet and protecting threatened cultures. Reinforcing the connection to *La chèvre*, Veber recycles the character names Jean Campana for the straight man and François Perrin for the comic. Having switched to using the character name François Pignon starting with *Les compères*, Veber had not used the Perrin name since *La chèvre*, and it would not be used again after *Le jaguar*.

The film opens in Paris, where an Amazonian shaman, Wanù (Harrison Lowe) has traveled alongside the anthropologist and interpreter Jean Campana (Jean Reno) to raise awareness about the destruction of the rainforest. Wanù is entranced by François Perrin (Patrick Bruel), a self-absorbed poker player who he meets by chance in an elevator. Sharing a sacred greeting with Perrin, Wanù then follows him home and performs a ritual that Perrin brushes off as mere superstition. Falling ill in a Paris hospital, Wanù informs Campana that Perrin has been chosen to return to the Amazon and find the shaman's lost soul. An academic, Campana is also a strong believer in Wanù's spirituality and attempts in vain to convince Perrin to travel with him to South America. When he is later threatened by Serbian mobsters over an unpaid gambling debt, Perrin takes advantage of the opportunity to leave the country and tells Campana that he has reconsidered. Once in the Amazon, Perrin shows disinterest bordering on contempt for the mission to find Wanù's soul. Staying in a mining town as they wait to travel down river to Wanù's remote village, Perrin has a run-in with local gangsters and gets into a bar fight where he is endowed with supernatural powers of the jaguar that have been granted to him by Wanù. Asked to fight the gang leader Kumare (Danny Trejo) over control of the village and Wanù's soul, Perrin refuses to fight, only to draw courage at the last minute. Gaining the power of the jaguar and then literally transforming into the animal, Perrin kills Kumare, restores peace to the village, and saves Wanù's soul. Waking up from his hospital bed in Paris, Wanù walks out of his own accord and takes a plane back to the Amazon. Watching with pleasure as Perrin, now back to human form, and Wanù again exchange their sacred greeting on the tarmac, Campana explains in voice-over that Perrin never leaves the Amazon. He stays there and fights to defend its indigenous people and protect the rainforest.

Interest in deforestation caused by both developers and greenhouse gases increased dramatically in the late 1980s and throughout the 1990s, with the Amazon and Brazil in particular emerging as key sites in global debates.

Numerous conservation groups were founded within Brazil between 1986 and 1994, and major international environmental organizations established offices in Brazil between 1992 and 1996, including the Nature Conservancy, Friends of the Earth, Greenpeace, and the World Wide Fund for Nature.[7] Typically, cinematic depictions of the Amazon have fixated on the brutality and immensity of the jungle from the perspective of outsiders, be they explorers, industrialists, missionaries, or researchers.[8] The shift toward didactic depictions of the evils of deforestation coincided with growing concern about the rainforest in the 1980s, as seen in such films as *The Emerald Forest* (1985, John Boorman), *Medicine Man* (1992, John McTiernan), and the animated children's film *Fern Gully: The Last Rainforest* (1992, Bill Kroyer). Unlike these three films, *Le jaguar* avoids a pitched battle between a now conscientious outsider and encroaching developers, focusing instead on Perrin's journey toward understanding and appreciating the Amazon's people and geography.

The opening aerial shot of *Le jaguar* resembles the image of the man parasailing over Puerto Vallarta that opens *La chèvre*. Starting close on a canoe, the camera moves out and up to reveal the landscape surrounding the water. Often a form of recreation, the canoe is a parallel to the parasail, except that when placed in the context of the Amazon it is a necessary and timeworn form of transportation, not a tourist activity. The camera's overview of the landscape furthers the reversal of *La chèvre*'s opening, revealing a vast rainforest and mountain ranges untouched by industry. The aerial shots of Puerto Vallarta, on the other hand, show lush green hills set against the overdevelopment of coastal hotels and resorts. The undisturbed river surrounding the canoe in *Le jaguar* is the opposite of the intersecting motorboats and sailboats in the water in *La chèvre*. In image and in scale, the opening shots of the Amazon find Veber returning to Latin America as a sincere observer, not a glib tourist. Reinforced by Vladimir Cosma's lush orchestral score, which is far removed from the playful flute music he composed for *La chèvre*, the tone of *Le jaguar* is sincere to the point of sentimentality.

Guiding the sincerity of the film is Veber's approach to language. Whereas *La chèvre* imagines a Mexico in which nearly everyone speaks fluent French, *Le jaguar* is multilingual. Portuguese is used for characters in Brazil, as is Spanish for those in southern Venezuela. To generate conversation as Perrin explores the mining town, the film introduces a French countryman named Moulin (Roland Blanche) who is there as a laborer hoping to find riches. It may not be particularly believable, but it is more plausible than the majority of Mexico speaking French. Having to navigate language barriers forces Perrin to confront his difference and the limitations of his first world privilege. Taking the time to learn how to communicate with locals, Campana reflects the deepened understanding and sense of shared humanity that comes of respectfully engaging with languages other than his native tongue.

One contradiction in Veber's approach to language comes with Wanù's tribal dialect. First, the film includes subtitles for the Spanish and Portuguese spoken in the film but chooses not to provide subtitles for Wanù's dialogue. While Campana often translates, *Le jaguar* follows a long tradition of selective subtitling being used to other only select groups. For example, Steven Spielberg uses this approach in *Amistad* (1997), providing subtitles for the Spanish navigators of a slave ship but denying the audience understanding of what the enslaved Africans are saying. Expressing difficulty in casting the character from indigenous Amazonians, Veber instead hired the American actor Harrison Lowe to play the part.[9] Lowe, a Navajo Indian who had appeared in a few television Westerns before *Le jaguar*, speaks the Navajo language as Wanù. Veber dismisses the discordant effect of Wanù speaking a North American dialect in the Amazon, saying that there are not a lot of "Navajos frequenting French multiplexes."[10] The flippant comment undercuts Veber's new approach to language, but from his perspective it was a decision based on expediency, not disrespect. Assuming that the incongruity would go unnoticed, a character from the Amazon rainforest speaking Navajo is less consciously incongruous than the introduction of gorillas and king cobras into the jungles of Mexico. Regardless, it shows that some of the imperialist undertones from *La chèvre* are still present in *Le jaguar*. That said, the film attempts to lend credence to belief systems and perspectives outside of the purview of its European characters.

Perrin's uncanny bad luck in *La chèvre* challenges Campana's reason-based thinking. In *Le jaguar* it is the Campana character who is a believer and Perrin who must be convinced that there are aspects of the world that transcend logical understanding. When placed in the context of the entire film, the initial encounter in the elevator between Perrin and Wanù is predestined, not accidental. Larger forces are at work in Perrin's life, and he must open himself up to accepting what cannot be explained by science or logic. Wanù's slight frame, towered over by Campana and Perrin, obscures the physical power he possesses. When Perrin is granted Wanù's jaguar powers he begins to understand that strength is not always outwardly recognizable. The contrast between scientific logic and spiritual phenomenon is reinforced by juxtaposing Wanù, still in his tribal garb, lying in a hospital bed in Paris, hooked up to tubes and wires. In a coma following his heart attack, Wanù flatlines during Perrin's fight with Kumare in the Amazon, then is fully restored once the fight is over. As he sits up in the hospital bed, removes the wires from the monitors, and walks out of the hospital, nurses and doctors watch in astonishment. Their sense of medical reality is incompatible with Wanù's sudden and unexplained recovery, yet they see with their own eyes an event for which science cannot account.

The difference between Wanù and Perrin—and French culture in general—revisits the juxtapositions of *Un indien dans la ville*. From his first appearance, stepping out of a limousine barefoot across the street from Place de la Concorde to meeting Perrin in the hotel elevator, the exoticism of Wanù is used as a recurring punchline. When the elevator stops, presumably due to mystical powers being summoned, the concierge of the hotel calls down to the lobby and refers to Wanù as "you know who" as he reports the outage. Although his tour of France is meant to raise awareness about deforestation, his image within the film recalls the Sioux Indian in *Le jouet*. Beyond the fact that he speaks in Navajo, the connection is made explicit when Perrin calls Wanù "Geronimo," conflating all indigenous American people into a pre-packaged stereotype. Even when he is being spoken of with reverence, there is a sense of condescension in how Europeans (aside from Campana) address Wanù. During a photo opportunity with Wanù a government Minister dryly proclaims that "France cares about the rainforest." It is a passing moment, but is central to establishing the film's overall message. Perrin's selfishness and indifference recur throughout the film, often expressed in extreme terms, such as when he responds to Campana's question "Do you know what it's like to be an Indian?" with a simple and defiant "Who cares?" But it is the Minister saying the right thing with a total lack of commitment that pinpoints the problem of first world indifference to the plight of the planet and threats to marginalized cultures. For the Minister, Wanù is a human prop used to create a false impression of compassion. His treatment may not be as crass and dehumanized as a toy-store Indian or a World's Fair showcase of exotic otherness, but he is a prop nonetheless. That Veber cuts directly from Perrin's "Who cares?" to the Minister makes the connection all the more evident in that it regards open hostility and feigned sympathy as one and the same.

Le jaguar is Veber's most direct political statement as a director, but its sincerity, ambition, and use of talent often undercut the comedy. The recurring gag of Wanù exchanging gifts with unwitting recipients, be it giving a necklace for Perrin's overcoat or a doctor's stethoscope, is more of a gentle misunderstanding than the foundation of a film's humor. Elsewhere, Perrin's uninformed description of the mob boss he is indebted to as being "Serb, Croat, or Bosnian" is a clumsy conflation that not only lacks charm, but comes across as grossly inappropriate in light of the film being released concurrently with the Yugoslav Wars. The key visual gags in *Le jaguar* are out of place in Veber's body of work, consisting of either cartoonish excess or grotesqueness. Taking on the power of the jaguar in his first bar fight, Perrin throws one attacker across a large room before picking another one up above his head, throwing him to the ceiling, and then batting him across the other side of the room like a volleyball. Later, Kumare performs acts of violence that stretch the bounds of humor, at least within Veber's usual parameters. Approaching Moulin, Kumare cuts off his arm with a machete and the camera focuses on the dismembered limb lying in the mud, the hand still clutching a can of beer. Taking the gross-out shot one step further, the fingers contract, crushing the can and spilling beer. The moment seems more at home in a George Romero film than a Veber comedy. Later, when he cuts off the head of a local priest and throws it out of a plane at Campana and Perrin, Kumare's violence seems so sadistic that it disrupts the sense of comedy in the film as a whole. Kumare is played by Danny Trejo, and the character's choice of weapon presages the actor's star turn a decade later as *Machete*—the only aspect of his performance that, in retrospect, lightens the mood.[11]

The subdued humor in the film stems largely from the pairing of Jean Reno and Patrick Bruel as Campana and Perrin. At the height of his international stardom following his title role in *Léon* (1994, Luc Besson, *The Professional*), Jean Reno's Campana is a subdued and moralistic straight man who lacks the expressiveness of Gérard Depardieu's Campana in *La chèvre*. As written, it is an unrewarding part that fails to let the actor build on his proven comedic performance in *Les visiteurs* or the playfulness of his previous films for Besson in *Subway* (1985) and *Le grand bleu* (1988). The flatness of his character could be forgiven had Reno been cast opposite a masterful comedian, but Patrick Bruel is unable to carry the film as Perrin.

A popular singer in France who started to act early in his career, Bruel portrays Perrin as young, arrogant, and good-looking: a far cry from Pierre Richard's performances or the idea of Perrin/Pignon as a common man. The narrative plays on his celebrity by using Bruel's real-life third career as a professional poker player as an inside joke, crafting Perrin as a degenerate gambler running from debts he has amassed playing cards. By and large, though, Veber's construction of the character does not do Bruel any favors. Perrin's continued resistance to helping, caring, or even being friendly to Campana is taxing. His ultimate transformation rings false, as it is not supported by anything at the core of his character. The voice-over explanation of Perrin deciding to live in the Amazon is rushed and nonsensical, with Bruel failing to convey much in the way of warmth or sincerity until the film's denouement. Placed alongside the similar transformation of Lucas in *Les fugitifs*, which is hinted at early on and is clear by the halfway mark of the story, Perrin's salvation in *Le jaguar* is absurd.

Released in October 1996, just shy of ten years removed from Veber's last French film, *Le jaguar* was only a modest success. Selling 2.4 million tickets in France, the film finished well below the heights he had achieved with the Depardieu-Richard comedies and failed to come close to the box office success of *Les visiteurs* or *Un indien dans la ville*. Compared to the creative and commercial disaster of *Out on a Limb*, however, *Le jaguar* was a smashing success. Having avoided consecutive flops and reestablished himself in France, Veber could look forward to new projects and try to find a way to match his political commentary with a genuinely funny movie. Luckily for him, he had been regularly watching that very project performed on stage since 1993.

NOTES

1. *JP's Box-Office*, <http://www.jpbox-office.com/charts_france.php?filtre=datefr&infla=0 &variable=1990> (accessed January 5, 2019).
2. Yves Robert did not direct a theatrically released feature film between 1984 and 1990, but in 1986 he made the television movie *L'été 36* for France 2 and co-directed the short film *Les petites magiciennes* alongside Vincent Mercier.
3. No film had topped thirteen million entries at the French box office since *Once Upon a Time in the West* (1969, Sergio Leone).
4. *JP's Box-Office*, <http://www.jpbox-office.com/charts_france.php?filtre=datefr&infla=0 &variable=1993> (accessed January 5, 2019).
5. *JP's Box-Office*, <http://www.jpbox-office.com/fichfilm.php?id=4247&view=2> (accessed January 5, 2019).
6. *Gazon maudit* translates to "cursed grass." Miramax renamed the film *French Twist* for its U.S. release.
7. Luiz C. Barbosa, *Guardians of the Brazilian Amazon Rainforest: Environmental Organizations and Development*, p. xiv.
8. Examples include *Aguirre, der Zorn Gottes* (1972, Werner Herzog, *Aguirre, the Wrath of God*), *Fitzcarraldo* (1982, Werner Herzog), and *The Mission* (1986, Roland Joffé).
9. Veber, *Que ça reste entre nous*, p. 274.
10. Ibid. p. 275.
11. First appearing in one of the fake trailers between the two feature halves of *Grindhouse* (2007, Robert Rodriguez and Quentin Tarantino), the character became the basis for *Machete* (2010, Robert Rodriguez) and *Machete Kills* (2013, Robert Rodriguez).

CHAPTER 9

The Art of Canned Theatre:
Le dîner de cons (1998)

The aesthetic tension between stage plays and films can be seen clearly in the first decade of French cinema. Breaking from the static camera and proscenium vantage point of Edison's Kinetoscope, the introduction of the Cinématographe by the Lumière brothers freed the camera from the confines of a single studio and stage, expanding the possibilities of the new medium by allowing for camera movement and location shooting. For all of their inventiveness, the films of Georges Méliès were also deeply connected to the traditions and aesthetics of the theatre. Shooting inside his custom-built studio in Montreuil, the narrative developments of Méliès's films were accompanied by innovations in editing and special effects. His camera, though, remained static and recreated the proscenium view of his pre-cinema stage shows. From a visual standpoint, the films of Méliès have more in common with the movies shot at Edison's Black Maria studio than they do with the liberated camera of the Lumières. Méliès's background as a stage performer, his penchant for creating elaborate set pieces, and the need to control variables to create cinematic illusions explain his limited use of the camera, but on the surface his replication of a theatre aesthetic seems to contradict his overall inventiveness.

The divide between the visual dynamism of a supposedly "pure" cinema and ties to theatre—both aesthetically and in terms of source material—have informed critical debates throughout the medium's history. André Bazin's comment that "'filmed theater' still frequently passes as heresy" is as true today as it was when he wrote it in the 1950s.[1] If a stage play is to be accepted as the source for a screenplay, the director must adapt the material "cinematically" in order to sidestep criticism. Otherwise, the director's film runs the risk of being labeled with the dreaded pejorative "canned theatre." Film comedy has developed as a move away from theatrical trappings, both in the silent era and again after the advent of synchronous sound. Comparing the limited settings and static camera of Max Linder comedies to the expansive visual worlds of Charles Chaplin and Buster Keaton, the move away from stage aesthetics in the silent era is evident. Bazin points out that great American comedies from the 1930s and 1940s, built on dialogue and situation, are primarily made up of interiors and use editing (shot-reverse-shot) to translate stage setups into cinematic language.[2] In a returning to theatre sensibilities that was caused by the advent of talking pictures, the grandiose location shooting of late silent-era Keaton would give way to the one- or two-room interior settings of many screwball comedies.

In France, comedies in the 1930s coincided with the rise of *théâtre filmé* (filmed theatre), which was popular but derided by intellectuals.[3] Film comedies, then, looked like stage plays and were often simply adaptations of popular theatre. Adaptations of Marcel Pagnol's plays in France as well as Hollywood remakes of stage comedies placed action indoors and foregrounded dialogue and performance. Films may have moved away from long takes with a single static camera setup, using close-ups and editing to guide the attention of the spectator, but they remained closely tied to the stage through setting and situation.[4]

The construction of film comedies would begin to change dramatically in the 1950s, as television situation comedies co-opted limited studio settings and big-screen comedies began to move outside the confines of the studio. In the 1930s, even a film with no direct connection to theatre like *My Man Godfrey* (1936, Gregory La Cava) could easily be conceived of as a stage play.[5] The location shooting and visual humor of *Les vacances de Monsieur Hulot* (1953, Jacques Tati, *Monsieur Hulot's Holiday*) or *The Bellboy* (1960, Jerry Lewis), on the other hand, would be impossible to translate to the stage. Of course, there are exceptions to the limited interiors of the 1930s and the expanded visual makeup of film comedies since 1960, but the differences hold as a broad generalization.

Coming off the production of *Le jaguar*—a comedy where the primary pleasures are wrapped up in location shooting—Veber was suspicious of the feasibility of adapting his stage play *Le dîner de cons* for the screen. Having written the play three years before making *Le jaguar*, Veber had already rebuffed Alain Poiré's suggestion of making *Le dîner de cons* into a film. The play was still unfinished at the time, and Veber told Poiré that the story was "inadaptable" because the majority of the narrative consists of conversations between men sitting on a couch.[6] The likelihood of Veber painting a mental image of the finished film as a static proscenium shot focused on this couch for an hour and a half explains his reservations. His work as a director had been defined by location shooting. Veber uses space to create meaning through the jungles of *La chèvre* and *Le jaguar*, the highways of France in *Les compères* and

Les fugitifs, and the business and personal properties of Rambal-Cochet in *Le jouet*. Even Veber's Hollywood films make it a point to foreground the natural scenery of the Puget Sound and Northern California. To go from this to setting the majority of a film inside a single apartment must have dredged up in Veber deep-seated notions about the differences between theatre and cinema. He had, of course, written for both mediums, and viewed film adaptations of his plays *L'enlèvement* and *Le contrat* as failures. Confining the majority of the action to a gangster's hideout in one and adjoining hotel rooms in the latter surely played a role in his low opinion of *Appelez-moi Mathilde*, *L'emmerdeur*, and *Buddy Buddy*.

Despite these reservations, Veber eventually agreed to adapt *Le dîner de cons* and it became the biggest critical and commercial success of his career. The film sold 9.2 million tickets in France and would have been the number one film at the French box office had it not been released the same year as the international sensation *Titanic* (1997, James Cameron).[7] Is there a way to reconcile the apparent contradiction of Veber's signature cinematic achievement being his least "cinematic" film? As with any comedy, *Le dîner de cons* relies on performance. Playing François Pignon, Jacques Villeret gives a performance that led to him being one of the rare comic leads awarded the César for Best Actor. Daniel Prévost would win the César for Best Supporting Actor for *Le dîner de cons* as well. Yet, there is something more than performance that explains the film's value. Veber finds ways to use the supposed limitations of the story's theatricality to craft a film that realizes Bazin's calls for a closer relationship between the two mediums.[8] As Fournier-Lanzoni suggests, Bazin's promotion of stage adaptations provides a foundation for cinema to translate performance through new tools (close-up, "middle shots") and deeper psychological identification with the characters.[9] Veber provides an experience in *Le dîner de cons* that transforms and complements the stage play, retaining the energy of its dialogue and performances while utilizing the camera to add an emotional layering to the film that would be impossible from a fixed seat at the Théâtre des Variétés.

LE FILM

With its title translating literally to "The dinner of idiots," the film is built around a game devised by wealthy and elitist friends who regularly host dinner parties where they compete with each other to invite the biggest idiots and eccentrics. Pierre Brochant (Thierry Lhermitte) runs into a friend, Jean Cordier (Edgar Givry) at a country club and confesses he does not have an idiot for his upcoming dinner. Taking a train the following day, Cordier sits next to a short and excitable accountant named François Pignon (Jacques Villeret)

Figure 9.1 François Pignon (Jacques Villeret), Pierre Brochant (Thierry Lhermitte), and the couch-based setting of *Le dîner de cons*.

who begins to show him photographs and launch into long explanations of the matchstick models he builds as a hobby. Cordier shares his "discovery" with Brochant, who then invites Pignon to the dinner party. A successful publisher, Brochant uses the guise of being interested in publishing a photo book of Pignon's matchstick models to woo him to the party. Eager to impress Brochant, Pignon arrives at his apartment ahead of the party only to find that the publisher has thrown out his back playing golf and can barely move. In an attempt to help, Pignon overstays his welcome and throws Brochant's life into chaos. During the span of the evening Brochant misses the dinner, further injures his back, is left by his wife, has his extramarital affair exposed, and unwittingly sets himself up for a tax audit. Pignon eventually learns that he was invited as an idiot by Brochant, but in an act of sincere kindness, he tries to salvage the man's marriage despite his anger and embarrassment at being used. Building tension to the point of emotional explosion, the films ends with Brochant expressing his respect for Pignon, only to have the bumbling guest make a final error that leads Brochant to call him an idiot once more. Returning to a device he had not used since *Three Fugitives*, the film ends in a freeze frame of Pignon and Brochant mid-argument.

Le dîner de cons incorporates a number of elements that by the time of its release had become staples of Veber's writing. Repetition generates humor and functions as a plot device, keeping Pignon in the apartment through a series of near-departures. Reflecting back on dialogue, the script lays the foundation for later jokes. When Pignon talks about his wife leaving him for another man who he deems to be an idiot because he only talks about windsurfing, Brochant feigns interest in the sport, hoping to meet someone who may be even more of an idiot than Pignon. Ten minutes pass in the film, and Brochant tells of how he stole his wife from another man. Not missing a beat, Pignon exclaims, "You windsurfers are all the same!" This joke requires patience and nuance in the repetition compared to immediate paired dialogue during the restaurant meetings in *Les compères*, for example, but the payoff is increased by the distance. *Le dîner de cons* also returns to familiar themes and dramatic beats from previous Veber films. The meeting on the train that sets the narrative in motion harks back to the themes of happenstance and luck that are seen in a number of Veber's screenplays, most markedly in *La chèvre*. Recalling the same film, Pignon's realization that he was invited to serve as an idiot for a dinner party matches Perrin's eventual understanding that he was chosen to be an investigator because of his uncanny bad luck.

The narrative remains largely unaltered from the stage play, save for a few moments that venture outside the claustrophobic setting of the apartment and visuals provided for the opposite end of telephone conversations. The tight quarters of the film place the juxtaposition of Brochant and Pignon into sharp relief. Much as the Depardieu-Richard comedies use physical stature to emphasise the differences between the characters in class and temperament, the casting of Thierry Lhermitte and Jacques Villeret reinforces the opposition of Brochant and Pignon. Tall, tan, and handsome, Lhermitte radiates health and privilege. Villeret, a full seventeen centimeters shorter, overweight, and bald, is diametrically opposed to Lhermitte. Recalling the production history of *La chèvre* (discussed in Chapter 3), the fact that Villeret was Veber's initial choice for the buddy comedy version of François Perrin in 1981 underlines how closely the actor's physical appearance matches the character.

Like Depardieu's Lucas and Campana characters, Lhermitte's Brochant functions as the straight man, portraying a somewhat normal person who serves as a barometer for the clownish exuberance of Pignon. However, there are key differences between Brochant and previous straight-man characters in Veber films. For one, the physical strength of Lucas and Campana (including Jean Reno's performance in *Le jaguar*) is stripped from Brochant by his back injury. The appearance of physical dominance, then, is illusory, as Pignon is the more physically capable one throughout the evening. More importantly, whereas fate thrusts Pignon/Perrin into the lives of Lucas and Campana, Brochant invites Pignon into his life. Since his intentions are mean-spirited to begin with, the havoc caused by Pignon is Brochant's just reward. This is rein-forced when his wife Christine (Alexandra Vandernoot) calls the dinner party "sinister." Ultimately, Brochant lacks the morality of other Veber straight men and, instead, functions as a symbol of derision akin to the millionaire Rambal-Cochet in *Le jouet*. The comic structure of the story forces moments of identification with Brochant, which in turn makes the audience complicit in judging Pignon. Nevertheless, the ethical corruption of Brochant situates him as an object of scorn.

The casting of Thierry Lhermitte, with whom he was working for the first time, brought Veber into contact with a performer whose rise had paralleled his own over the previous twenty-five years. While Villeret had played Pignon on stage for hundreds of performances beforehand, Lhermitte was not part of the stage play's cast. Taking the part previously played by Claude Brasseur and Michel Roux, Lhermitte brings a sense of youth and sexuality to the character that was absent on the stage.[10] Lhermitte's appearances in hit films like *Les ripoux* (1984, Claude Zidi), *La totale!* (1991, Claude Zidi), and *Un indien dans la ville* (1994, Hervé Palud) added a level of screen stardom to his casting, but his background in theatre is the most compelling aspect of his being cast in *Le dîner de cons*.[11] Having transitioned to cinema from *café-théâtre* in the 1970s, Lhermitte gives a performance as Brochant that reflects the political dimensions of his stage beginnings. As Fournier-Lanzoni points out, "*café-théâtre* tended to involve comic plays that set out to mock the habits of the petit-bourgeoisie."[12] Brochant is a perfect distillation of this tendency. Insecure to the point of callousness and surrounded by outer trappings of wealth that are tenuously owned, Brochant aspires to be part of the *haute bourgeoisie* and engages in rituals like the dinner party in order to feel superior.

The initial conversation between Brochant and Cordier at the country club and the eventual back injury playing golf set up intersections between masculinity, corporate culture, and leisure. Cordier's reservations about the dinner—and Brochant's implication that his father's collecting of ladles would qualify him to be an invitee—expresses a sense of peer pressure and acquiescence that make Cordier a participant in the demeaning ritual against his better judgment. There is a need to belong accompanied by a derision of difference that permeates the film. Outliers are continuously targeted as subjects for ridicule. The pervasiveness of this brand of cruel gamesmanship among elites is found in a conversation between Brochant and his physician. During a house call, Christine admonishes her husband by telling the doctor about the dinner before leaving in a huff. Embarrassed, Brochant looks at the doctor, who hesitates, smiles, and admits that in college he and his friends played a similar game by choosing ugly girls instead of idiots. Soft-spoken and unemotional, the admission of the doctor comforts Brochant and normalizes his bad behavior. As Brochant admits, he also competed to find ugly girls with his friends in college. Coming after Christine has left, the doctor's sharing of this disturbingly sexist game speaks to the secrecy and protective umbrella of male homosocial groups.

Instead of opening the film with an image of Brochant or Pignon (or a pedestrian establishing shot like those in his two Hollywood films), Veber begins with visual misdirection. Across a cloudy sky, the camera tracks the movement of a boomerang flying through the air. There is a cut as the boomerang descends past a tree line, and the second image is a long shot of a man in a brown suit catching the boomerang, standing in a grass field. The camera pans to the right across a line of trees bordering the field and reveals a series of office buildings. The scene is clearly in a city park, and the Australian outback iconography has been placed out of its natural setting. The third shot reveals a case overflowing with boomerangs and the man in the brown suit bending over to pick out a new one. Moving around to see the man's face for the first time in a medium shot, we see him seriously preparing to throw a new boomerang, repeating the arm motion needed for a perfect throw. The man is middle-aged, wearing glasses, and not very athletic. His throw is awkward and childlike. Behind him is another man jogging in the distance past rugby goalposts. As the first man moves to catch the boomerang his cell phone rings, he answers, and it is clear that he is being invited to a dinner party.

This character is not a major part of the subsequent film, but by starting with another one of the "idiots," Veber is able to make connections to the types of difference and eccentricity that are deemed unacceptable by people like Brochant. The rugby pitch (which recurs as a symbol in Veber's next film, *Le placard*) is meant for demonstrations of masculinity, not childish hobbies. The man's repurposing of the field and lack of sportswear distinguish him as an outlier and nonconformist. Placing him alone on the field emphasizes the difference between valid forms of masculine expression and eccentric ones, but it also highlights the difference between homosocial groups and solitary endeavors. Individuality, be it unique interests or social isolation, is a shameful marker. More than just setting up the eccentricities of the character and the tensions surrounding masculinity that run through the film, the boomerang also functions as a metaphor for karma. Throughout the film, whether for Brochant, Pignon, or the tax auditor, the ill will shown towards others is continually repaid in misfortune.

In his historical analysis of the film, Fournier-Lanzoni uses *Le dîner de cons* as a more recent example in a long line of French comedies that follow the tradition of Molière blending "comedy and serious reflection."[13] Placing the film alongside the approaches of auteurs like Jean Renoir and Sacha Guitry, Fournier-Lanzoni points to Veber's use of the recurring plot device of the stranger, or "an intruder, ignorant of the rules, who will legitimately produce an effect of surprise and comedy."[14] Deflecting the sensitivities of political commentary by masking it in comedic performance, the intrusion of Pignon into Brochant's world may make him the clownish subject, but it also creates a juxtaposition that accentuates class difference. Renoir does this in *La règle du jeu* (1939, *The Rules of the Game*) through the poacher Marceau (Julien Carette), but Veber's social commentary is far less caustic than Renoir's upstairs/downstairs comedy of manners. The contentious initial release of *La règle du jeu*, marked by low attendance, angry reviews, and state censorship, is a far cry from the commercial success and awards that Veber's film would generate, but both films are nonetheless organized around similar class analyses.[15]

The class divisions at the heart of the film are multiplied a little over halfway through when Brochant is joined by his friend Juste Leblanc (Francis Huster) and Pignon enlists a work colleague to help track down Christine. The introduction of Pignon's colleague from the tax office, Lucien Cheval (Daniel Prévost), results in a paranoid rush by Brochant to hide his belongings. Brochant's luxurious apartment is overpopulated with paintings and statues that ostentatiously proclaim his wealth. Obviously unclaimed, the rush to hide them from the tax auditor is evidence that Brochant's fortune is tenuous. Cheval's suspicions create a dual tension in that it plays on general fears and distaste for taxation while also providing a method for humbling and punishing the cruelties of Brochant. His being a tax cheat and accumulating wealth without paying his share back into the state system parallels capitalist greed with his other transgressions. Simultaneously condemnatory and sympathetic, Veber avoids simple characterizations to interrogate the push and pull of moral choices. Splitting into pairs, Brochant and Leblanc struggle to control their laughter at Cheval's misfortune when he finds out his wife has been cheating on him. Pignon, standing next to his colleague, is crestfallen and disgusted by Brochant and Leblanc's laughter. For a moment, though, he slips and joins in the laughter, catching himself and feeling guilty for indulging in superior and mean-spirited humor at the expense of others. Throughout the film Pignon expresses judgmental humor, calling others idiots without knowing how he is perceived by Brochant.

In pairing Brochant and Leblanc opposite Pignon and Cheval, the creative class and the working class are separated in appearance, interests, and wealth. The banter between Pignon and Cheval over their favorite football clubs marks a working-class investment in sports, whereas the connection to creative labor between the publisher Brochant and the writer Leblanc is evidence of their sophistication. They are both unaware and uninterested in the match between Auxerre and Marseille that preoccupies their guests from the tax office. The choice of teams is also evidence of the regional identities of Pignon and Cheval. Both support teams far outside of Paris (Burgundy and Marseille, respectively), presumably due to where they were born and raised. This sense of Paris and belonging recurs throughout the film. As Pignon is introduced on the train, he drops a photo of his prized matchbook model of the Eiffel Tower. The obsessive detail he has used in recreating the structure in miniature reflects a childlike reverence suggesting it is more of a distant symbol than a daily site. Brochant, on the other hand, has a view of the real Eiffel Tower from his apartment window, so close that the elevators can easily be seen moving up and down. When Pignon offers to call a physical therapist from Courbevoie to help treat his ailing back, Brochant brusquely rebuffs the offer. The insinuation is that Pignon's friend from an outer commune could not possibly be as good as the doctor he can afford to hire in the city center.

Beyond being expansive and ornate, the most noticeable aspect of the Paris apartment is that it is a constructed set, not a real location. Veber does not preoccupy himself with realism, choosing to stay close to the story's theatrical origins instead. The camera stays on one side of the living room couch at all times, maintaining the vantage point and blocking of the stage play for large portions of the film. However, Veber strives for cinematic expression as well. *Le dîner de cons* is shot in an aspect ratio of 2.35:1, making it the first use of anamorphic widescreen in Veber's directorial career. Having avoided the extreme widescreen format for the visually lush location shooting of films like *La chèvre* and *Le jaguar*, his decision to use it for the mostly interior action of a stage adaptation is not simply an overcompensation to avoid the "canned theatre" label. The widescreen format alters the proscenium while retaining the spectator's ability to scan the shot. The aspect ratio creates a hybrid form that looks cinematic, yet functions like a stage play. Instead of using 1:1.85 or the common European aspect ratio of 1:1.66, the anamorphic widescreen of *Le dîner de cons* emphasizes set design and turns the apartment into a character in its own right. The visual ambition of the film is evident in Veber reuniting with Luciano Tovoli, the cinematographer responsible for Veber's two most image-centered movies in *Les fugitifs* and *Le jaguar*.

Working mostly on a constructed apartment set, the visual design of *Le dîner de cons* walks a fine line of stage-to-film adaptations. As Fournier-Lanzoni points out, there has been a long tradition of criticizing film adaptations of novels or stage plays for their lack of fidelity to the original source.[16] In the case of a novel the lack of fidelity is often due to length, causing screenwriters to omit narrative elements, conflate characters, or manufacture new scenarios. For stage plays, issues of fidelity focus more on the altering of stage devices that would be awkward in a film (monologues and cross fades, for example). The specificity of each medium makes some differences inherent, showing that true fidelity in adaptation is impossible. Other differences are practical, stemming from the best practices of film production and the realization that what works on stage may not work on screen. Returning to Bazin's belief in what cinema can bring *to* stage plays, as opposed to widely held assumptions that film adaptations only take *from* their source material, Veber's use of close-ups does much more than direct the spectator's attention and break up the monotony of a wide-angle shot. Moving the camera in closer adds emotional depth and allows for performances that fluctuate from broad comedy to subtle despair. The interiority of Villeret's Pignon would be far more difficult to locate in a stage performance, particularly from the back row of a theatre. In using film language, Veber constructs an adaptation that adds to the source material without drawing attention to technique.

In arguing that cinema and theatre are complementary mediums rather than oppositional arts where the former threatens the viability of the latter, Bazin discusses the idea of presence. Cinema cannot replace the immediacy of live theatre, leaving only a "tracing" of performance.[17] Instead of regarding film as an inferior medium, however, Bazin explains, "The cinema does something strangely paradoxical. It makes a molding of the object as it exists in time and, furthermore, makes an imprint of the duration of the object."[18] The film works cinematically without thoroughly altering the theatrical elements of the original play, owning and celebrating the once pejorative label of "canned theatre." To see Villeret in the film is not the same as having seen one of his hundreds of stage performances as Pignon between 1993 and 1997, but in capturing the actor at a given moment the film provides a perpetual presence. When Villeret died in 2005 at the age of fifty-three from complications due to his alcoholism, his obituary in *Le Parisienne* read "François Pignon est mort."[19] Pignon had also been embodied by Pierre Richard (twice), Jacques Brel, and Daniel Auteuil by the time of his death, but Villeret's performances on stage and screen in *Le dîner de cons* had become iconic to the point of being definitive.

LE REMAKE

Released in the United States under the gentler title of *The Dinner Game*, the film grossed $4 million during a limited art house run for the distributor Lion's Gate in the summer and fall of 1999.[20] Although its initial release in France came six years after *Out on a Limb*, the proximity of Veber's Hollywood experience to the writing of *Le dîner de cons* informs the tone of both the play and the film. Taking the story idea from a conversation Veber overheard while walking the hills of Los Angeles, the narrative focuses on cruelties that are deeply embedded in aspirational wealth and the corporate culture of Hollywood.[21] The success of the film in France and abroad would make it a natural candidate for "le remake" treatment, but the fact that Veber wrote the original play from his home in California makes its American adaptation, set in Los Angeles no less, fitting. Unfortunately, Veber's story and sense of humor proved out of step with the sensibilities of American screen comedy in 2010, the year that Jay Roach's adaptation *Dinner for Schmucks* was released.

Starring Steve Carell and Paul Rudd in the roles inhabited by Villeret and Lhermitte respectively, the film plays off of the pair's established chemistry in *Anchorman: The Legend of Ron Burgundy* (2004, Adam McKay) and *The 40-Year-Old Virgin* (2005, Judd Apatow). Aside from the basic premise and a

Figure 9.2 The elusive titular dinner of Veber's film is realized for the Hollywood remake, with Barry (Steve Carell) at the center of the spectacle in *Dinner for Schmucks*.

few rehashed gags, though, *Dinner for Schmucks* is a near-total reworking of *Le dîner de cons*. Previous Hollywood adaptations of Veber's films strained to stay close to the source, often to their detriment. The nearly shot-for-shot remakes *Three Fugitives* and *Pure Luck* are lifeless in comparison to their French originals, whereas the altered historical and political context of *The Toy*, *Father's Day*, and *The Man with One Red Shoe* turn Veber's story concepts into largely incoherent American imitations. *Dinner for Schmucks* looked to escape this tendency by looking at Veber's optioned script as a story treatment, essentially. In its place, director Jay Roach and screenwriters David Guion and Michael Handelman hoped to craft a film that matched the energy and improvisational framework of *Anchorman* and *The 40-Year-Old Virgin*.

The influx of actors trained through improv theatre, from Elaine May and Mike Nichols to the Second City comedians who transitioned from *Saturday Night Live* to Hollywood in the 1970s and 1980s, largely found a way to apply their training to the traditional confines of film production by taking an alternate route to the deep, emotionally resonant performances of actors steeped in Stanislavski's method. With Judd Apatow and Adam McKay, however, the feature-length narrative, as opposed to the standard improv mockumentary, became a canvas for improvisation. The screenplay for their films became a loose framework for improvisation much in the same way that Thelonious Monk's bebop compositions were a guide for players, not a rule. The screenplays for *Anchorman* and *The 40-Year-Old Virgin* outline narrative direction, but the films were actualized by the improvisations of the cast and off-camera suggestions from the directors mid-scene, using alternate takes and multi-camera setups to facilitate creation. *Dinner for Schmucks* has a similar feel of actors riffing, but with very different results.

David Guion and Michael Handelman had been hyped as an up-and-coming screenwriting team for nearly a decade by the time *Dinner for Schmucks* was released. Meeting at Yale, the two were part of the university's improv troupe The Purple Crayon before reconnecting in New York a few years later, and they began writing screenplays together while performing in yet another improv troupe, Circus Maximus.[22] Selling their spec script *Mondo Beyondo* only a few months after deciding to try their hand at screenwriting, Guion and Handelman looked poised to find success in Hollywood. Aside from the critically panned financial flop *The Ex* (2006, Jesse Peretz), none of the pair's screenplays had been produced before they were hired to adapt *Le dîner de cons*. Jay Roach, on the other hand, was in the midst of a hot streak after directing *Austin Powers: International Man of Mystery* (1997), its two sequels (1999, 2002), *Meet the Parents* (2000) and its sequel *Meet the Fockers* (2004).

The final result of a collaboration between ambitious screenwriters and an experienced comedy director, *Dinner for Schmucks* is an odd mélange of Veber's original, a standard studio comedy, and rogue improv practices. Along the way, Guion and Handelman dismantle Veber's script to the point where its meaning is nearly reversed. *Dinner for Schmucks*, in many respects, is the moral antithesis to *Le dîner de cons*. Paul Rudd plays Tim, a kindhearted finance executive stuck in the middle rung of his company. Invited by his boss to take part in their regular "dinner for winners," Tim struggles to overcome his moral objections in hopes of moving up the corporate ladder. Having promised his girlfriend (Julie, played by Stephanie Szostak) that he will not attend the dinner, Tim changes his mind when he hits a man with his car. Barry (Steve Carell), an eccentric I.R.S. accountant whose hobby is making dioramas with dead mice, is a perfect choice for the dinner. Like Pignon, he is also accident-prone and soon throws Tim's life into chaos. Finding out that he has lined up an idiot for the party, Julie leaves Tim. While begging her to come back, Tim is pulled to the ground by Barry, hurting his back.

Rather than setting the rest of the film on the couch in Tim's apartment, he is soon placed in a back brace so he can leave the apartment with Barry to investigate Julie's whereabouts. After their first adventure snooping around the studio loft of Kieran (Jemaine Clement), a lothario artist Julie works with, Barry magically cracks Tim's back into shape and frees him to go on more adventures. The pair get into a series of misadventures with Kieran, a former one-night stand of Tim's named Darla (Lucy Punch), and Barry's I.R.S. colleague Therman (Zach Galifianakis), a workplace rival who has also stolen Barry's wife. All of this takes place while trying to score a major deal that will lead to a surefire promotion for Tim. While *Le dîner de cons* is premised on Brochant and Pignon never making it to the dinner party, the final quarter of *Dinner for Schmucks* takes place at the "dinner for winners." Somehow the event turns into a triumph for Tim and Barry, scoring revenge against Therman, humiliating Tim's bosses, and leading to new prosperous careers and stable romantic relationships for both men.

Staging the dinner in and of itself violates the very essence of Veber's original, with the supposed humor of Roach's film coming via the spectacle of the party's eccentric guests. One of the most prominently featured guests is Marco (Chris O'Dowd), a blind swordsman whose only comedic function is his physical disability. The extended dinner scene makes the audience virtual participants in the mean-spirited party. This is a sentiment that is not effectively erased by the film's easy and rushed moral lesson at the end. Veber begins his film by establishing sympathy for the invitees. Empathy is established by opening the film with the boomerang enthusiast and then showing another man at a bar who tells his friends about his upcoming dinner, to which they respond, "Why would they invite an idiot like you?" *Dinner for Schmucks* directs its sympathies toward Tim, arranging the narrative around his professional and romantic fulfillment. Because Tim is well-meaning and gets caught up in the momentum of events, he can be forgiven for exploiting Barry. Besides, Barry remains oblivious to exploitation, insults, and simple logic. Unlike Pignon, Barry is not merely fumbling and overzealous in his attempts to impress others. He really is an idiot, and has a warped understanding of the world that essentially repackages Carell's Brick Tamland character from *Anchorman*. As the Tamland character cheerily explains in a direct address to the audience in *Anchorman*, "Years later a doctor will tell me that I have an I.Q. of 48 and am what some people call 'mentally retarded.'" Carell's Barry is cut from the same cloth in terms of his random thought process and inability to process the surrounding world. This is a far cry from Villeret's tender and sympathetic portrayal of Pignon.

Comparing Tim to Brochant underscores the dramatic departure in both characterization and meaning between the two films. Tim's hesitancy to take part in the dinner is his own, and is then reinforced by Julie. He knows that it is wrong from the start, but only considers participating out of financial insecurity and his desire to convince Julie to marry him by becoming successful. Brochant, to the contrary, never hides his participation in the dinner and is unapologetic about the joy he gets out of laughing at others. Tim's eventual participation is due to peer pressure and the need to play the masculine power role to move up the corporate ladder, while Brochant's stems from sadistic pleasure and his wholehearted aspiration to be part of the *haute bourgeoisie*. By displacing the critique toward the marginal executive characters, *Dinner for Schmucks* makes a toothless and unfocused social commentary. When Therman threatens Tim with a tax audit, it carries with it the promise of an inconvenience. There is no real sense that Tim has been evading taxes. The film goes so far as to alter the details of the other woman to preserve Tim's dignity. Darla, whose appearance makes Julie believe Tim has been cheating on her, is a one-night stand from before they started dating; there is no ongoing affair like the one Brochant is having behind Christine's back. Tim even sincerely likes Barry's photos of his dead mice dioramas.

Veber is credited as an executive producer, but his creative input appears to have been minimal. It is hard to imagine a writer actively signing off on so many changes that upend the humor and tone of something so painstakingly crafted. Changing elements of the original that cannot be translated is certainly understandable, such as the complicated wordplay at the heart of a number of Veber's jokes, but other additions and subtractions speak to the overblown nature of *Dinner for Schmucks* and cultural incompatibility. Before *Dinner for Schmucks* was released, Veber spoke in good humor about being perplexed by the American writers' decisions in adapting his script, relaying a conversation where producers told him "we're trying to open up the movie" by curing Tim of the back ailment and taking the majority of the action outside of his apartment.[23] To get there, Barry needs to have a hidden chiropractic talent that, in some ways, is suggested by the subtitling of *The Dinner Game* and not the intent of Veber's dialogue. Pignon suggest to Brochant that he can call a *kiné*, which gets translated to "chiropractor" in *The Dinner Game*.[24] The Americanization of the dialogue turns into an Americanization of the treatment, as Tim's injured back no longer requires physical therapy. He just needs a good kick from Barry to realign his spine and make everything as good as new. It is symbolic of the quick and easy fixes applied throughout the adaptation that are ultimately more harmful than helpful.

There are changes that expand the film but undercut the comedy, like developing the suspected lothario only heard off screen in the original into a full-fledged character. Other changes shift the tone of the film to such an extent that a repeated joke becomes almost unrecognizable. When Pignon is forced to say "Allez l'OM" to coax Cheval into helping him, the humor lies in how indignant Pignon is to simply utter the supporter's chant from a rival football club. In *Dinner for Schmucks*, Therman forces Barry to say, "You can eat my pudding." Convinced by Tim to say this seemingly nonsensical sentence, Barry later confides that "pudding" was his pet name for his ex-wife, making the forced statement a deeply personal form of humiliation. The scene is symptomatic of the contempt that Guion and Handelman have for their characters (Tim and Julie are exceptions). The mean-spirited humor that runs throughout the film somehow coexists with the sappy sentimentality of a romantic comedy, a continuous attempt to mine comedy out of discomfort modeled after Roach's *Meet the Parents*, and a failed attempt to utilize Carell and Rudd's improvisations as effectively as McKay and Apatow.

The film grossed what would have been a respectable $73 million at the domestic box office if not for the fact that its production budget was a staggering $69 million.[25] Like the bloated *Father's Day*, a major studio decided to overspend on what should have been a tautly paced and simply staged comedy. The opening and closing of the film uses The Beatles' song "Fool on a Hill" as a bookend, with Paramount needlessly flexing its muscle by showing that they can afford the licensing rights. The furthest removed adaptation from Veber's source material, *Dinner for Schmucks* is also, to date, the last Hollywood remake of one of his screenplays. Of course, the possibility of more is always there, especially in an industry so prone to remakes and reboots. Should there be more remakes in store, *Dinner for Schmucks* serves as a cautionary tale of straying too far from the source material, as opposed to the equally frustrating process of listless repetition that Veber himself was guilty of with *Three Fugitives*.

Of all the American remakes of Veber's screenplays, only Mike Nichols's 1996 film *The Birdcage* successfully strikes a balance between respecting the source material and reinventing the story for American context and comedic sensibilities. More than simply swapping out Saint Tropez with Miami and including references to the Republican Revolution of the mid-1990s, *The Birdcage* melds the original film with the improv theatre foundations that have shaped American screen comedy since the late 1970s. Not coincidentally, the film's primary American authors are arguably the two most important figures in the history of improv theatre: Nichols is reteamed with his former comedy partner, Elaine May. Nichols's direction and May's screenplay do not reinvent the story as much as they transform the possibilities for performance. Although Durham argues that *La cage aux folles* and *The Birdcage* are so similar that they are hardly distinguishable from each other, Nichols and May reimagine the original without needing to blow up their source.[26] The improv team of Guion and Handelman, on the other hand, throw out the soul of *Le dîner de cons* in the pursuit of cheap laughs in *Dinner for Schmucks*. The film, in many respects, is symbolic of the American improv theatre's decline, trading in creative discovery for the desperate pursuit of laughs.

NOTES

1. André Bazin, *What is Cinema? Vol. 1.* Berkeley: University of California Press, 1967, p. 76.
2. Ibid. p. 77.
3. Fournier-Lanzoni, *French Comedy*, p. 19.
4. Ibid. p. 22.
5. *My Man Godfrey* was an adaptation of Eric Hatch's novel *1101 Park Avenue*. It has been performed on radio and been published in play form, but to date has not been staged on Broadway.
6. Veber, *Que ça reste entre nous*, p. 259.

7. *JP's Box-Office*, <http://www.jpbox-office.com/charts_france.php?filtre=datefr&infla=0&variable=1998> (accessed January 5, 2019).
8. Bazin, *What is Cinema?*, pp. 115–17.
9. Fournier-Lanzoni, *French Comedy*, pp. 20–21.
10. Lhermitte is sixteen years younger than Brasseur and twenty-three years younger than Roux.
11. *La totale!* is yet another film that received "le remake" treatment, becoming *True Lies* (1994, James Cameron), with Arnold Schwarzenegger taking on Lhermitte's role.
12. Fournier-Lanzoni, *French Comedy*, p. 132.
13. Ibid. p. 5.
14. Ibid.
15. V. F. Perkins, *La règle de jeu*. London: British Film Institute, 2012, pp. 8–21.
16. Fournier-Lanzoni, *French Comedy*, p. 22.
17. Bazin, *What is Cinema?*, p. 96.
18. Bazin, *What is Cinema?*, pp. 96–7.
19. Veber, *Que ça reste entre nous*, p. 279.
20. *Box Office Mojo*, <http://www.boxofficemojo.com/movies/?id=dinnergame.htm> (accessed January 5, 2019).
21. Veber, *Que ça reste entre nous*, p. 258.
22. Scott Macauley, "25 New Faces of Independent Film." *Filmmaker*, Summer 2001, <https://filmmakermagazine.com/archives/issues/summer2001/features/25_faces1-5.php> (accessed January 5, 2019).
23. *A Conversation with Francis Veber.*
24. *Kiné* is short for *kinésithérapuete*, a physiotherapist. In France, as in most of the world, chiropractic clinics are seen as marginalized sites of alternative medicine.
25. *Box Office Mojo*, <http://www.boxofficemojo.com/movies/?id=dinnerforschmucks.htm> (accessed January 5, 2019).
26. Durham, *Double Takes*, p. 194.

CHAPTER 10

Closet Conservatives:
Le placard (2001)

<hr>

Again using the François Pignon character to situate a narrative around unspoken judgments and the veneer of social niceties, Veber's ninth film *Le placard* (The Closet) appears to be closely linked to its predecessor, *Le dîner de cons*. Dialogue-heavy, and mostly filmed with constructed interiors that could easily transfer to the stage, *Le placard* shares a sense of theatricality with Veber's previous film. Although it did not originate as a play, *Le placard* would be adapted for the stage in 2014. Reversing the order of adaptation from *Le dîner de cons*, the transfer of the story to the stage emphasizes their shared structure. Even the posters for both films are remarkably similar, placing the main characters against an all-white background and the title in bold red sans serif lettering. Thematically, though, *Le placard* follows in the footsteps of two other Veber projects by tackling issues of queer identity and complicating progressive readings of his body of work. Veber's work on the screenplay for the adaptation of Jean Poiret's *La cage aux folles* (1978, Édouard Molinaro) is arguably the most high-profile film on his résumé. The other, Veber's first foray working for a Hollywood studio, is the forgettable low-budget police comedy *Partners* (1982, James Burrows). Together, the films attest to Veber's interest in exploring queer identity and also foreground the complicated and often contradictory politics that are at the center of *Le placard*.

Despite being credited for the screenplay to *La cage aux folles* along with the playwright Jean Poiret, the film's producer Marcello Danon, and the director Édouard Molinaro, Veber's track record as a screenwriter led to his contributions to the adaptation being singled out for praise. *Cahiers du cinéma*, for example, refers to Veber as a gifted writer in its review of *La cage aux folles*.[1] The four credited writers would share an Academy Award nomination for best adapted screenplay, but being the lone participant whose background was primarily as a screenwriter, Veber has been assigned a significant portion of authorial credit for the film. Stylistically, *La cage aux folles* combines his signature dialogue with Poiret's scenario and Molinaro's penchant for hand-held camera to create a hybrid of three distinct sensibilities that is somehow coherent. The commercial reception of the film has often been pointed to as a turning point for queer representation, with Fournier-Lanzoni making the case that *La cage aux folles* helped to push forward new ways of thinking about homosexuality and removed the cinematic topic from the primary domain of the avant-garde.[2] In terms of a risk-averse industry that looks to precedent, the film's success certainly fostered future investment in projects with queer characters.

The relationship between the characters and persistent stereotypes, however, complicates progressive responses to *La cage aux folles*. The film is an antithesis to most screen images of queerness in the preceding years, in that it depicts a loving and committed relationship between two men. At the same time, as Harry M. Benshoff and Sean Griffin note, the film "invite(s) straight audiences to laugh at the swishy antics of effeminate gay men and drag queens."[3] This sense of *La cage aux folles* being constructed for a straight audience is reinforced by noting that all of the principles in the film—Veber, Molinaro, Poiret, Danon, and the film's stars Ugo Tognazzi and Michel Serrault—self-identify as straight. The liberating "positive" depiction of a gay male couple is further complicated by the characters' need to pass for being straight. As Vito Russo astutely observes, "the film is about passing for straight and the accommodations gays make, large and small, each day of their lives in order to meet the expectations of the straight world."[4] The film is accepting of difference, but it also reinforces heteronormativity and largely finds its humor in sissy stereotypes.

Veber's screenplay for *Partners* does not share the complex queer representations of *La cage aux folles*, as it is bereft of Poiret's saving graces in his original story. Made at Paramount, *Partners* was not based on an existing French screenplay but, instead, marks Veber's first assignment working directly for a Hollywood studio (he is also credited as executive producer). Ultimately, it is the only original screenplay of Veber's career written exclusively for Hollywood. The story follows Los Angeles detective Benson (Ryan O'Neal) as he goes undercover as a gay man with an effeminate police filing clerk named Kerwin (John Hurt) as his partner to investigate a serial killer attacking gay men. Echoing *Cruising* (1980, William Friedkin), Benson's descent into the gay underworld includes him dressing up in leather and presenting himself as a sexual object to other men in order to find the killer. The jokes in the film consist of well-worn stereotypes that are emphasized through Benson's disgust and discomfort with gay men. Here, the passing narrative from *La cage aux folles* is reversed, with the plight of the straight male cop taking precedence over a community that is under attack. The ending of the film has Benson begrudgingly express a sense of care and respect for Kerwin, but the partnership of the title is never fully realized.

Unlike *La cage aux folles*, *Partners* fared poorly at the box office. Its failure, however, was chalked up to Paramount's unique production strategy rather than the deficiencies of Veber's screenplay or the shortcomings of veteran television director James Burrows's foray into feature films.[5] One of seven features rushed into production by the studio to beat an impending director's strike in 1981, *Partners* was a test case for making movies outside of the big budget and long development model that had become the norm in Hollywood.[6] Budgeting a series of films between $4 million and $8 million each, cutting down on the time spent in preproduction, and eliminating third party production companies, *Partners* only needed to be made fast and cheaply to help Paramount test its theory.[7] That most of the seven films failed to turn a profit did not matter to the studio in the long run, because one of those seven releases was *An Officer and a Gentleman* (1982, Taylor Hackford). Its $129.7 million box office gross more than made up for the shortcomings of the other six Paramount films.[8] As a guinea pig for cost-cutting, *Partners* had a clear function, but compared to other mainstream American releases from that year its depiction of queer identity is wildly outmoded. Although both would be subject to their own criticisms, *Personal Best* (1982, Robert Towne) and *Making Love* (1982, Arthur Hiller) show a level of sincerity in depicting queer identity akin to the racial problem pictures of the late 1940s and 1950s. *Partners*, by contrast, simultaneously traffics in sissy stereotypes and envisions gay subcultures as both empty and violent. If *Cruising* had been made as a comedy it would have been *Partners*.

Reconciling Veber's work on *La cage aux folles* with *Partners* is difficult, much in the same way that William Friedkin being the director of both *The Boys in the Band* (1970) and *Cruising* is inexplicable. As with *The Boys in the Band*, the problematic elements of *La cage aux folles* have not diminished its place as a central text in the history of queer cinema. Both films present images of gay men that were not consciously destructive, and the clumsiness of both films is somewhat mitigated by their boldness in countering the dominant discourses of the 1970s. *Partners*, like *Cruising*, foreshadows the growing fear and hostility toward gay men that would immediately follow with the diagnosis, definition, and spread of HIV/AIDS in the 1980s. The increased visibility of gay communities through political activism and the use of art and entertainment to address issues of queer identity in the 1980s and 1990s has made the problematic representations in both *Cruising* and *Partners* particularly conspicuous. For Veber, his films following the release of *Partners* were noticeably devoid of gay characters for nearly two decades. Aside from a few allusions to homosexuality played for laughs—namely the shower sequence in *Les compères* and the cross-dressing and dual male parent-ing at the end of *Les fugitifs*—Veber's films would avoid gay characters until *Le placard* in 2001.

The development of antiretroviral drugs that led to declining mortality rates in Europe and North America placed the film at a safe distance from the politically charged context of queer representation during the height of the AIDS crisis in France. *Le placard*, instead, examines an era where safe sex education has been legitimized and standardized, gays and lesbians have been granted a number of legal rights that had been denied just a few decades earlier, and the identity politics that were a major component of AIDS activism have begun to be incorporated into mainstream consciousness. The film may be part of a dramatically changed cultural and political climate, but making sense of Veber's perspective in *Le placard* recalls the contradictions in his previous depictions of queer identity.

LE FILM

Daniel Auteuil plays François Pignon in *Le placard* as a simple, boring, and lonely accountant who finds out that he is about to be laid off by his company. A divorced father of a teenage son who avoids him, Pignon contemplates suicide on the balcony of his high-rise apartment before being coaxed inside by his new next-door neighbor Belone (Michel Aumont). Talking through his troubles, Belone hatches a plan for Pignon to keep his job. By leaking a doctored photo suggesting that Pignon is gay, rumors of his sexual orientation make the execu-tives at his company avoid laying him off out of fear that they may be perceived to violate anti-discrimination laws. Belone, a gay man in his sixties who has lived through discrimination and been fired over his sexual orientation, uses Pignon

Figure 10.1 François Pignon (Daniel Auteuil) as an unwitting corporate symbol for gay pride in *Le placard*.

as a way to exact an unfocused revenge. Pignon keeps his job and in passing as gay transforms the way he is perceived at work. Working at a condom manufacturer, he even becomes a symbol for the company to use in promoting their inclusivity and connecting with gay customers. Some employees find the once boring Pignon to now be intriguing, while others see him as disgusting. Félix Santini (Gérard Depardieu), captain of the company rugby team, is particularly distressed by Pignon's supposed gay identity. Fearful that his penchant for homophobic jokes will get him fired, Santini tries to befriend Pignon and, in the process, suffers a nervous breakdown. Discovered to be straight when the company's director (Jean Rochefort) stumbles upon Pignon having sex with a female colleague (Michéle Laroque) on the factory floor, Pignon keeps his job despite the ruse. By pretending to be gay he has shown that he is not the drag he was presumed to be and, along the way, has attained new self-confidence that allows him to get over his ex-wife, reconnect with his son, make friends, develop a stable romantic relationship, and succeed at work.

Opening on an exterior shot of a suburban corporate headquarters, the majority of the film takes place inside the condom factory. The cold and sterile modern architecture along with its conservative corporate culture stand in opposition to a product associated with sex and progressive politics. If *Le jouet* is a commentary about the growing corporate influence in France during the 1970s, *Le placard* is a reflection on that shift a quarter-century later. The factory floor, replete with men in lab coats and assembly-line machinery reminiscent of *Modern Times* (1936, Charles Chaplin), is unfeeling and automated. The factory facilitates a punchline near the end of the film when Pignon begins to have sex with his female colleague and she asks, "Do you have any protection?" as they lie on an assembly-line belt littered with condoms. The need for a condom abruptly stops them in the throes of passion, while the consideration of practical health concerns in the scene foreshadows the growing "condom fatigue" that followed the height of the AIDS crisis in Europe and North America.

The glass walls of the offices may promote transparency, but they also erase privacy, facilitate surveillance, and make the factory floor visible at all times. Above all, the glass walls reinforce the need for constant productivity, or at least the appearance of productivity. The *culture du travail* in France, where colleagues eat together in a cafeteria, engage in shared recreation, and create a collective identity around their shared labor, becomes as regimented as the assembly line itself. Pignon's daily nicety toward the two women in his office is programmed, asking "Quelqu'un veux café?" (Anyone want coffee?) the same way every day, with the same negative response from his colleagues. The repetition eventually pays off with a signature Veber joke as Pignon's later deviation points out the monotony and predictability of office life. Still, in getting coffee he heads to a Nescafé vending machine, furthering the sense that all aspects of corporate life are mechanized.[9]

Placing a story about sexual identity into this corporate setting is a telling choice on the part of Veber. *Le placard* is a comedy of manners and a meditation on the climate of political correctness in France, rather than a genuine exploration of queer experiences. The only self-identifying queer character of any note in the film is Belone, and he never sets foot in the company offices. Instead, the film focuses on straight people discussing and deliberating amongst themselves on the shifting landscape of identity politics in and out of the workplace. When Santini makes a homophobic joke at a board meeting, the director reprimands him by explaining that certain jokes are not acceptable ("Il faut éviter certaines plaisanteries. Je ne vous le redirai pas"). Later that day in the cafeteria, when Santini sits to talk rugby with two blue-collar colleagues, they make a crack about Pignon's sexuality and he snaps into action, repeating the director's admonition word for word. Clearly, he has not dramatically overhauled his belief system within the span of a few hours. Still, Santini cannot afford to be perceived as accepting of his colleague's humor or complicit in their homophobia. The company director himself has a similar turnaround before his reprimand of Santini. In a closed-door meeting an executive suggests that the leaked photograph of Pignon makes his firing dangerous from a public relations standpoint. Protesting, the director says, "J'ai rien contre les homosexuels moi" (I have nothing against homosexuals) before pausing and exclaiming "Fait chier ce pédé!" (Damn that faggot!).

Santini's narrative function is to represent the painful cultural transition around identity politics. Whereas his two blue-collar colleagues feel victimized by Pignon's acceptance and later attack him in a parking garage, Santini makes an earnest effort to connect with him and overcome his own homophobia. Santini ultimately loses himself in the process. The impetus for this effort is not self-generated, but instead is orchestrated by two colleagues (played by Thierry Lhermitte and Edgar Givry) who are having fun with the least progressive and intelligent member of the company's executive board. Santini's rigid gender definitions are apparent when he explains that he knew that Pignon was gay because he broke his collarbone playing rugby. Unable to compete with others on the pitch, Sanitini reasons, Pignon's masculinity is obviously deficient. When coaching the rugby team in a scrum, Santini shouts out expletives at the players, including "On dirait des tantes!" (You look like sissies).[10] When called out on this, Santini gets flustered, saying it is "le vocabulaire de rugby!" and complains that he cannot say anything anymore. To fit into the modern world, it seems, he has to reinvent himself from the ground up. Unsure how to relate to a homosexual, Santini struggles to befriend Pignon. He awkwardly tries to start conversations by discussing vegetables, and later buys Pignon a pink cashmere sweater. Santini's eventual breakdown leads to his confinement in a mental institution, coming after he makes a bizarre plea for Pignon to live with him that cascades into a physical assault. Wearing the cashmere sweater for his visit to the mental treatment facility, Pignon invites Santini to return to work after having straightened everything out with the company. Throwing a welcome back party, Pignon takes Santini's hand in a nonsexual form of physical intimacy between men, leading Santini into the factory party and symbolically pulling him into the twenty-first century.

Reflecting on the past, Santini, the company's director, and a number of other factory workers are forced to come to grips with the rapidity of change. Belone's sense of history, however, is very different. Having lived through state-sponsored bigotry that is only now being addressed, he explains his motivation for helping Pignon by telling a story about being fired from his job in the past. Belone sees the possibility of Pignon using queer identity as a way to *keep* his job as a form of poetic justice. Belone's firing, twenty years prior to 2001, would predate the adoption of anti-discrimination laws in France. Passed in 1985, the prohibition on workplace and housing discrimination based on sexual orientation was made possible by alliances between gay rights groups and feminist, anti-racist, and socialist organizations.[11] These progressive connections are shown in the film through a black colleague taking part in humbling Santini. Realizing that race and sexual identity would be shared targets of the unenlightened man's jokes and bigotry, he agrees to help his colleagues in pushing Santini to make dramatic changes in his behavior. That Belone chooses to help Pignon, a straight white male, suggests the socialist dimensions of this alliance, using queer identity politics to help a threatened employee fight back against the cost-cutting whims of a corporate executive.

Publicizing visible diversity to offset criticism, the company looks to make a spectacle of Pignon's supposed homosexuality much in the same way that women and people of color are often prominently used in corporate advertising. Using him as a corporate mascot, the director enlists Pignon to ride on the company's float in the Paris Gay Pride parade. Apparently the company's only openly gay employee, Pignon sits expressionless at the center of the float wearing a t-shirt and a condom-shaped hat. The t-shirt reads *Sortez couvert* (literally, 'go out covered'), a popular French idiom used to promote condom use in the fight against AIDS that also could be used in a nonsexual context to tell children to bundle up before going outside. The transference or interchangeability of homespun wisdom with combating sexually transmitted diseases reflects the conflation of past and present that the company is trying to promote. Pignon's temperament on the float, expressionlessly looking out at the crowd and awkwardly waving, is typical of the passing narrative of *Le placard*.

Auteuil's reputation as the most celebrated French dramatic actor since Depardieu is used humorously when Pignon protests to Belone that he cannot pretend to be gay because he is "no actor." More than having fun with Auteuil's professional stature, the statement also foregrounds Pignon's non-performance. Unlike the overt playacting at the heart of Veber's previous queer-focused projects, Pignon's pass*ing* is pass*ive*. When Renato attempts to teach Albin to "act straight" in *La cage aux folles* by instructing him to "essaie de marcher comme (try to walk like) John Wayne," there is an assumption that sexual identity requires an outward physical performance. Similarly, the straight cop Benson in *Partners* must be trained to dress like a homosexual: wearing low-cut tank tops, leather vests, and eventually a cowboy costume help him to pass as gay. Pignon, conversely, remains unchanged in dress and mannerisms. His passing is based solely on the perception of others who are reading him through the prism of the circulating photograph and rumors. In *Le placard*, Pignon functions along the lines of Lev Kuleshov's experiments in editing, with his impassivity allowing for projections based on preconceived notions and provided context. Daniel Auteuil's Pignon is a far cry from the manic energy of Pierre Richard and Jacques Villeret or the cocky insouciance of Patrick Bruel. Auteuil's Pignon is boring to the point of being annoying to others around him. Although he is unlucky in life, it never approaches the uncanny manner of François Perrin in *La chèvre*. Previous versions of Pignon are either human wrecking balls or outsized characters; here, he is an idiot through timidity and circumstance.

In *Le placard* Pignon is a blank slate who is as boring and nondescript while he is passing as he was before. Colleagues search for meaning in small actions and project attributes onto him, such as the suspicion of a female colleague that Pignon may be passing because he lacks the culture and refinement to know how to use chopsticks. Veber ultimately deconstructs the association of outward markers with sexual orientation by guiding Auteuil's understated performance. Pignon can be read as either straight or gay, regardless of his performance. In a way, a similar deconstruction of outward markers is present through a comparative analysis of *La cage aux folles* and *Partners*, as the cowboy serves alternately as an icon of straight and gay identity. Still, *Le placard* avoids the primary investment in the outward performance of sexual identity that defines *La cage aux folles* and *Partners*. In bypassing the barrage of sissy stereotypes that are the foundations of his comedic approach to the other two films, Veber is at once conscious and critical of the boundaries in regard to political correctness.

In recalling the construction of the film, Veber writes, "Traiter en comedie un sujet sur lequel il est politiquement incorrect de plaisanter est risqué" (Comedic treatment of a subject which it is politically incorrect to joke about is risky), suggesting that the very project of *Le placard* walks a fine line between being funny and tastelessly offensive.[12] Changes in representation from *La chèvre* in 1981 to *Pure Luck* a decade later are evidence of the growing impact of identity politics on comedy in the years separating the original film and its remake. That Veber uses the term "politically incorrect" is telling.

The conservative co-opting in the late 1980s of a phrase that originated as a self-critical commentary of the left in the 1970s implies that Veber, by using the term, is a writer longing for "simpler times" when jokes could be told free of repercussions.[13]

In the workplace, the focus on political correctness in *Le placard* upsets existing order and power dynamics, but is largely an outward utterance rather than a genuine paradigm shift. For most employees, from the company director to gossiping secretaries, actions and utterances are changed, but not basic assumptions or ways of thinking. They are essentially closeted themselves, in that they hide their intolerance and conservatism. Only Santini and Pignon experience profound transformations of character. Santini nearly loses his sanity in becoming more accepting, while Pignon's passing instills a newfound confidence and assertiveness that is only accompanied by a marginal boost in cultural understanding. Comparing the passing narrative of *Le placard* to an American comedy corollary like *Soul Man* (1986, Steve Miner) clarifies the film's modest aims. In *Soul Man* a white college student (C. Thomas Howell) pretends to be black in order to gain a scholarship to Harvard Law School. Along the way he learns about his privilege and the burden of race. In passing as gay for his own professional benefit, Pignon may listen empathetically to Belone's life story and feel the judging gaze of his colleagues, but he has no such revelation about queer identity.

Regardless of its hesitant political statement, the film was generally lauded for its portrayal of issues related to sexual identity.[14] The film, however, is a product of its time, as anyone who has tried teaching it within the past decade can attest to through the confused and concerned responses from students. Coming on the heels of *Le dîner de cons* and featuring what Veber describes as a "dream" cast, *Le placard* was another commercial success for Veber, selling 5.3 million tickets at the French box office.[15] Released by Miramax as *The Closet*, *Le placard* outperformed its predecessor by grossing $6.6 million at North American box office, the most for any of Veber's French-language films.[16] Stylistically and commercially, the film marks the end of an era for Veber. The first frame of the film following the Gaumont production logo is a black screen with simple white lettering in the bottom right-hand corner reading "à Alain Poiré." As well as being Veber's longtime friend, Poiré was the producer on each of his French-language directorial efforts. When he passed away during the preparation for *Le placard* it marked the end to both a fruitful professional partnership and a deep friendship.[17] Moving forward, Veber's films would be fostered by a different set of perspectives and expectations. The creative freedom that he had long enjoyed in France did not disappear, but without Poiré he would be navigating the French film industry alone.

NOTES

1. Durham, *Double Takes*, p. 193.
2. Fournier-Lanzoni, *French Comedy*, p. 140.
3. Harry M. Beshoff and Sean Griffin, *Queer Images: A History of Gay and Lesbian Film in America*, p. 184.
4. Vito Russo, *The Celluloid Closet: Homosexuality in the Movies*, p. 263.
5. Released on April 30, 1982, *Partners* marks a notable crossroads in Burrows's career. It coincided with the airing of the last of his seventy-five episodes directing *Taxi* during the spring schedule before he moved on to co-create and serve as the primary director for *Cheers*, which debuted in the fall of 1982. *Partners* remains the only theatrical released feature for Burrows.
6. Aljean Harmetz, "How Paramount 'Seven' Fared at the Box Office." *New York Times*, May 23, 1983.
7. Ibid.
8. *Box Office Mojo*, <http://www.boxofficemojo.com/movies/?id=officerandagentleman.htm> (accessed January 5, 2019). The other films produced by Paramount that made up their so-called "Magnificent Seven" were *Young Lust* (1984, Gary Weis), *White Dog* (1982, Samuel Fuller), *I'm Dancing as Fast as I Can* (1982, Jack Hofsiss), *Jekyll and Hyde . . . Together Again* (1982, Jerry Belson), and *Some Kind of Hero* (1982, Michael Pressman). The latter was a minor hit for Richard Pryor.
9. Auteuil seems to be drawn toward coffee vending machines, as they are a key element to his performance in *Caché* (2005, Michael Haneke) as well.
10. *Tantes* literally translates to "aunts," but in the scene's context it is closer to "sissies."
11. Scott Gunther, *The Elastic Closet: A History of Homosexuality in France, 1942–Present*, p. 83.
12. Veber, *Que ça reste entre nous*, pp. 280–1.
13. Stuart Hall, "Some 'Politically Incorrect' Pathways Through PC," in Sarah Dunant (ed.), *The War of the Words*, pp. 164–84.
14. Lynn A. Higgins, "The Liberating Power of Laughter: *Le Placard* and *Gazon maudit*." *L'Esprit Créateur* vol. 51, no. 3 (Fall 2011): 118–19.
15. *JP's Box-Office*, <http://www.jpbox-office.com/fichfilm.php?id=2079&view=2> (accessed January 5, 2019).
16. Veber, *Que ça reste entre nous*, p. 281. *Box Office Mojo*, <http://www.boxofficemojo.com/movies/?id=closet.htm> (accessed January 5, 2019).
17. Veber, *Que ça reste entre nous*, p. 279.

CHAPTER 11

Repetition and Revision: *Tais-toi!* (2003)

Veber's productivity from the early 1970s until the mid-1980s is astonishing. From 1972 to 1986 Veber wrote the screenplays for twenty films, not including the Hollywood adaptations of his work. From 1987 to 2001 Veber is only credited on the final screenplay for six films, two of which are English-language translations of French originals (*Three Fugitives* and *My Father the Hero*). Veber's largely unfruitful sojourn in Hollywood explains part of this drop-off, but the greatest difference between these two eras is his growing tendency to write without any collaborators. Never working with a traditional writing partner, Veber nevertheless shared screen credit for a number of films in the 1970s even though his contributions were made in isolation. In the 1970s and early 1980s Veber wrote adaptations, developed sequels, composed dialogue for existing stories, and intermingled his story contributions with those of the director. As a director, however, Veber never shared writing credit. With the exception of *Out on a Limb*, the only project of his directorial career that he did not write, Veber's process would typically begin with developing his own concept and writing a screenplay by himself. In doing so, Veber's films exhibit an authorial control and consistency that reflect his sensibilities and aesthetics. Outside influences can be seen at times, such as the similarities between *Un indien dans la ville* and *Le jaguar*, but by and large his directorial efforts are connected by the dominant presence of Veber's personal voice.

Based on Serge Frydman's story concept, Veber's screenplay for *Tais-toi!* is the only French-language film in his directorial career on which he worked with a collaborator. Why Veber chose to depart from his usual method of story development is open to speculation, but in Frydman he may have seen both a reflection of his younger self and a reprieve from the early creative struggles that accompany any writing project conceptualized from scratch. Like Veber in the 1970s, Frydman worked in a number of capacities as a screenwriter in the years prior to *Tais-toi!* He shared writing credit with directors, provided dialogue for other writers' screenplays, and worked alone on screenplays.[1] Most notably, Frydman's collaborations with director Patrice Leconte helped expand the reach of his films outside of France in the 1990s, particularly with *La fille sur le pont* (1999, Patrice Leconte, *The Girl on the Bridge*). Veber did not need Frydman's help breaking into markets outside of France, but the writer's track record of success surely made him more appealing as a collaborator.

If Veber looked to Frydman's story idea as a way to expedite the screenwriting process, the distance between the release of *Le placard* in January 2001 and *Tais-toi!* in October 2003 suggests otherwise. The nearly three-year gap between directorial projects had become standard for Veber, with the exception of the year-and-a-half gap between the release of *Le jaguar* and *Le dîner de cons*. In that case, the bulk of the writing for the latter film had been completed five years earlier when Veber staged *Le dîner de cons* in Paris. Perhaps the story concept for *Tais-toi!* simply struck Veber's fancy, but the departure from his usual method of developing projects to direct is curious. Veber's choice to use another writer's story concept seemingly complicates his authorship, but in looking at the finished film, *Tais-toi!*, Veber's voice is as present as ever. Better put, the film recalls specific elements from past films to the point where he appears to be referencing himself throughout.

LE FILM

Returning to the antagonistic buddy pairings of the three Depardieu-Richard comedies, *Tais-toi!* uses Jean Reno as the straight man opposite Gérard Depardieu's unrestrained comic performance. The title (which translates to "Shut Up!") references Depardieu's character Quentin, an unhinged petty criminal who never stops talking. When he is sent to prison following a failed bank robbery, Quentin's need to make friends is offset by his ceaseless banter and lack of social grace. He is running through cellmates on a daily basis until the prison decides to room him with Ruby (Reno), a hardened criminal who refuses to speak to the police or anyone else. Ruby's willpower to remain silent and expressionless ends up endearing him to Quentin, who finally meets someone who allows him to talk as much as he wants. Ruby is plotting to escape from prison in order to seek vengeance on Vogel (Jean-Pierre Malo), a gangster who killed his girlfriend and is demanding money that he has hidden away. As part of his plan, Ruby fakes a suicide attempt in order to be moved to the less secure medical ward of the prison. Quentin, who regards Ruby as his first true friend, cuts his own wrists in order to join him on the medical ward. Eventually they escape together, and the film follows Ruby and his

Figure 11.1 Quentin (Gérard Depardieu) and Ruby (Jean Reno) as a fugitive odd couple in *Tais-toi!*

unwanted companion as they run from Vogels's henchmen and the police. Allowing himself to be taken hostage and brought to Vogel, Ruby attempts to kill the gangster, only to be shot in the leg. Vogel, with a gun pointed to Ruby's head, demands to know where the money is, but is shot dead by Quentin, who has unexpectedly arrived at the mansion. Injured in the exchange, Ruby and Quentin sit on the floor together as the police arrive. The film ends with a freeze frame of the unlikely friends, giving the impression that they will be joined together in prison for years to come. Again, as in earlier Veber films, the freeze frame is less of a resolution in the narrative than it is a signal that the paired men will continue their hijinks, inextricably linked forever.

The most noticeable difference between *Tais-toi!* and all of Veber's previous French films as a director (as well as most of his screenwriting credits) is that he abandons the François Perrin/Pignon character name for the comic lead. As Veber explains, he chose to use Quentin instead of Pignon because he was not the author of the original idea.[2] The choice of character name may hint at a collaboration surpassing a simple story idea being developed by Veber, but the connections to previous films make it likely that Serge Frydman did little more than provide a narrative outline. Otherwise, Veber's choice of the project must have been due to its direct references to his body of work. As a whole, though, the naming difference appears to be merely superficial. The Quentin character may not be named François Pignon, but he functions in a nearly identical fashion.

The Ruby and Quentin pairing (which is emphasized in the U.S. release title *Ruby & Quentin*) follows Veber's formula for buddy comedy by coupling an unhinged comic with a hardened tough guy.[3] Depardieu had played iterations of the tough guy character three times opposite Pierre Richard, but the origins of the character can be seen as early as Veber's 1969 play *Le contrat* (adapted for the screen in 1973 as *L'emmerdeur*). Jean Reno fills the same role as he does in *Le jaguar*, playing the exasperated straight man. Depardieu, on the other hand, is asked to radically transform his performance as the comic lead. The centrality of comedy to Depardieu's stardom, according to Ginette Vincendeau, is a shared attribute with other male stars throughout the history of French cinema.[4] He had proven himself to be adept at comedy, but entering the 2000s Depardieu began to refashion his performances as a clownish lead. As Quentin, Depardieu's manic expressivity is placed at the center of the film, as opposed to subtle gestures working opposite a comic co-star. It is nearly impossible to imagine former straight men like Bing Crosby or Dean Martin making such a transition in the latter stage of their careers. Depardieu's move toward a wackier comic style is evident in *Le placard* when he works opposite the impassive Daniel Auteuil, and has become a defining characteristic of his performances as Obélix in *Astérix & Obélix contre César* (1999, Claude Zidi, *Asterix and Obelix vs. Cesar*) and its numerous sequels. To have him utilized in a reversed role from his first three Veber films merely stresses Depardieu's comic range.

Tais-toi! recycles a number of elements from previous Veber films, beginning with the failed bank robbery. Echoing Pignon's amateurish attempt in *Les fugitifs*, Quentin's criminal incompetence is taken a step further when it turns out that he is not actually robbing a bank, but an exchange bureau that only has Yen and Canadian dollars on hand. Taking the exchange teller's suggestion, Quentin heads across the street to try again at a savings bank, only to be surrounded by police. Later, the film reuses two gags from *Les fugitifs* by costuming the fugitive Ruby and Quentin in women's clothes (like Pignon during the final escape to the Italian border) and then stealing clothes from two tough youths, mirroring the scene with a failed mugging of Lucas in the abandoned warehouse. The primary function of the scene is a simple gag in which the tables are turned on unsuspecting hoodlums, but Veber embellishes the payoff from *Les fugitifs* by showing the would-be attackers walking into a police station wearing the women's clothing that was previously donned by Quentin and Ruby. There is thematic weight to the scene, as the attacking youths see cross-dressing as clear sign of weakness, playing with ingrained notions about masculinity that Veber had explored in *Le placard*. However, this is a fleeting moment that is unrelated to any broader commentary in *Tais-toi!*

Although there are reflections of previous films throughout *Tais-toi!*, the film lacks an organizing critical perspective. Instead, there are fragmented commentaries that are never fully developed. While Quentin and Ruby are hiding out in an abandoned café they stumble across Katia (Leonor Varela), a young immigrant from Albania. Ruby takes a special liking to her, becomes protective, and gives her money to start a new life for herself in France. The introduction of this character more than two-thirds of the way into the film reflects back on the murder of Ruby's girlfriend. Ruby shows tenderness toward Katia because she physically resembles his murdered girlfriend (Varela plays both characters, actually), but the relationship remains platonic and paternal. There is also a shared sense of suffering between Katia and the escaped prisoners, as all three of them are on the run and forced by circumstance to the margins. The inclusion of Katia's national origin, however, opens up the possibility of a broader commentary on migration, political instability, and the hope placed in the European Union by Albania in the 2000s, but this is a hint rather than a point of emphasis.[5] The film has other fragmented commentaries on street crime and psychiatry, but they are similarly underdeveloped.

After making direct political commentaries, particularly in *Le placard* and the didactic *Le jaguar*, Veber constructs *Tais-toi!* around gags instead. In providing a rationale for Ruby and Quentin to cross-dress Veber returns to the type of simple joke based on physical stature that he used in both *Les fugitifs* and *Three Fugitives*, when Pignon demands a bank teller come out from behind his desk to retrieve a bag hanging from a light fixture. In *Tais-toi!* the fugitives break into a luxurious apartment and find a man sitting on the couch reading a magazine. Still wearing robes from the psychiatric ward of the prison, they demand the man's clothes. Finding a sports jacket lying on a chair, Quentin picks it up to try it on, only to realize it is a child's size. Standing up when Ruby approaches, the man only comes up to the middle of Ruby's chest. The apartment's décor, overflowing with oil paintings and statues of racehorses, makes it apparent that the man is a jockey. When his extraordinarily tall wife walks in wearing a red pantsuit, it becomes apparent that the fugitives only have one option. Using an elliptical edit, Veber cuts to Ruby and Quentin stealing a car, both dressed in the woman's pantsuits and shoes.

Other comedic bits are premised on Quentin's incompetence, recalling the perpetual sense of disaster surrounding Pignon/Perrin. When Ruby sends him out to steal an escape vehicle, for example, he comes back with a police squad car. Their prison escape, orchestrated by Quentin, is one of the best visual gags of the film. Enlisting the help of a bumbling friend, Ruby and Quentin are lifted out of the prison by a crane, only to move back and forth over the prison wall as the man fumbles with beer can at the controls. Veber returns to the cartoonish sensibility of *La chèvre* by punctuating the scene with the escaping prisoners jumping onto the roof of a stranger's minivan, leaving perfectly molded indentations of their feet. This excessive flourish at the end of the scene nearly obscures the visual inventiveness of the crane sequence.

Elsewhere, Veber undercuts the impact of his gags by failing to frame the action properly. On the run, Ruby and Quentin break into a costume and novelty store. Quentin steals a whoopee cushion and a can that makes a cow's "moo" sound when it is tipped over. Reinforcing Quentin's childlike nature, the items become an annoyance to Ruby, who has to deal with the sounds of both toys as he drives and negotiates with Vogel over the phone. Throwing the can out the car window in frustration, Veber employs a slight pan as Quentin steps out of the car and moves sneakily around the trunk to retrieve his toy. While the comedic intent would be perfectly apparent with a static take, Veber forces the camera's perspective to guarantee that the audience follows the action. The pan is overkill, dictated by an arbitrary decision to begin the scene with a two-shot of Ruby and Quentin framed around the car's windshield. Much like the medium shot of the bank teller in *Three Fugitives* undoing the physical gag that works in *Les fugitifs*, the incompatibility of camera placement and physical comedy in *Tais-toi!* undercuts Veber's writing and the performances of his cast.

The adoption of action genre conventions further dampens the comedy. The film is littered with car chases and gunfights that play out with grave seriousness, only to be juxtaposed with cartoonish sequences where Quentin beats people up with a superhuman strength that is never explained. There are real consequences to most of the violence in *Tais-toi!*, yet Veber never reconciles this with the cartoonish violence of Quentin. The first French film of Veber's directorial career not featuring a Vladimir Cosma score, its action sequences are accompanied by a serious score from Marco Prince that recalls Hollywood action and heist movies more than it does popular comedy. Most striking, the murder of Ruby's girlfriend, which takes place off screen, is communicated to the audience with a close-up of her lifeless face underneath clear plastic wrapping as dirt begins to be shoveled over her dead body. This is an especially gruesome scene for Veber, even in comparison to the dismemberments in *Le jaguar*. Those moments of violence in *Le jaguar*, while out of character for Veber, nevertheless are handled humorously. In contrast, the death of Ruby's girlfriend is somber and becomes far more jarring and disturbing than anything else Veber had committed to celluloid in his directorial career. The difference is in tone, not content, as Veber has long been preoccupied with the criminal underworld and has often handled death in a flippant manner (such as with the gunning down of Arbal at the side of the road in *La chèvre*). Gangsters appear in a number of the films he had previously directed, but there is a tonal departure in *Tais-toi!* that is removed from the mob assassins of *Les compères*, the immigrant hustlers of *Les fugitifs*, or the Latin American underworld figures in *La chèvre* and *Le jaguar*.

Veber's use of gangsters can be seen as early as his work for television in the late 1960s on the series *Agence Intérim* and continues in *les policiers* from the 1970s like *Adieu Poulet*, but his conception of the underworld balances two competing traditions within French cinema. The prominent use of gangsters in the 1930s via poetic realism films, and the noir-inspired films of Melville, Godard, and others in the 1950s and 1960s, run counter to the surge of noir parodies in the 1950s and 1960s that are best exemplified by *Les tontons flingueurs*.[6] Veber's films show a clear inspiration from both traditions, yet never fully cohere to the tone or function of either. Too comedic to present as underworld figures with total earnestness, Veber's gangsters depart from the iconography of poetic realism or the *nouvelle vague*. Not incompetent or one-dimensional enough to count as parody or spoof, the underworld figures that populate his crime films retain an existential inner turmoil, begging to be taken seriously. In *Tais-toi!*, Ruby's deep sense of suffering and loss run counter to the joyful chatterbox Quentin, but rather than strengthening the oppositional banter that defines the Depardieu-Richard comedies, this mismatch in overall tone supersedes the intended contrast in character type. Just as fragmented commentaries run through *Tais-toi!*, the film shifts in mood, style, and even genre from one section to the next.

One fragment that aims to add depth and connects to broader contexts in ways both artful and crass comes early in the film, as Quentin runs from the police after his failed bank robbery. Running into a multiplex, he backs into a dark theatre only to become transfixed by the movie, which is the computer-animated children's film *Ice Age* (2002, Chris Wedge and Carlos Saldanha, *L'âge de glace*). Watching it, Quentin immediately breaks into a smile and sits down amongst a group of small children to laugh and cheer as prehistoric animals slide down an icy tube. The moment of unbridled joy not only supports Quentin's childlike innocence, but it also brings to mind the final scene of *Sullivan's Travels* (1941, Preston Sturges), reveling in the power of film comedy to provide laughter and comfort regardless of the spectator's lived circumstance. At the same time, the lifeless exterior of the multiplex and the use of a big-budget Hollywood import as the vessel for this joy come across as calculatingly consumerist. To make matters worse, Quentin runs into the UGC Ciné Cité Bercy, an eighteen-screen multiplex owned by the same company that distributed and coproduced *Tais-toi!*[7] The shamelessness of this synergistic self-promotion, coupled with the banal commercialism of the multiplex, strips away the moment's tenderness.

Tais-toi! sold a respectable 3.1 million tickets in France, falling just outside of the top ten at that year's box office, but third amongst films produced domestically.[8] The response was a far cry from *Le placard* and *Le dîner de cons*, but Veber proved with *Tais-toi!* that he could make a commercially viable film simply by rehashing his past work. Their fifth film together, *Tais-toi!* marks the final collaboration between Veber and Depardieu. Capturing the actor's comedic range, the film avoids the self-parody that characterizes the latter career comedies of Robert De Niro, Depardieu's one-time American corollary. In subsequent years his personal tragedies, scandals, and disputes with the French government would begin to overshadow his acting, but from the mid-1970s up until the early 2000s Depardieu's performances and persona came to symbolize the national mood. That such a long span of that era was connected with Veber is not to be taken lightly. Veber helped Depardieu connect to an audience on a different level than his dramatic roles, solidifying his importance. As Ginette Vincendeau writes, "In French comedy, stars establish and perpetuate a closeness to their audience, and signs of social identity."[9] For Depardieu, *Tais-toi!* marks the end of that shared journey with Veber. In renouncing his French citizenship, Depardieu's closeness with French audiences also ended in the years that followed. For his next project, Veber would look to a new generation of performers who could connect with the national mood and comedic tastes.

NOTES

1. Frydman shares screenwriting credit with Leconte on *Les grands ducs* (1996) and *Rue de plaisirs* (2002, *Love Street*), is credited only for the dialogue on *Chambre à part* (1989, Jacky Cukier), *1 chance sur 2* (1998, Patrice Leconte), and *Amazon* (2000, Philippe de Broca), and is the lone writer credited for *La fille sur le pont*.

2. Veber, *Que ça reste entre nous*, 209.

3. In the U.K. the film was released as *Shut Up!*

4. Vincendeau, *Stars and Stardom in French Cinema*, 217.

5. Albania began negotiations to join the E.U. in 2003, the same year that *Tais-toi!* was released.

6. Fournier-Lanzoni, *French Comedy*, 98–103.

7. UGC is the top billed production company on the film, although, like many contemporary French films, it is a collaborative production between a number of companies. UGC is one of eight French and Italian companies credited on *Tais-toi!*

8. *JP's Box-Office*, <http://www.jpbox-office.com/charts_france.php?filtre=datefr&infla=0&variable=2003> (accessed January 5, 2019).

9. Vincendeau, *Stars and Stardom in French Cinema*, 218–19.

CHAPTER 12

Modern Times: *La doublure* (2006)

Defining standup comedy is almost as difficult as charting the art form's origins, but the influence of the American standup boom in the 1970s on global comedy is hard to overstate. It can be seen in the spread of American-style comedy clubs, televised one-man shows, and the use of standup as a springboard to film stardom. Whereas music halls, cabarets, and *café-théâtre* have long functioned as training grounds for French film comics, since the late 1970s the majority of Hollywood comedians have either come from improv theatre (as discussed in Chapters 6 and 9) or from standup. Major American film stars who began as standup comedians include Robin Williams, Billy Crystal, Richard Pryor, Steve Martin, Eddie Murphy, Adam Sandler, Whoopi Goldberg, and Cheech and Chong. Collectively, they form a strong argument that the solitary stage performance of a standup can translate to film, or at least to box-office success. France had never established a similar pipeline for comedic talent, but the growth of French standup in the 1980s and 1990s has been followed by a number of comics moving into narrative films.

The difference in reception between Gad Elmaleh's feature-length screen debut *Salut cousin!* (1996, *Hi Cousin!*) and *Chouchou* (2003) situates the comedian's increased celebrity, the growth of standup in France, and the political thrust of his one-man shows. Both films are directed by Merzak Allouache and revolve around immigrant characters adjusting to life in Paris, but *Salut cousin!* hardly garnered an audience, selling only 73,598 tickets in France.[1] Seven years later, *Chouchou* sold 3.8 million tickets in France and ended up outpacing Veber's *Tais-toi!* at the domestic box office.[2] In the interim, the circulation of Elmaleh's one-man shows both on stage and through home video release turned him into a household name in France. His first one-man show in 1997, *Décalages*, articulates a personal and confessional brand of comedy akin to that of Richard Pryor's recollections of his childhood in Peoria, Illinois. Premised on his backstory of growing up in Morocco, moving to Canada, and eventually arriving in France, the long-form routine in *Décalages* is much more than a series of jokes. It is a collection of character sketches and social commentaries that created both a following and mythology around the comedian. Beginning in small clubs, Elmaleh soon graduated to selling out large theatres and arenas.

Regardless of Elmaleh's success, Veber had reservations about casting him as François Pignon in *La doublure*.[3] Veber was considering casting two standup comics in the film (the other being Dany Boon) despite the fact that he had never worked with a standup before. Veber saw both men perform in person, but was unsure if the interactive nature of their live performances could translate to the screen.[4] Veber does not mention the experience of working with Martin Short on *Three Fugitives* in relation to this new endeavor, but his concerns about Elmaleh echo the shortcomings of his approach to utilizing American comic talent. Like Short's improv background, standup is grounded in interactivity and improvisation. The connection is evidenced in one of the central comedy clubs in the American standup boom being named The Improv. Routines can be written and rehearsed, but there is a spontaneity found through the interaction between a standup comedian and an audience during a live performance that is absent in most narrative film productions. Veber's affection for retakes and repetition certainly makes an awkward match for the improv or standup comedian. Still, Veber decided to try his hand working with standups after seeing Elmaleh and Boon perform in person, casting Elmaleh as Pignon and Boon in a smaller role as his roommate and coworker.

Recalling the public reaction to Elmaleh being cast as the next Pignon, Veber points out the recurring criticisms of Elmaleh being "too attractive" and "not enough of a common man."[5] Pignon, through the repetition of the character name being used in Veber films, had become something of a symbol of the French everyman. Unlucky and put upon by those in power, Pignon invites empathy and identification from the audience. Embedded in the claim that Elmaleh is not enough of a common man is the implicit critique that he is not French enough. Born in Morocco, Elmaleh was part of a wave of French standup comics in the early 2000s whose work addressed issues of immigration and ethnicity. His imaging as the surrogate for a national experience is part of the subtext to negative responses to his casting in *La doublure*. Another factor, however, is the confidence exuded in Elmaleh's standup. Far from the neurotic and insecure stage personas of countless standups, Elmaleh exhibits a swagger and authority in his routines that is antithetical to previous depictions of Pignon as an unlucky (Pierre Richard), overbearing (Jacques Villeret), or impotent (Daniel Auteuil) fool. Only Patrick Bruel's arrogant and self-absorbed François Perrin in *Le jaguar* is a less "common" lead than Elmaleh.

Ultimately, the retrospective doubts that Veber expresses in his memoir about Elmaleh transitioning from standup to narrative film comedy ring false. By the time that *La doublure* was released in 2006 Elmaleh had been acting in films for over a decade, with seventeen feature-length credits ranging from supporting to starring roles. In fact, immediately preceding *La doublure* he had a starring role in *Olé!* (2005, Florence Quentin) that paired him opposite the venerable Gérard Depardieu. If Veber was unaware of Elmaleh's screen performances, it would have taken a concerted effort to avoid hearing, seeing, or reading about them. Perhaps Veber had been checked out of popular culture, but it seems unlikely that he would have cast the actor based solely on seeing one live performance. In summing up his impression of Elmaleh on and off camera, Veber writes, "Gad gave the impression that each moment of his life not spent being funny is a second lost."[6] While this is certainly a tendency that runs through the worst screen performances of Robin Williams (including the Veber remake *Father's Day*), attributing this solely to being a standup is a cop-out. Never going so far as to disparage his performance, Veber acknowledges the difficulty in portraying the *clown blanc* role of Pignon and expresses admiration for the "progress" Elmaleh made as an actor while working on the film.[7] A decade into making movies, praising Elmaleh's progress as an actor reads as a backhanded compliment that, at its core, is acknowledging the shortcomings of *La doublure*. Perhaps Veber saw in the restrained performance of Elmaleh that the actor was fighting against his performative instincts to portray Pignon.

LE FILM

As is the case with other Pignon films, *La doublure* shows the character getting into a situation that is out of his depth. Parking cars as a valet for a high-end restaurant across from the Eiffel Tower, Pignon lives in a modest apartment with Richard (Dany Boon), a roommate and fellow valet. He is also planning to ask his childhood sweetheart Émilie (Virginie Ledoyen), a bookstore owner struggling to stay in business, to marry him. Crosscutting with Pignon's failed proposal is an extramarital tryst between Levasseur (Daniel Auteuil), a rich industrialist, and his supermodel mistress Elena (Alice Taglioni). Stating her disappointment that he has not left his wife as promised, Elena leaves, and Levasseur follows her outside to beg for her to come back. While they are on the sidewalk together, a paparazzo takes their photo together at the very moment that a dejected Pignon walks next to them. When the photo is published the next day in the tabloids, Levasseur is confronted by his wife Christine (Kristin Scott Thomas), a major stockholder in his company and the source of his wealth. He denies the affair.[8] Levasseur and his lawyer (Richard Berry) concoct a plan to make it seem that he was the innocent bystander in

Figure 12.1 Oblivious corporate executive Levasseur (Daniel Auteuil) engulfed by labor protest in *La doublure*.

the photo, and that Pignon is in fact Elena's lover. As part of this plan, Pignon and Elena are paid to pretend to live together in order to deceive Christine and the press. Pignon attends a fashion show in order to be seen with Elena and becomes a mainstay in the tabloids as their supposed romance becomes public, piquing Christine's suspicions and prompting Levasseur's jealousy. Becoming close platonic friends through it all, Pignon and Elena help each other to find happiness: Elena helps Pignon finally win over Émilie, and Pignon assists Elena in getting even with the duplicitous Levasseur.

Most of the humor in the film is situational, built around the improbability of a famous fashion model falling in love with an unexceptional working-class man. *La doublure* literally translates to "the lining," tying in the fashion angle of the story while also symbolizing Pignon's role as a buffer between Levasseur and the truth. The film's English title, *The Valet*, places the emphasis instead on Pignon's profession and, in turn, class difference.[9] The opening sequence of the film shows Richard driving a silver Porsche, coming to a stoplight, and acknowledging Pignon as a stranger when he pulls up next to him in a red Ferrari. The two feign indifference toward their expensive sports cars, trading banter about how they easily tire of their toys before revving their engines and speeding off. Cutting to the red Ferrari pulling up in front of the fountains and entrance of the Les Jardins de Chaillot restaurant, the camera moves in for a medium shot of Pignon exiting the car, only to show him turning around to open the door as another man steps inside. The back of Pignon's white collared shirt reads in clear black letters "voiturier" (valet), with the word placed at the center of the frame. The shot holds for a few moments to capture the silver Porsche pulling in behind, to show the same exchange with Richard and another restaurant customer. Taking place without any context, the scene is a simple piece of comedic misdirection. Cutting from the valet stand to Pignon driving his own personal car, a mid-1980s Peugot hatchback, Veber adds a point of emphasis to the initial false impression of wealth to underline the fanciful imaginations of Pignon and Richard.

The playacting of the valet drivers foregrounds the class divisions at the heart of the narrative. Veber dedicates a number of scenes to contrasting Pignon's modest life with the wealth of Levasseur, including the crosscutting of the failed proposal with Émilie and the executive's rendezvous with Elena. Pignon's humble engagement ring is compared to the diamond bracelet offered to Elena, and both of the women's refusals of the jewelry are rooted in a financial consideration. Elena wants to be loved, not purchased, whereas Émilie needs to focus on her failing bookstore and the debt she owes (32,450 euros, which is later the exact amount that Pignon requests from Levasseur's lawyer to take part in the ruse with Elena). Typical of the type of parallelism and repetition that mark his films, Veber does more than simply juxtapose characters from different economic strata in subsequent scenes. In *La doublure*, Veber makes his most direct commentary on big business since *Le jouet* by using Levasseur as a stand-in for corporate greed, dishonesty, and indifference.

Although it becomes a mere afterthought to the unfolding drama and jealousy developing around Pignon, Elena, and Christine, the professional obligation that should be Levasseur's primary concern is a labor strike at a factory. Sent to Lille to negotiate with union delegates, Levasseur is instead preoccupied with Elena. Leaving in the middle of the meeting to take a call from one of his hired spies, Levasseur walks away from negotiations to hear his detectives describe the way Pignon appears to be making sexual overtures to Elena. Had Veber set it in an isolated office or conference room, the scene could merely have conveyed Levasseur's state of mind. Instead, Veber employs hundreds of extras to articulate his political commentary. The first shot of the negotiations begins at a window facing outside to show hundreds of protesters chanting and holding signs that read "Levasseur menteur!" (Levasseur is a liar!). Craning down slowly as a voice of one of the labor leaders speaks, the camera adjusts to a medium close-up of Levasseur, now engulfed by the protesters outside as they fill the rest of the frame. Levasseur's expression blends his detachment with an unconvincing smile meant to appease his critics. Returning to the meeting after his phone call, the camera tracks in to a close-up of Levasseur as he finally responds to the union's comments on the human cost of the impending layoffs he has proposed. "I'm thinking," Levasseur says gravely, "it is a painful situation. A very painful situation." Reinforcing his self-absorption and callousness, it is clear that he is talking about his feelings for Elena and not the plight of the workers. Indicating its thematic importance, the shot is one of the most elaborately staged of Veber's career, far surpassing the number of extras employed for any scene in his previous films and utilizing them only as background for Auteuil's performance.[10]

The class and corporate commentaries of *La doublure* coincide with Veber's observations on modern life. The financial pressure that becomes the undoing of Pignon's proposal is not arbitrary. Émilie's bookstore, once an integral part of the neighborhood, has become an outmoded passion project rather than a viable business. The introduction of Pascal (Patrick Mille), a sleazy and empty-headed suitor who runs a thriving cell phone store, becomes an annoyance to Émilie in more ways than one. He not only exhibits characteristics of a predatory male, but his business and personal affinity for his own cell phone is an inversion of Émilie's earnest bookstore venture. Pascal sees the bookstore as a hopeless enterprise that is resisting the coming dominance (and lucrative financial possibilities) of digital technology, yet it is shown as an essential part of the community through Émilie caring for an old man with dementia. The fact that the store is antithetical to a modern economy suggests a deterioration of community and neighborhoods.

This localized observation coincides with the film's broader commentaries on modern celebrity and media. The entire narrative is put into motion by the presence of paparazzi and tabloid newspapers. Contemporary media may be a means of humbling Levasseur, but it also disrupts the lives of the kindhearted Pignon and Elena. Veber uses the culture surrounding tabloids and gossip magazines to implicate the public at large, as consuming the story of Pignon and Elena separately shapes the impressions of Émilie, Richard, Pignon's parents, and other co-workers and acquaintances. Rumors take on a life of their own, spread both by newspapers and secondhand accounts; Pignon's mother rushes home from the beauty parlor to tell her husband the false news that their son is set to marry the famous model Inès de la Fressange.[11] Poking fun at the public fascination with celebrity, *La doublure* also indulges in the tendency by shooting a sequence of the film (with a jarring difference in film stock) at an actual Karl Lagerfeld fashion show. Having known Lagerfeld since the 1960s, Veber crafts a small cameo for the designer that places the film within the very real world of high fashion and celebrity culture.[12]

Commentaries aside, the Pignon character is often displaced by the machinations of the narrative. Between Levasseur, Christine, Émilie, Pascal, Richard, and a separate story involving Pignon's parents and Émilie's ailing father (Michel Aumont), there is little left for Elmaleh to do in the film, aside from a few moments where he is able utilize his standup-style delivery for jokes within the dialogue. As in *Le placard*, Pignon is a kind and gentle figure trapped in a broad deception. Only showing a sense of empowerment in the final scene when he confronts Levasseur, Elmaleh's Pignon lacks the comedic highs of Pierre Richard or Jacques Villeret, or the spiritual rebirth experienced by the character as played by Daniel Auteuil (or by Patrick Bruel as Perrin). The confrontations between Pignon and Levasseur did manage to amuse Veber, with the circumstance of Auteuil acting opposite Elmaleh causing the director to remark, "For the first time in a film I had two Pignons face to face."[13]

La doublure includes other references and echoes of past Veber films, although never as blatant or recurring as those from *Tais-toi!* Returning home to see his parents, Pignon gifts his father an antique corkscrew for his impressive collection. Recalling the eccentric obsessions with ladles, boomerangs, and matchstick models, the collecting of corkscrews would make Pignon's father a candidate for an invitation from Brochant in *Le dîner de cons.* Elsewhere, the stakeout and surveillance of Levasseur and Christine's detectives recalls the police, assassins, and spies that populate numerous Veber screenplays including *L'emmerdeur* and *Le grand blond avec une chaussure noire.* A troubling echo comes in the final shot of the film, as Levasseur stands on the side of the road and has his picture taken by a paparazzo just as a transsexual prostitute steps out from behind a tree and takes his arm. The freeze-frame image disappears in a hard cut and reappears as the cover image of a gossip magazine. The bold headline reads "Levasseur piégé!" (Levasseur trapped!). The ending is supposed to show justice coming to Levasseur, but it is mostly a reminder of Veber tastelessly and lazily using queer identity as a punchline.

Stylistically, the film returns to the aesthetics of Veber's French films prior to *Tais-toi!*, despite employing a new cinematographer in Robert Fraisse.[14] Using a playful animated opening credit sequence of a style that had become standard for Veber starting with *Le dîner de cons*, the light tone of the film is evident from the start. Although the film contains serious commentaries, there is a confectionary tenor that permeates the film. From the blatant product placement of Pom'lisse potato chips, with Dany Boon unnaturally holding the bag to prominently display the logo, to composer Alexandre Desplat's goofy off-brand score version of Roy Orbison's "Oh, Pretty Woman," a number of the elements of the film are crass and inconsequential.[15] Still, the commentaries in *La doublure* remain consistent and prominent enough to combat the film's empty packaging.

La doublure finished in twelfth place at the annual French box office, with just over three million tickets sold.[16] It was a respectable if not overwhelming showing, well behind four other French comedies that year. The final original screenplay of Veber's career, *La doublure* represents the passing of the popular French comedy torch. Although Gad Elmaleh is the headlining star, Veber's kindest comments about the making of the film are reserved for Dany Boon, who he observed to be a far more natural actor.[17] In 2006, Boon performed in *La doublure* and also made his directorial debut with *La maison du bonheur*, a modest success with just over 1.1 million tickets sold.[18] Boon's second directorial feature, *Bienvenue chez les Ch'tis* (2008, *Welcome to the Sticks*) became the highest grossing domestic film in the history of France, selling over twenty million tickets.[19] The film's use of linguistic and regional humor specific to a French audience represent the sort of cultural touchstones that can never be replicated or remade elsewhere, although there were reports of Boon's film receiving Hollywood's "le remake" treatment at one point.[20]

A year before Boon's breakout hit, Veber cast him to play François Pignon in the new stage version of *Le dîner de cons*, this time with Veber directing his own play at the Théâtre de la Porte Saint-Martin in Paris. Perhaps understanding that Boon had more of a "common man" charm than Elmaleh, the stage play gave Veber a chance to amend a casting mistake. In any event, the characteristics of Pignon are certainly evident in Boon's performance in *Bienvenue chez les Ch'tis*. After having written for the stage, it took thirty-six years for Veber to finally direct for the theatre. His 2007 staging of *Le dîner de cons* marked his second outing as a director. Two years earlier, he had decided to make his stage debut as a director with *L'emmerdeur*, a retitling of his 1969 play *Le contrat*. This play had been staged by another director the first time around, and Veber now decided to tackle it himself. Following the same logic, he subsequently decided to direct his own film adaptation in 2008.

NOTES

1. *JP's Box-Office*, <http://www.jpbox-office.com/fichfilm.php?id=10702> (accessed January 5, 2019).
2. *JP's Box-Office*, <http://www.jpbox-office.com/charts_france.php?filtre=datefr&infla=0&variable=2003> (accessed January 5, 2019).
3. Veber, *Que ça reste entre nous*, p. 299.
4. Ibid.
5. Ibid. p. 300.
6. Ibid.
7. Ibid. p. 301.
8. British by birth, Kristin Scott Thomas has lived primarily in France for most of her adult life. Her first film appearance, although not in a French-speaking role, came in *Under the Cherry Moon* (1986), Prince's directorial debut shot in and around Nice.
9. The various ways that translated titles frame the story prove fascinating. Italy's *Una top model nel mio netto* (A Top Model in My Bed) alters the profession of interest; Brazil's *Contratado para Amor* (Hired to Love) fixates on the transactional aspect of the pairing; and Spain's *El juego de los idiotas* (The Game of the Idiots) seems like a leftover title from *Le dîner de cons*.
10. The final fight in *Le jaguar* would come closest in terms of Veber's use of extras.
11. In an attempt to universalize the joke, *The Valet*'s subtitles replace the name of French model Inès de la Fressange with Naomi Campbell.
12. Veber, *Que ça reste entre nous*, p. 295.
13. Ibid. p. 300.
14. Luciano Tovoli had served as cinematographer on all of Veber's French films since their first collaboration on *Les fugitifs*.

15. Among a host of corporate partners, the end credits acknowledge the participation of Pom'lisse's parent company Multi-Marques through their product placement agency Marques & Films.

16. *JP's Box-Office*, <http://www.jpbox-office.com/charts_france.php?filtre=datefr&infla=0&variable=2006> (accessed January 5, 2019).

17. Veber, *Que ça reste entre nous*, p. 301.

18. *JP's Box-Office*, <http://www.jpbox-office.com/fichfilm.php?id=360> (accessed January 5, 2019).

19. *JP's Box-Office*, <http://www.jpbox-office.com/fichfilm.php?id=10042> (accessed January 5, 2019).

20. "Le projet de remake US de 'Bienvenue chez les Ch'tis' abondonné!" *Allocine*, September 3, 2012, <http://www.allocine.fr/article/fichearticle_gen_carticle=18616421.html> (accessed January 5, 2019). The remake project was reportedly attached to Will Smith and Steve Carell.

CHAPTER 13

The Last Picture Show: *L'emmerdeur* (2008)

In addition to being his final film as either a director or screenwriter, *L'emmerdeur* is also a project that represents a number of firsts in Veber's career. The play originated as *Le contrat* in 1969, staged by Veber in the same year that his first film adaptation, *Appelez-moi Mathilde*, premiered. *Le contrat* became Veber's first buddy comedy, and is the foundation for subsequent mismatched pairings of a tough straight man and a manic, disaster-prone comic that he would revisit and rework in *La chèvre*, *Les compères*, *Les fugitifs*, *Le jaguar*, and *Tais-toi!* The play also marks the first use of the François Pignon character name. The name does not appear in one of Veber's own films until 1983, but actually predates the François Perrin character that dominates his screenplays from the 1970s and early 1980s. Made as a film in France by Édouard Molinaro in 1973, *L'emmerdeur* was the first Veber film to receive "le remake" treatment in Hollywood, becoming Billy Wilder's *Buddy Buddy* in 1981. Finally, *L'emmerdeur* would also mark Veber's first time directing for the theatre, when he restaged the play in 2005 with Richard Berry and Patrick Timsit in the lead roles. Reprising their stage performances, Berry and Timsit returned three years later for Veber's final film. The number of firsts connected to *Le contrat/L'emmerdeur* did nothing to make the 2008 iteration fresh or inspiring. Looking back on forty years in his career by touching on key themes and characters, the concluding version of *L'emmerdeur* signifies Veber's creative exhaustion and declining interest in filmmaking.

Both coda and catastrophe, the failures of *L'emmerdeur* are largely contextual. Being such a key part of his œuvre, the motivation to finally make *L'emmerdeur* on his own terms is understandable. Just as Veber charts his creative rebirth with the decision in 1976 to direct his own material, the eventual decision to direct a project that had passed through the hands of two other filmmakers appears to be an attempt to amend past frustrations. Still, Veber's decision to dedicate his final project to a story he had written forty years earlier is a curious final statement for such an inventive writer. The public's lack of enthusiasm for the 2008 screen version can easily be explained by the fact that the story had already been filmed twice and had just recently been revived on stage a few years earlier. Moreover, what Veber would find out by making the film was just how connected the project would be to its cinematic forerunners. 2008's *L'emmerdeur* stands in the shadows of the 1973 version and shares unfortunate similarities with the 1981 Hollywood remake.

The plot of *Le contrat/L'emmerdeur* (The Contract/A Pain in the Ass) remains largely unchanged across the various stage and film iterations aside from character names in the Hollywood version. Milan is a professional assassin hired to kill a key witness before he can testify against a powerful mobster. Checking into an adjacent hotel overlooking the entrance to the courthouse, Milan's preparations for the killing are complicated when Pignon, the guest in the next room, attempts suicide. His wife having left him for a shady psychiatrist, Pignon ties himself to a water pipe in the hotel bathroom and tries to hang himself, only to have the pipe give way and seep water into Milan's room. Not wanting to have the authorities called and disrupt the assassination, Milan convinces a bellboy to let him take responsibility for Pignon. Stuck with the clumsy depressive, Milan feigns helping Pignon to win back his wife, but ends up becoming caught up in their drama when the psychiatrist sneaks into the hotel and accidentally injects Milan with a tranquilizer intended for Pignon. With Milan's body failing him as the arrival of the witness draws near, Pignon learns the truth about his new friend's profession and they wrestle over a rifle as the moment arrives. The details of the ending change from the French and American versions, but all three films end with the presumption of an interminable connection between the assassin and his unwanted companion.

LE FILM DE MOLINARO

Starring Lino Ventura as Milan and Jacques Brel as Pignon, Édouard Molinaro's adaptation of Veber's stage play is heavy on handheld cameras and the use of zoom lenses, both of which are typical of the aesthetic approach throughout the director's body of work. Molinaro began his career making documentaries, and his penchant for handheld camera infuses gritty realism into his narrative work that, in the case of comedies like *L'emmerdeur* and *La cage aux folles*, adds a frenetic and anxious tone that is absent from the stage versions of each. The handheld camera also requires that his films be shot on location as opposed to the constructed sets of Wilder and Veber's subsequent remakes. Because of his camera's impact on tone, it takes a long while for anything resembling comedy to happen in the film. Still, there are gags that are typical of Veber's writing, such as Pignon bypassing gas stations when his tank is running low because he only uses one corporate chain to fill up in order to accumulate trinkets. Pignon's lack of awareness is present as well, showing an inability to filter his thoughts by confessing to a traffic cop that he always gets out of paying his fines. Being honest and open in spite of himself, this obliviousness to self-interest and expediency is an essential characteristic of most iterations of Pignon. When picking up an American hitchhiker, Pignon launches into a long monologue in French despite the fact that the American has told him that he only speaks English.

L'emmerdeur also incorporates happenstance as the dominant form of narrative motivation. Despite being strangers, Pignon and Milan travel the same stretch of highway together and eventually end up in adjoining rooms through sheer coincidence. Arriving at the hotel to take a life, Milan instead finds himself saving one by taking responsibility for Pignon after the failed suicide attempt and, later, rescuing Pignon from the window's ledge of the hotel. Taking this a step further, Milan helps to bring a life into the world when the pair stumble upon a woman going into labor and end up driving her to the hospital to deliver the baby. The balance between life and death within the narrative is central to the moral tension for the audience.

Organized around an impending assassination, Veber's script makes the audience complicit by structuring the narrative around Milan's singular goal. Without humanizing the witness, the assassination remains an abstraction and, therefore, becomes a task that helps create sympathy for Milan in the face of the chaos created by Pignon. There is a sense that the audience is meant to root for the witness to be killed, or at the very least understand that it is merely part of Milan's professional obligation. In the end, Pignon accidentally shoots Milan in the arm as the witness arrives, thwarting the assassination and prompting a wounded and stumbling Milan to flee the hotel as the police descend. Grateful for the kindnesses shown to him and sorry to have shot him, Pignon risks his life to chase after Milan and save him. As they walk away together in an alley, Pignon promises to take Milan to his house, only to have the film cut to a prison yard where both men march in a circle with other inmates. Whispering to Milan, Pignon cheerfully informs the jailed hit man that he has requested that they be placed in the same cell together.

The unwanted friendship and perpetual connection between the characters foregrounds the buddy comedies of Depardieu and Richard, as well as being explicitly recycled in the prison sequences of *Tais-toi!*, but Molinaro's *L'emmerdeur* departs from the emotional polarity of subsequent pairings. Rather than the contrast in characters, both Ventura's stoic assassin and Brel's depressive Pignon come across as somber. This is the mood that pervades the entire film. The subtlety of Brel's performance foregrounds pathos over broad comedy. Even when he is chattering at a fast pace it reads as a deeply troubled man working through his emotions, not a wacky caricature meant to be the object of laughter. Brel's Pignon is sympathetic and exudes a depth of emotion that is either absent or fleeting in subsequent performers' takes on the character.

Like other singers-turned-actors, audience responses to Brel's screen performances are informed by the broader context of his music. Rather than superimposing a star persona onto his role, however, Brel's career as a singer brings with it a seriousness and reverence that Veber later found to be so sacred amongst people in France that a filmed remake of one of his roles was found to be essentially heretical. Along with Georges Brassens and Léo Ferré, Brel forms a musical trinity at the center of the "golden age" of *la chanson française*.[1] More than a beloved singer and songwriter, the depth of Brel's emotion coupled with the serious political subtext of his music give his screen performances a distinct aura that supersedes the scripting of a character. Chris Tinker's analysis of Brel and the *chanson* is an indication of the transcendent nature of the singer, arguing that in order to approach an understanding of Brel, a scholar needs to move beyond biography and lyrical analysis to account for the almost indefinable aspects of voice, cadence, gesture, and sincerity.[2] To watch Brel's 1966 television performance of the song "Ne me quitte pas" is to experience a profound moment of emotional honesty. Shot in a single uninterrupted close-up with only a black background behind him, Brel's ability to be mesmerizing in this performance without the use of anything except for voice and expression is a crystallization of his art. To have Brel play Pignon, then, not only transforms the character but reshapes the entire film.

LE REMAKE DE WILDER

The success of *L'emmerdeur* at the box office in 1973, when it sold 3.3 million tickets in France and another 1.7 million tickets in Germany, made it an obvious candidate for a Hollywood remake.[3] That it would be made by a Hollywood icon like Billy Wilder was perhaps less obvious. In his mid-seventies, the height of Wilder's career was in the rearview mirror by the time he started work on *Buddy Buddy*. Like Veber, Wilder spent a number of years writing screenplays for others before transitioning to the director's chair full-time in the early 1940s.[4] Also like Veber, Wilder was himself a transnational filmmaker, albeit under very different circumstances. Born in Austria in 1906, he began working in the film industry in Berlin during the 1920s before moving to Paris in 1933 and eventually emigrating to the United States.[5] Directing a number of iconic Hollywood films such as *Double Indemnity* (1944), *Sunset Boulevard* (1950), *Some Like it Hot* (1959), and *The Apartment* (1960), Wilder shares a writing credit on all of his commercial Hollywood films between 1942 and 1981.[6] Through most of the 1960s and 1970s, however, Wilder lacked critical and commercial success.

With his prospects dwindling in Hollywood as the 1980s arrived, Wilder had trouble getting studios to green-light his projects.[7] When producer Jay Weston at MGM invited Wilder to direct *Buddy Buddy*, Wilder agreed to take on the project despite not having any personal connection to the material.[8] Remembering his resignation in agreeing to direct, Wilder would say of *Buddy Buddy*, "Maybe I was a little tired of hitting my head against the wall."[9] The impetus for Weston to offer the project to Wilder was the producer's desire to use the project as a vehicle for Jack Lemmon and Walter Matthau. However, the friends and frequent collaborators would only agree to sign on if the studio hired Wilder to direct.[10] Having appeared together in Wilder's comedies *The Fortune Cookie* (1966) and *The Front Page* (1974), the teaming of the stars with the director had already proven successful and allayed some of the persistent industry fears related to Wilder's recent flop with the drama *Fedora* (1978). Although he rushed through adapting the screenplay with co-writer I. A. L. Diamond, biographer Gene D. Phillips is still able to point out a number of parallels between *Buddy Buddy* and Wilder's previous films.[11] Looking at the finished film, however, Wilder retains so many elements from Veber's original to suggest that the script was chosen because it is built from Wilder's comedic legacy rather than a work that the writer-director transformed to match his sensibilities.

Far from a faithful remake, however, there are key alterations in *Buddy Buddy*. For the most part, the alterations are additions, with Wilder tacking on additional jokes and details to Veber's original screenplay. When he sent Veber a copy of the final draft of the adapted screenplay, Veber recalls thinking that "it was very bad." He tried in vain to suggest a few changes that could improve it.[12] What Wilder had written and would eventually shoot is a film that seems transported from another age in Hollywood. The film looks and feels like a stiff soundstage studio comedy from the 1950s or early 1960s. Even the principals seem out of place and time. Matthau plays the hit man Trabucco, a curmudgeonly cheapskate looking for a big payday on a final job that will allow him to retire. He is also a master of disguise, dressing up as a milkman and a priest while also posing as a salesman when checking into the hotel. Lemmon plays the suicidal guest in the next room, Victor Clooney. Transforming Brel's depressed shirt salesman into a tightly wound network television censor, Wilder adds chronic stomach trouble to the Clooney character for good measure.

The most dramatic addition to the story comes in the transformation of Veber's psychiatrist character. Casting Klaus Kinski and playing off his deranged energy, the character no longer runs a traditional practice. Instead,

Buddy Buddy's Dr. Hugo Zuckerbrot is a fringe behavioral scientist who owns and operates the Institute of Sexual Fulfillment, which is a cultish outgrowth of the sexual revolution replete with sitar music playing in the lobby. Having stolen Clooney's wife, the doctor has had her wedding ring melted down and recast into a penis-shaped pendant that he wears on a necklace. The character and the sequences at the Institute are eye-rolling examples of an elderly Wilder clumsily taking aim at contemporary culture. Later, when Trabucco and Clooney pick up a woman in labor who is stranded on the side of the road, she turns out to be half of a hippie couple who name their kid Elvis Jr. To provide such a broad, uninformed, and unfunny caricature of hippie culture more than a decade removed from Woodstock shows just how out of touch Wilder had become. Other additional characters, such as a Mexican maid who is oblivious to Lemmon sitting in the room bound and gagged, are equally odd and offensive.

The biggest change in Wilder's film comes in the conclusion. The set-up remains the same, with the doctor accidentally injecting Trabucco with a tranquilizer rather than Clooney, making it impossible for the assassin to carry out the hit. Instead of having Clooney confront the assassin and foil the job, Wilder has the innocent hotel neighbor decide to help out his new friend and carry out the shooting in his place. Unbeknownst to Clooney, the police have changed clothes with the mobster witness to allow him to enter the courthouse anonymously. When the incompetent Clooney shouts out to Trabucco, "I think I shot a cop!" it is clear that luck has guided the bullet toward the witness and fulfilled the singular goal of Trabucco. In the process, the film erases care for human life from the character makeup of both Clooney and Trabucco. Not to be outdone, the film ends with Matthau relaxing on a Polynesian island with a number of servants and a topless girl waiting on him hand and foot while he watches football on television. Clooney washes up onto the beach in a ragged sailboat and proposes that he stay with Trabucco in the tropical paradise. Having parted ways with Trabucco after killing the mob witness, Clooney explains that he then firebombed the Institute of Sexual Fulfilment, presumably killing everyone inside. With the change from Pignon as a hapless but kindhearted common man to the prudish, jealous, and apparently sociopathic Clooney, *Buddy Buddy* destroys the tenor of Veber's screenplay.

Wilder called the film a "misfire" after it lost money and was ravaged by critics.[13] Blending good humor and bitterness, Wilder said of the film, "I didn't know that was going to be my swan song; if I'd known, I would have bet on a different swan."[14] Comparing the film to the far more successful Matthau-Lemon pairing *The Front Page*, Wilder biographer Richard Armstrong writes, "A much lesser film, *Buddy Buddy* is nevertheless significant for dramatizing Wilder's growing sense of redundancy."[15] Veber, who expressed open admiration for Wilder in interviews and in his memoir, was unable to avoid the same pitfalls and ignominious end to his career as a filmmaker. In making *L'emmerdeur* and rehashing the past, Veber found himself equally redundant and doomed to repeat Wilder's mistake by betting on the wrong swan.

LE REMAKE DE VEBER

Considering the subtle symbolic power of opening shots throughout Veber's directorial career, the first shot of *L'emmerdeur* is noticeably uninspired. A low-angle shot of a courthouse, the camera tilts downward and then pans right to show a black police car driving down the street in a rather mundane establishing shot. There are hints at a broader commentary on state power throughout, but the use of the opening shot to convey this idea is unclear and underdeveloped. The first scene of the film follows a police sweep of the hotel where one of the officers plants a rifle in a hotel room for Milan, giving the film a conspiratorial edge that is missing from its predecessors. The GIGN tactical unit (France's equivalent of a SWAT team) and a largely militarized police force throughout the film present one of the biggest differences between Veber's film and those of Molinaro and Wilder. Rather than bumbling cops, there is a sense that modern France is an occupied territory. What Veber is trying to say about this and how it relates to the film's central characters remains unclear, providing a fragmented comment instead of a coherent political statement.

Figure 13.1 Milan (Richard Berry) bumps into a pedestrian (Francis Veber) in the director's swan song, *L'emmerdeur*.

The narrative mostly adheres to Molinaro's 1973 version, although there are some slight deviations and additions that impact the tone of the film. Rather than presenting the politician witness as an anonymous target, the film spends time cutting away from Milan and Pignon to develop him; recurring Veber player Michel Aumont is cast in the role. The character is given his own subplot, and his scenes in transit to the courthouse where he talks to the police in the back of a van distract from the Milan/Pignon story. Oddly enough, this subplot flies in the face of Veber's own stated distaste for "second actions," which he says are uninteresting and get cut out of his films and screenplays.[16] Perhaps he regarded it not as a subplot, but as a device for making the film less tied to the theatre. Much of the film's action takes place on the road; the addition of scenes with the witness are accompanied by additional characters outside of the hotel, such as a pair of young lovers traveling together on a scooter. It is an understandable tendency to expand the visual world of a film, but just as with *Dinner for Schmucks'* deviations from the interior setting of *Le dîner de cons*, opening up the story also distracts from what makes the characters and dialogue work in the first place. Other changes come from casting, performance, and era. The omnipresence of cell phones in 2008, for example, allows for an ease of conversation across physical distance that is ultimately detrimental to narrative flow. The challenges of balancing digital technology's internality with the exterior needs of drama have become even more precarious in subsequent years (for example, the recent trend toward displaying text messages on screen), but it is apparent in *L'emmerdeur* that Veber is struggling to find ways to adapt a forty-year-old script to a modern setting.

The biggest difference from Molinaro's version is Veber's departure from realism. Instead of using handheld camera and real locations, the 2008 version has a constructed air, with a hotel room set and green screens placed behind windows to establish its position across from the courthouse. The decision to use a set is rooted in the production's theatrical background, but the amount of crosscutting between the hotel and real exteriors creates a distraction that is not present in the equally clear sound stage design of *Le dîner de cons*. The film looks cheap, and carries with it a television aesthetic. The broad comedy is supported by the well-lit sets and smooth camera movements, but the performances of Berry and Timsit solidify the departure from Molinaro's moody take on Veber's script. With far more dialogue than the 1973 version, Timsit's Pignon never shuts up, becoming more like Quentin in *Tais-toi!* than Brel's vision of the character. Pignon's room number is repeated throughout the film, with the symbolism of Room 53 reinforcing that he is the joker in a deck of cards.[17] The continued use of the noose after the failed suicide, with Milan pulling and prodding Pignon for minutes afterward with the rope, transforms the trauma of Molinaro's treatment of the scene into a cartoonish episode akin to the suicidal phone call in *Les compères*.

The joke that recurs most throughout Veber's film is, once again, premised on queer identity and the embarrassment of men being caught in compromising positions. Milan grabs Pignon by the crotch to lift him up from the window's ledge, drawing on overly broad slapstick and homoerotic embarrassment that is absent from the 1973 ledge scene. Landing on top of each other, Pignon and Milan's mouths are precariously close to each other, adding insult to injury for Milan. Veber also constructs multiple scenes where the bellboy walks in on what appears to be rough gay sex, forcing the employee to embarrassingly excuse himself from the room. It is comedy from another era that is both unfunny and unbelievable, rooted in the impression that any physical contact between men is innately sexual.

Despite its rushed and uninspired look, *L'emmerdeur* includes a few details that show Veber placing more of himself into the film than he had in the past. As always, Veber uses a virtual repertory of actors, but one appearance stands out as an explicit inter-textual reference with Stéphane Bierry's small role as a photographer recalling the actor's only other appearance for Veber as the runaway teen in *Les compères*. Another scene, which seems superfluous, is rooted in Veber's biography. Using a news report to situate the plot's court appearance and impending testimony, Veber shows real-life journalist Élisabeth Martichoux reading the report from her RTL (formerly Radio Luxembourg) desk. Serving no necessary function, going to the trouble of shooting on location at the RTL studio and cutting to it in a standalone shot rather than simply have the news report heard from a radio or television within the hotel room can only be explained as Veber having fun referencing his past working as a journalist for the radio network. In his most blatant and uncharacteristic piece of self-reference, Veber makes a cameo in *L'emmerdeur* when he bumps into Milan outside of the hotel. There is a momentary pause and a shared glance that draws attention to Veber in case the audience may have missed his appearance. The only other screen cameo of Veber's career came as a TV presenter in *Appelez-moi Mathilde* in 1969, the first of his screenplays to be made into a film. These first and final cameos serve as bookends to his career, with Veber's lingering appearance offering strong evidence that he was aware during filming that *L'emmerdeur* would be his swan song as a director.

If Veber imagined the film as an authorial corrective or a triumphant final act, the response to *L'emmerdeur* surely cured him of such fanciful notions. The film sold a paltry 240,720 tickets in France, over a million fewer than any other film from Veber's career as a director.[18] Making sense of the failure, Veber acknowledges, "It was my mistake" for not taking into account the public's fondness for the 1973 Molinaro version and the legendary status of Lino Ventura and Jacques Brel.[19] "It was my first flop in ten movies," Veber recalls, only considering his French films.[20] Explaining his reaction to the flop in a 2009 interview, he self-deprecatingly confessed that the failure of the film was "why I'm writing my memoir."[21] If this statement is to be taken at face value, the failure of *L'emmerdeur* caused a retreat from cinema just as his only other flop as a director, *Out on a Limb*, prompted him to return to writing for the theatre. This time he never returned to the cinema. Another comment from the same 2009 interview expands on his bitterness, wounded pride, and the realization that his time as a writer and director had come to an end. "There are two things that French people don't like," he explains. "Success and funny movies."[22] Because it is Francis Veber, even his most vitriolic comments are wrapped in humor.

NOTES

1. Chris Tinker, *Georges Brassens and Jacques Brel: Personal and Social Narratives in Post-War Chanson*, p. 1.
2. Ibid. pp. 2–4.
3. *JP's Box-Office*, <http://www.jpbox-office.com/fichfilm.php?id=8524> (accessed January 5, 2019).
4. Wilder's debut behind the camera happened in France, co-directing *Mauvaise graine* with Alexander Esway in 1934. His second film as a director, 1942's *The Major and the Minor*, marked his permanent transition from being a writer for hire. After 1942 Wilder only wrote one screenplay for a film he did not also direct, coming with his co-writing credit on *A Song is Born* (1948, Howard Hawks).
5. Gene D. Phillips, *Some Like it Wilder: The Life and Controversial Films of Billy Wilder*, pp. 2–12.
6. The only film Wilder directed without also sharing a writing credit is his 1945 film *Death Mill*, which was made for the U.S. Department of War.
7. Phillips, *Some Like it Wilder*, p. 332.
8. Ibid. p. 333.
9. Ibid.
10. Ibid.
11. Ibid. p. 334.
12. *A Conversation with Francis Veber*.
13. Phillips, *Some Like it Wilder*, p. 339.
14. Ibid.
15. Richard Armstrong, *Billy Wilder, American Film Realist*, p. 131.
16. A Conversation with Francis Veber.
17. The room number is less pronounced in the 1973 film, but is prominent enough to have been noticed by Wilder, who oddly changed the room number but wrote a line of dialogue acknowledging Veber's intent, with the bellboy stating, "Room 359, Victor Clooney . . . That's the joker!"
18. *JP's Box-Office*, <http://www.jpbox-office.com/fichfilm.php?id=9963> (accessed January 5, 2019).
19. *A Conversation with Francis Veber*.
20. Ibid.
21. Ibid.
22. Ibid.

The Precarious State of National Cinemas

Pierre Nora's massive three-volume set of books, *Les Lieux de Mémoire* (released in English as *Realms of Memory*), explores French culture and sites of national memory in an attempt to figure out what it means to be "authentically" French.[1] Published between 1984 and 1997, Nora's search for the meaning(s) of national identity and the ensuing debates amongst readers coincides with a key decade of Francis Veber's career. At the same time that Nora was exploring how national identity is defined and constructed, Veber was complicating his definition as a French filmmaker by splitting his time between France and the U.S. Nevertheless, Veber is an ideal filmmaker through whom to explore national identity precisely because of the complications in his body of work. His career simultaneously and paradoxically prompts optimistic visions of a culturally specific French cinema maintaining far into the future while also supporting cynical views of the economic and aesthetic pervasiveness of Hollywood across the globe. That Veber's career can reconcile these contradictions is not a symbol of his uniqueness. It is a function of how much his career reflects the modern state of global cinema.

France's preoccupation with its national culture comes first from a sense of there being such a thing as a definitive or authentic French identity. Second, the preoccupation with culture demands that it be cultivated and preserved. As opposed to other European nations that both fund domestic art and sponsor foreign artists to work/perform/exhibit in their country in order to enrich the lives of their citizens, France's Ministry of Culture has traditionally been more focused on the promotion of its own national identity than it is on the work of artists outside of its borders. This inward promotion has been a boon to French filmmakers. The resiliency of French cinema in the face of Hollywood's growing dominance in the global film marketplace has been a rare exception amongst national cinemas, especially within Europe. As Jonathan Buchsbaum points out, the responsiveness of the French state to the globalizing push of Hollywood helped to save a struggling national industry in the 1980s and beyond.[2]

While neighbors such as Italy have seen their once proud film cultures marginalized and overrun by American imports, France has maintained a consistent level of domestic production and distribution through the state financing of French filmmakers and a strict quota system that mandates exhibitors dedicate a fixed percentage of their total screens for homegrown releases. If French cinema has remained financially resilient to Hollywood and celebrates its independence as a distinct national culture, the aesthetic makeup of popular films produced in France since the 1980s often complicates the idea of cultural boundaries. As Susan Hayward notes in discussing the rise of mainstream cinema in France since the late 1980s, "the spectacular genre film . . . unashamedly takes many of its cues from American cinema (and thus problematizes the notion of French national cinema that has traditionally defined itself *against* Hollywood)."[3] Luc Besson's French-financed films, for example, share as many American attributes as his multinational co-productions, reinforcing Hayward's observation. Moreover, the bleeding over of American aesthetics into French cinema is not relegated to popular or "spectacular" genre films, but can also be seen in the high art films that the *avances sur recettes* system is designed to support.

The combativeness of France's then Minister of Culture Jack Lang to America's "cultural imperialism" in the 1980s was simply a reiteration of a broader project to define and promote national identity that expands far beyond the age of mass media.[4] Migration, expedition, conquest, and travel prove that the impossibility of complete cultural insularity was apparent long before the arrival of cinema. The movement and adoption of culture can be voluntary or imposed, but every corner of the world is subject to cultural and linguistic intermingling. Cultural nationalism, then, is not always premised on a delusional sense of insularity. It can be a resistant effort geared toward self-definition. In France, the fixation on culture and language in defining and promoting a national identity was a major component in the establishment of the First Republic in 1792. It informed the rebellious spirit of the Paris Commune in 1871 as well as the reconciliatory aftermath of World War II. The contested definition of France as both a nation and an identity played an outsized role the events of May 1968. As difficult as it may be to define, Lang's project of maintaining a vibrant national cinema is premised on the idea that French cinema has a distinct look and feel. The influence of Hollywood films is apparent throughout the work of Jean-Pierre Melville and Jean-Luc Godard, for example, but their films have an unquestionably French *feel*. The same argument can be made for subsequent filmmakers like Luc Besson, although the markers of cultural difference are less pronounced. Still, there is a sense of anxiety on the part of most national cinemas that the dominance of Hollywood films is not isolated to the distribution of American films.

Bollywood is a prime example of a film industry that has flourished and resisted Hollywood imports, yet Mumbai productions are beginning to reflect the style and sensibilities of America. Since India's economic liberalization in the early 1990s, the themes and formal structures of Bollywood films have gradually moved closer to Hollywood sensibilities, as evidenced most clearly in films with shorter running times, fewer (or sometimes no) musical numbers, and avoidance of tonal shifts. Films are still financed in Mumbai and geared primarily toward audiences throughout South Asia (or diasporic Indian populations elsewhere), but they increasingly *feel* American. At the same time, the influence of Bollywood can be seen across the globe, demonstrating that cultural bleeding is not a one-sided phenomenon of America imposing its will on the rest of the world.

Aside from his two films made in Hollywood, Veber's body of work as a director *feels* French. Even *Les fugitifs*, which dramatically departs from the tone and visual composition of his previous films, is more reflective of French drama and action films than it is of anything coming from the United States. The inability of Hollywood to capture the essence of Veber's screenplays is evidence enough that his films embody uniquely French sensibilities. The remakes of Veber's films, including his own *Three Fugitives*, prove in reverse the value of comedy in making national cinemas resistant to globalization. If comedies cannot be remade or even effectively dubbed into another language without losing both meaning and humor then, logically, the only way to reach an audience with a comedy is to specifically tailor it for them linguistically and geographically. The dominance of Mandarin-language productions in Hong Kong cinema, for example, has posed a danger of erasing Cantonese from the screen, but comedies require that Cantonese be used to match the sensibilities and linguistic traditions of local audiences.[5] As essential as language is to comedy, however, what is lost in the translation of Hollywood remakes is more than the meaning and nuances of dialogue. The common Hollywood strategy for remaking foreign comedies is to repeat gags from the original and build around the situational premise of the narrative, but humor is premised on sensibilities that are unique from one country to the next.

Gad Elmaleh, Veber's Pignon from *La doublure*, was part of a reversal of "le remake" when he hosted the premiere episode of the French version of *Saturday Night Live* in January of 2017.[6] Simply titling the show *SNL* (the premiere aired on a Thursday, after all), the French version departs from basic logic by restaging successful sketches from the four-decade run of the American show rather than having a team of French writers and performers create a show with new material each week in the model of the American program. Remaking the famous "More Cowbell" sketch from 2000 in the first episode, Elmaleh replaces Will Ferrell as the overeager percussionist during Blue Öyster Cult's recording session for "(Don't Fear) the Reaper." The French version of the sketch has only one function, which is to have Elmaleh ridiculously dance around and make flailing gestures in a curly blond wig. Gone are all of the elements that make the original sketch iconic. Elmaleh's mugging excess is the opposite of the slow build of Ferrell's performance and obscures the premise of the sketch, which is rooted in the actual song's overuse of cowbell. Unlike the original sketch, the French version ditches the found footage visual device to treat the recording session like a standard comedy routine. Coupled with breaks where Ferrell, Jimmy Fallon, and Chris Kattan struggle to regain their composure, the original sketch is famous for the energy of that specific moment, not for goofy dancing. For an American viewer, though, the most bizarre aspect of the remade sketch is the camera work. Using wide shots of the large audience sitting in front of the stage, the French *SNL*'s variety show format is the antithesis of *Saturday Night Live*'s intimacy in Studio 8H.

It would be nice to think that Elmaleh consciously sabotaged the show as an act of revenge for Veber and all of the other French directors who have seen their work ruined by American reinterpretations. Perhaps the entire project of France's *SNL* is a high-concept commentary on the impossibility of translating humor. Anything is possible. The more likely reality is that the show is earnest but ill-conceived. It may be a classic example of comedy lost in translation, but it represents something more. It exemplifies a number of the reasons that so many transnational comedic remakes fail, while also signifying how the allure of great material can prompt misguided adaptations. In the case of Veber, his career is frustrating on a number of levels. Many of the reasons are rooted in the impossibilities of transnational comedy, such as the sheer number of poorly executed remakes of his screenplays and the lost decade in which he was inactive in the French film industry; but they do not play a role in other disappointments such as his latter career redundancies, intermittent bad taste, and moments of dispassionate labor. Regardless, the endearing aspects of Veber's career far outweigh the frustrations. There is a reason he remains popular in France and has generated an unparalleled interest from Hollywood over the years. His nuanced dialogue, inventive scenarios, cultivation of performance, political commentaries, and subtle formal technique all play a part in crafting comedies that, at their best, are so genuinely funny that they work for audiences both in France and abroad. Hopefully some of the magic that can be found in his films has been conveyed in this book.

NOTES

1. Pierre Nora, *Realms of Memory Vol. 1, Vol. 2, Vol 3*.
2. Jonathan Buchsbaum, *Exception Taken: How France Has Defied Hollywood's New World Order*.
3. Susan Hayward, *French National Cinema*, p. 298.
4. Samuel G. Freedman, "French Minister Cites U.S. Cultural Influence." *New York Times*, November 16, 1984.
5. Jenny Kow Wah Lau, "Besides Fists and Blood: Michael Hui and Cantonese Comedy." In Poshek Fu and David Desser (eds.), *The Cinema of Hong Kong*, pp. 158–75.
6. Grégor Brandy, "Nos sketchs préférés du 'SNL' de Gad Elmaleh étaient des adaptations." *Slate.fr.*, January 6, 2017, <http://www.slate.fr/story/133574/saturday-night-live-gad-elmaleh> (accessed January 5, 2019).

Bibliography

Alkhas, Anita Jon. "DVD for Dummies: Lessons in Technology from *Le Dîner de cons.*" *The French Review* vol. 79, no. 6 (May 2006): 1252–64.

Armes, Roy. *French Cinema*. New York: Oxford University Press, 1985.

Armstrong, Richard. *Billy Wilder, American Film Realist*. Jefferson, NC: McFarland, 2004.

Barbosa, Luiz C. *Guardians of the Brazilian Amazon Rainforest: Environmental Organizations and Development*. New York: Routledge, 2017.

Barker, Martin. *The New Racism: Conservatives and the Ideology of the Tribe*. London: Junction Books, 1981.

Bazin, André. *What is Cinema? Vol. 1*. Berkeley: University of California Press, 1967.

Beshoff, Harry M., and Sean Griffin. *Queer Images: A History of Gay and Lesbian Film in America*. Lanham, MD: Rowman & Littlefield, 2006.

Beylie, Claude. *Une histoire du Cinéma Français*. Paris: Larousse, 2000.

Buchsbaum, Jonathan. *Exception Taken: How France Has Defied Hollywood's New World Order*. New York: Columbia University Press, 2017.

Chutkow, Paul. *Depardieu: A Biography*. New York: Knopf, 1994.

Custen, George F. *Bio/Pics: How Hollywood Constructed Public History*. New Brunswick, NJ: Rutgers University Press, 1992.

Durant, Philippe. *Jacques Villeret, le comique angoissé*. Lausanne: Favre, 2005.

Durham, Carolyn A. *Double Takes: Culture and Gender in French Films and Their American Remakes*. Dartmouth, NH: University Press of New England, 1998.

Faludi, Susan. *Backlash: The Undeclared War against Women*. New York: Crown, 1991.

Finburgh, Clare, and Carl Lavery. *Contemporary French Theatre and Performance*. New York: Palgrave Macmillan, 2011.

Forrest, Jennifer, and Leonard R. Koos (eds.). *Dead Ringers: The Remake in Theory and Practice*. Albany: State University of New York Press, 2001.

Foucault, Michel. *Discipline and Punish: The Birth of the Prison*. New York: Vintage, 1977.

Fournier-Lanzoni, Rémi. *French Cinema: From Its Beginnings to the Present*. New York: Bloomsbury, 2002.

Fournier-Lanzoni, Rémi. *French Comedy on Screen: A Cinematic History*. New York: Palgrave Macmillan, 2014.

Fox, Alistair, Michel Marie, Raphaëlle Moine, and Hillary Radner (eds.). *A Companion to Contemporary French Cinema*. Malden, MA: Wiley Blackwell, 2015.

Frey, Hugo. *Nationalism and the Cinema of France: Political Mythologies and Film Events, 1945–1995*. New York: Berghahn, 2016.

Gordon, Rae. *Why the French Love Jerry Lewis: From Cabaret to Early Cinema*. Palo Alto: Stanford University Press, 2002.

Grant, Barry Keith (ed.) *Auteurs and Authorship: A Film Reader*. Malden, MA: Blackwell, 2008.

Guerrero, Ed. *Framing Blackness: The African American Image in Film*. Philadelphia: Temple University Press, 1992.

Gunther, Scott. *The Elastic Closet: A History of Homosexuality in France, 1942–Present*. New York: Palgrave Macmillan, 2009.

Hall, Stuart. "Some 'Politically Incorrect' Pathways through PC." In Sarah Dunant (ed.), *The War of the Words: The Political Correctness Debate*. London: Virago, 1994, pp. 164–84.

Hayward, Susan. *French National Cinema*. Second edition. New York: Routledge, 2005.

Higgins, Lynn A. "The Liberating Power of Laughter: *Le Placard* and *Gazon maudit*." *L'Esprit Créateur* vol. 51, no. 3 (Fall 2011): 118–33.

Humbert, Brigette E. "Films français et remakes américains." *The French Review* vol. 82, no. 5, April 2009: 962–80.

Judt, Tony. *Postwar: A History of Europe since 1945*. New York: Penguin, 2005.

Kershaw, Ian. *Hitler, 1936–1945: Nemesis*. New York: W. W. Norton, 2001.

King, Geoff. *Film Comedy*. New York: Wallflower, 2002.

Krebs, Katja (ed.). *Translation and Adaptation in Theatre and Film*. New York: Routledge, 2014.

Kuisel, Richard F. *Seducing the French: The Dilemma of Americanization*. Berkeley: University of California Press, 1993.

Lane, Jeremy F. "Parody of political correctness or allegory of 'Immaterial Labour'? A second look at Francis Veber's *Le Placard* (2001)." *French Cultural Studies*, vol. 26, no. 4 (2015): 404–14.

Langford, Barry. *Film Genre: Hollywood and Beyond*. Edinburgh: Edinburgh University Press, 2005.

Lau, Jenny Kow Wah. "Besides Fists and Blood: Michael Hui and Cantonese Comedy." In Poshek Fu and David Desser (eds.), *The Cinema of Hong Kong: History, Arts, Identity*. New York: Cambridge University Press, 2000, pp. 158–75.

Marie, Michel, and Sally Shafto. "French Cinema in the New Century." *Yale French Studies* no. 115 (2009): 9–30.

Mazdon, Lucy. *Encore Hollywood: Remaking French Cinema*. London: British Film Institute, 2000.

Muir, John Kenneth. *The Unseen Force: The Films of Sam Raimi*. New York: Applause, 2004.

Neveux, Olivier. *Théâtres en lute: le theater militant en France des années 1960 à aujourd'hui*. Paris: Découverte, 2007.

Nora, Pierre, and Lawrence D. Kritzman. *Realms of Memory: The Construction of the French Past, Vol. 1: Conflicts and Divisions*. New York: Columbia University Press, 1996.

Nora, Pierre, and Lawrence D. Kritzman. *Realms of Memory: The Construction of the French Past, Vol. 2: Traditions*. New York: Columbia University Press, 1997.

Nora, Pierre, and Lawrence D. Kritzman. *Realms of Memory: The Construction of the French Past, Vol. 3: Symbols*. New York: Columbia University Press, 1998.

O'Donnell, Pierce, and Dennis McDougal. *Fatal Subtraction: The Inside Story of Buchwald v. Paramount*. New York: Doubleday, 1992.

Palmer, Tim. *Brutal Intimacy: Analyzing Contemporary French Cinema*. Middletown, CT: Wesleyan University Press, 2011.

Perkins, V. F. *La règle de jeu*. London: British Film Institute, 2012.

Phillips, Gene D. *Some Like it Wilder: The Life and Controversial Films of Billy Wilder*. Lexington: University Press of Kentucky, 2010.

Powrie, Phil (ed.) *The Cinema of France*. New York: Wallflower, 2006.

Prédal, René. *Le Cinéma français contemporain*. Paris: Les Éditions du Cerf, 1984.

Provencher, Denis M. *Queer French: Globalization, Language, and Sexual Citizenship in France*. New York: Routledge, 2007.

Richard, Pierre, with Jérémie Imbert. *Je sais rien, mais je dirait tout*. Paris: Flammarion, 2015.

Russo, Vito. *The Celluloid Closet: Homosexuality in the Movies*. New York: Harper & Row, 1987.

Salé, Christian. *Les scénaristes au travail: entretiens avec Jean Aurenche, Gérard Brach, Jean-Claude Carrière, Nina Companeez, Jean-Loup Dabadie, Jean Gruault, Jorge Semprun, Francis Veber*. Paris: Hatier, 1981.

Sarris, Andrew. *The American Cinema: Directors and Directions, 1929–1968*. New York: Da Capo, 1996.

Short, Martin. *I Must Say: My Life as a Humble Comedy Legend*. New York: Harper, 1994.

Smith, Alison. *French Cinema in the 1970s: The Echoes of May*. Manchester: Manchester University Press, 2005.

Sowerwine, Charles. *France Since 1870: Culture, Society and the Making of the Republic*. Second edition. New York: Palgrave Macmillan, 2009.

Stam, Robert. *Reflexivity in Film and Literature: From Don Quixote to Jean-Luc Godard*. New York: Columbia University Press, 2006.

Swamy, Vijay. *Interpreting the Republic: Marginalization and Belonging in Contemporary French Novels and Films*. Lanham, MD: Lexington, 2011.

Tinker, Chris. *Georges Brassens and Jacques Brel: Personal and Social Narratives in Post-War Chanson*. Liverpool: Liverpool University Press, 2005.

Turk, Edward Baron. *French Theatre Today: The View from New York, Paris, and Avignon*. Iowa City: University of Iowa Press, 2011.

Vanderschelden, Isabelle. *Studying French Cinema*. New York: Auteur, 2013.

Veber, Francis. *Que ça reste entre nous*. Paris: R. Laffont, 2010.

Vincendeau, Ginette. *Stars and Stardom in French Cinema*. New York: Continuum, 2000.

Vinen, Richard. *1968: Radical Protest and Its Enemies*. New York: Harper, 2018.

Wasson, Sam. *Improv Nation: How We Made a Great American Art*. Boston: Eamon Dolan, 2017.

Williams, Alan. *Republic of Images: A History of French Filmmaking*. Cambridge, MA: Harvard University Press, 1992.

Yakir, Dan. "Writers with Gaul." *Film Comment* vol. 18, no. 5 (September/October 1982): 26–31.

Index